Ernest L. Norman
**Author, Philosopher, Poet, Scientist,
Director-Moderator of Unarius Science of Life**

UNARIUS
UNiversal **AR**ticulate Interdimensional
Understanding of Science

TEMPUS INTERLUDIUM

PART ONE

by

Ernest L. Norman

UNARIUS PUBLICATIONS
145 S. Magnolia Avenue
El Cajon, CA 92020

TEMPUS INTERLUDIUM VOL. I

© Copyright 1978

By

Unarius Educational Foundation

Printed in China

ISBN 0-9724710-3-0

Third Edition

*

CONTENTS

Interdimensional Solar Mechanics
(Of Atoms and Astronauts)

PREFACE

The various and sundry articles in this volume, "Tempus Interludium" part 1, as well as part 2 of this same volume, were all given at various times throughout the many years by the (late) beloved Moderator, Ernest L. Norman. They were not written with any particular sequence in mind, but rather, as the need was realized were they received from his Higher Self, written down by myself to be later published—which is now, the middle of September, 1975. Many of these articles were written as early as 1960-1965, yet the most recent were written or voiced on the recorder within a few months before the Moderator left the physical plane in December, 1971.

The topics and interests in these two books truly run the gamut of great and varied interests, which again prove and show the truly Infinite Mind of He whom we call the Moderator, and which indeed is not doing justice to his full state of Consciousness for, in fact, the earthman could not conceive the vast Being that He is, living now in an entirely different universe.

The very important chapters "Atoms and Astronauts" as well as "Parallel Worlds" were written during a time when these interests and topics were at an alltime high pitch of interest, and I might say that the Beloved One himself, the Moderator, was most pleased with this information that it could be brought in before He did leave this, the Earth world. He realized how very much the Earth scientists needed this particular information, for it will help him to conceive that to gain the greatest possible power from the atom is not by smashing it to pieces, but rather, by tuning into the higher spiritual atom, as will be done with the generating system which we shall build in the immediate, oncoming years.

The articles in this book have been stored away for the many years and now that my Mission is being completed, I wish to make sure that these books get published, along with the others, and it is my highest recommendation that the student studies the vast material in these two books, along with "Tempus Procedium" and "Tempus Invictus" which likewise carry a vast collection of articles of similar, varied interests.

Now I have also included in part 2 of this book (and some may wonder why) pages and information that have been sent out to the student as introductory literature about Unarius or welcoming literature, but I did not wish to leave out one of his words from this, the almost last book to be published before leaving this Earth world. So, if some of you may feel that you have already read a few of these sheets, be not concerned; to mull it in your consciousness once again only serves to be beneficial, for each and every word uttered by this great and wondrous Being carries the great Radiations, the Infinite Power of the Inner World. Creative in nature are his words, and they do carry this very high attunement for the earthman.

Soon too, the new cycle shall enter wherein I shall contact the heads or the leaders of the various countries of this world and pass on to them the truth of this great work and teaching, that they shall know about our wondrous and beloved Avatar, Ernest L. Norman, who did come to this, your earth world in 1904 to deliver that which He did leave for you people—the great, new way of life, the books, and mainly, the meat course of all this study, the lesson course book titled "Infinite Concept of Cosmic Creation". And this title is most applicable, along with the other many volumes.

Dear ones, study with open mind; know that which we have brought to you is genuine; it is life-changing and will change your life for the better when you will study with the desire to gain greater understanding and to remove the inhibiting blocks that cause you to feel or to say (when you are not aware of some particular concept) that it "aint so," but rather, enter with the feeling, "I know so little. Teach me!" Then you can be helped and we can work with you from the Inner in a much more successful way.

The Radiations, the Light, the Infinite Powers and Love of the combined Brotherhood oscillating through this, our great and magnificent Lens that we have so often described to you, now come to you in the fullest measure and you, yourselves, can tune into this Lens for your help and in times when you so need to change your less positive bias. In your times of stress or your problems, your mere thought in the direction of the Lens will bring to you the relief and help so desired! So as we have related elsewhere, drink deeply of these Waters of Life, for this is the Eternal Wellspring, that you may live life more abundantly.

Uriel

Note

August 9, 1975

Although this book was titled "Tempus Interludium" by the Moderator, Ernest L. Norman, before He left the physical plane, and which means an interlude in time it was felt by myself now, after these intervening years, since his departure for the higher strata of life, that these two volumes—Part 1 and 2—could well be called additional lesson courses. Certain previous discourses by the Moderator have been placed in the large volume titled "Infinite Concept of Cosmic Creation—or Lesson Course #1 & 2".

The sincere student will find these various dissertations—although given in response to daily current events or news discussions—equally as interesting and important as the first two courses contained in the Lesson Course book. It is my personal feeling that the voluminous science, teaching and philosophy contained within these two volumes—Lesson Course #3 & 4 —is a stupendous, informational accumulation of infinite education.

A Discussion on the Russian Book, "Psychic Discoveries Behind the Iron Curtain" and Other So-Called Phenomena

Several months ago we ran across the book, "Psychic Discoveries Behind the Iron Curtain", and after due consideration, decided that it would be of some interest to the Unariun students and we began promoting its distribution. However, the reading of this book may present certain intangibles, unanswered questions and equivalents, or even seeming contradictions; therefore, some explanation is in order.

Generally speaking, the book is an extensive documentary of interest and research done by some Russian scientists, laymen and other protagonists of psychic phenomena, such as is currently classified as ESP, mental telepathy, psychokinesis and such. It is quite clear that Russia in particular is far ahead of the United States in such research, due principally to the restrictive religious bigotry which is redundant in this country but absent in the U.S.S.R.—a condition quite similar to that found in Europe during the Middle Ages when arts and sciences were so strongly repressed by the empirical Holy Roman Empire.

In their research, however, the Russians find themselves farther out on the proverbial limb and have precipitated themselves into that classical dilemma in finding out that it happens or exists but lack any suitable scientific hypothesis which would solve the enigma. The book reaches its climax, so to speak, in its description of a certain Russian woman who supposedly moves small objects around the table; salt shakers, matches, et cetera, all moved, supposedly by her concentrated mind powers (psychokinesis). Even motion pictures have been made (which we viewed on

1

television) showing her moving such objects around without help of her hands.

Of course, such an assumption is erroneous. As I have stated before, the human brain and the thinking process is not a mechanism which can project energy beams of sufficient strength and intensity to move objects, even a speck of dust; and there is a much more logical and factual explanation of this phenomena.

Did you ever hear of a poltergeist—an entity or a spirit body which can throw objects around a room, books, ornaments, dishes? There are literally thousands of authenticated cases of poltergeistic activities. You may ask, how is this done? Briefly, the entity draws on energies radiated by the house, objects, people in the room and such, and is able to polarize these energies in such a way that they can be discharged. Like powder behind a bullet, this energy charge from behind some object propels it across the room. The situation is very much the same with the Russian woman. She has a "captive" entity working with her, the entity drawing on her energies, and when polarized, is able to direct these energies against the object to be moved, and the polarized charge, if sufficiently strong, will move it.

The poltergeist or spirit generally is not conscious of what he is doing—much like a situation where two people meet, there is an oscillation or exchange of auric energies between these two people. They are not conscious of this interchange or "drawing"—so it is with the poltergeist; believing he is still alive and trying to do normal life activities, he may attempt to pick up a book or other objects and thus being "charged", the object is repelled from him. He may actually chase it across the room, attempting to catch it.

The proposition of auric interchange or the exchange of energies between two or more people is a very important fact of life. Many psychic, mental and physical diseases are transferred and propagated by this process; colds, headaches, many vague and undetermined diseases are transferred or "caught" from one person to another, who is a more positive polarity and draws, so to speak, these conditions to him. The interchange of auric energies is the basis for magnetic healing. Certain persons may have a very strong auric field radiating in certain frequencies more relative to the physical anatomy.

These strong radiated frequencies can, to a certain extent, cancel certain wave-form energies in another person's body. These energies, usually psychic in nature, have given rise or cause to the condition and a temporary adjustment or healing may occur. However, this is by no means a true healing or miracle—which always occurs in, and does take place within the psychic anatomy, and by the cancellation of a negative anomaly which gave rise to the condition.

Were all of these facts to be known by mankind—the true energy factors and all attendant interpolations—there would be a tremendous change in the life on this planet which would tremendously increase the effectiveness of any medical therapies now existent. All of these factors relative to healing, miracles, et cetera, are dealt with extensively in the "Tempus Procedium" book. Also remember, in your normal intercourse in life you cannot cause or instigate an increase in auric radiations, positive or otherwise, by attempting to concentrate. Your mind is not equipped to do this; moreover, such energies, could they be consciously generated, would be on the same level as your life. They would not be nor contain energies suitable to cancel malformations in the psychic anatomy.

Every person radiates an electromagnetic field or aura which extends several feet in all directions from his body. This electromagnetic field is a composite field —that is, it contains energy wave forms relative to all portions and organs of the physical anatomy, and a certain weak and limited field is radiated from the brain. However, most of these energies are radiated-subharmonics and it is virtually impossible to use these radiated energies as a means of telepathy or mind reading. Such telepathy occurs on a higher plane of transference; however, a well-trained mind, such as an Intelligent Being from a Higher World, can process these various auric radiations and make some sort of a diagnosis accordingly. A true and valuable diagnosis must always be made from the psychic anatomy which is the true cause and originating source of all the ills of mankind—except possibly pathogenically caused diseases from virulent bacteria forms. Wave forms as they radiate from any human are only symptomatic. They are also variable and change from moment to moment according to emotional and chemical changes in the mind and body.

A true relevance as to the cause of any disease must be made from the psychic anatomy and any corrective therapies likewise must be instigated in that psychic body.

In order to properly analyze and understand all energy spectrums involved in these numerous categories (under discussion), it is most necessary to make a proper differentiation. Any atom radiates an electromagnetic field. A group of atoms form a molecule radiating an even stronger EMF proportionate to the number of atoms and their atomic weights. A large number of molecules form a cell. The human brain may contain at least 50 million cells. A subsequent increase in the EMF generated by these atoms is relative to the atom itself, its composite wave forms, et-cetera. The brain, therefore, while it radiates an EMF, radiates information pertinent only to the atom-molecule information contained in the net structure, and very little if any other wave form energies which could be called the emotional content, could be super-imposed in this atomically generated EMF. A sine wave radiated from a television station contains four different superimposed bands of energy frequencies, sight, sound, picture and synchronization; however, this has been purposely designed to function this way. The wave forms radiated from the human brain are, atomically speaking, a heterogeneous assortment of frequencies, all intermixed, and the many thousands of these different wave forms are relative only to their particular atom-molecule-cell combination, and due to certain wide differences in frequency bands, are not suitable carriers for the transmission of thought which occurs on a different plane more closely fourth-dimensional in their spectral wavelengths. Now, in this fourth dimension, there is a certain band of cyclic energies which, like the television carrier, can transmit thought instantaneously, even to remote distances thousands of miles away.

Again, proper knowledge and training in a higher fourth-dimensional world is necessary before mental telepathy or any other paranormal function can be attained. All this will adequately explain why there are so many misconceptions, malpractices and derelictions in the field of paranormal functions and activities. The earthman simply does not understand, nor is he aware of all factors and elements involved; and here again is presented the absolute necessity of your evolution. You must, in the thousands of years and lifetimes to come, learn of all this to the extent that it will be your daily life in a Higher World; that is, presupposing you wish to live in a Higher World and you have the necessary desire and dedication to fulfill such an evolution.

In certain Unarius books and in the Second Lesson Course, the function of the human brain has been well described. The brain cells do not and cannot generate electricity even though electricity in the brain has been

5

measured in certain wave forms by the encephalo-graph, which is a very sensitive amplifier. Brain cells in the different cortical layers are similar to transistors or rectifiers. They can alter or change certain wave form characteristics or they can retain for a millionth of a second a certain electronic wave form facsimile. This retention is called purveyance.

In the net sum and total of all oscillations from the psychic anatomy to the surface exterior life, this process of rectification and purveyance, etc., in the brain cells creates the illusion of sight, sound, feeling and different emotions, etc., but in no case and without exception does the brain ever generate any electricity. Furthermore, any direction of energies would necessitate some kind of an antenna such as the dish-shaped antenna used in radar transmission. Any such radiating mechanism is however, entirely absent in the physical anatomy. Moreover, energies which oscillate in the brain are of such a high frequency that they would have to be transposed into much lower frequencies before they could be effectively used to move objects, and in a certain way, this is exactly what is done by the entity who works with this woman being discussed. By drawing on her energies and after a polarization or stepping down, they are used as a propellent charge by the entity to move objects.

Again, the book in its entirety should be thoroughly analyzed as you read it. You, as a Unariun student, have in your hands and contained in the Unariun liturgies, all the necessary elements and requisites to give you the correct answers to the many obvious questions posed in this book.

It should be interesting to note that Tesla, with his Tesla coil was able to perform numerous seemingly magical feats. High-frequency radiation from the coil could clear smoke from a room . . . propel corks through the air . . . light electric bulbs several feet away, or cause jagged lightning-like streaks of energy to flow from different protruding points of any human who stood close-by.

The Russians have advanced several theories to explain these different types of psychic phenomena, and with but one exception—all wrong. This one exception hits closely to the truth. They theorize an interdimensional energy field which they call bioplasma, an energy field which is, in its oscillating spectrum, beyond any known terrestrial oscillating fields—such as the gamma or delta rays which oscillate well over 500 million megacycles. Laser is said to oscillate at 750 million megacycles. The oscillating energies in the psychic anatomy and which are reoscillating in the brain cells, are well above any of these theoretically known fields.

The encephalograph measures only one or two subharmonics which have been regenerated in the net oscillating process. One in particular is said to have a frequency of 15 cycles per second and is the wave form most commonly used to make a medical or psychiatric examination to determine possible symptoms of paranoia, et cetera.

In its entirety, the book almost immediately suggests, yes, demands, the great universal scientific world of Unarius and all of the answers to these enigmatical problems which are presently confounding the so-called savants of this world at this time.

The interdimensional cosmos is the birthplace and originating source of all things, including solar systems and planets. Any and all such third-dimensional manifestations are merely one of many surface planes of expressions for this interdimensional cosmos, or as I have frequently called it—The Infinite or The Fountainhead.

As of today, man seems to be singularly unaware of the interdimensional cosmos, even though there are vague suppositions and hints such as were contained in Einstein's classical theory of relativity. However, far beyond that and far beyond the outermost reaches of the galaxy, and yet all contained within every atom, is this interdimensional cosmos—all represented as oscillating wave forms which, through the multiples of harmonics, portray the full facade of Infinity.

In my own experience and in expressing psychic phenomena at one time, from a distance of about four miles I drove a Cadillac car a distance of approximately one mile, negotiating an "S" turn and keeping the car well-controlled in spite of several efforts of the owner-driver to control the car. He said later, "The steering wheel turned in my hands with a will of its own," and he asked me how I did it. This is but one of countless thousands of types and kinds of psychokinetical expressions I have demonstrated. Others would include repairing radio and television sets . . . electronic and mechanical contrivances of all kinds . . . voltage regulators . . . preventing tire blowouts . . . bearing failures . . . different kinds of physical therapies such as relieving headaches and other aches and pains . . . locating hard-to-find clothing and food, etc.

Even the Unariun Mission is made possible due to different kinds of psychokinesis; in fact, my entire life is oriented around psychokinesis—all done without physical contact, mind consciousness or concentration, and all done from the more highly developed Higher Self in conjunction with others in the Higher Worlds who are likewise knowledgeable and capable in expressing themselves in infinite ways as well-directed polarized expressions—all of which, as of today, confounds the savants of this time.

Yes, the people on this earth, despite their affluences of electronic and mechanical inventions and developments, are still less than primitive savages in the eyes of those peoples who live in a constant and never-ending interplay of mind forces and energies, all of which oscillates with the infinite source of energy and supply and remanifests as individual polarized expressions.

The Russian book clearly indicates the abysmal ignorance of the earthman's intellectual status when it concerns itself with factors and elements outside the periphery of his little third-dimensional reactionary world.

It would be well at this point to objectify how certain transmissions such as mind reading, telepathy, clairvoyance, audio and other such similar transmissions occur. As stated, the brain does not radiate or broadcast these energy transmissions. There is an auric or electromagnetic field which surrounds the head and is part of the same body-field. However, this has nothing to do with telepathic transmissions which may occur over great distances—thousands of miles. All such transmissions occur as a result of tuned frequency fields which are a part of, and radiated by the psychic anatomy. As this psychic anatomy is more nearly fourth-dimensional, such attunements will therefore occur as cyclic transmissions. That is, the infinite so-called void being actually infinitely-filled with small and large cycles composed of oscillating wave forms, transmission or induction can take place instantly when radiated fields from the psychic anatomy are tuned and polarized at the receiving end of the transmission.

The transmission of energies in a fourth-dimensional field has been discussed in the "Tempus Invictus" book, an explanation which will also explain the transmissions of solar energies and their conversion into normal spectrums of heat and light found in the electromagnetic fields of the planet Earth. This will explain why ESP and other forms of thought transmission, so far as the earthman is concerned, are extremely variable because he lacks the knowledge to properly make necessary attunements in the fourth-dimensional cyclic fields.

As it is today, it's a hit and miss situation and also explains why certain scientific factions are still loathe to accept such transmissions from mind to mind, so to speak. Also indicated is the faculty of a highly trained mind which can tune in to the past, present or future, either as events that have transpired, that are taking place or that will occur in the future; also, the individual life history or akashic records.

In general and because of lack of training, even the most highly acclaimed reader has only fragmentary success usually, and delivered with the help of astral entities who, in the fourth dimensional world, may have easier access or adaptability to such necessary attunements.

Also, so far as a living earth person is concerned, the conscious mind does not readily and voluntarily oscillate in the necessary frequency bands, therefore blocking any conscious effort, as the conscious mind will regenerate or oscillate from the subconscious, and on the basis of positive-negative phase shifts, will cancel out any information being received from the psychic anatomy via the mental portion of this body.

So you see, it's very necessary and extremely important to understand the fundamentals of energy transmission. When you leave your earth body, possessing the knowledge or lack of it will determine whether you live a beautiful spiritual life, or one filled and cluttered with a psychedelic interplay of energy wave forms—all wildly gyrating—the sum and total of which will make your spiritual life a hell.

The Metamorphosis of Intelligence

In our previous discussion upon research in the field of psychic phenomena in Russia, we discussed certain (what would be to most people) rather astounding display of mind power—the actual moving of small objects around the table by what apparently seems to be through the power of mind, and as it was thoroughly explained, is an erroneous misconception popularized and accepted by those who were unfamiliar with the extraterrestrial or psychic world—the world of bioplasma, as it was called. It would be equally astounding to those people, as well as other members of the human race interested in any paranormal phenomena, or even sundry individuals, and laymen, etc., to know that all actions, reactions, emotions, the entire concourse of physical life as it is lived here on Earth by any individual throughout his lifetime, that this entire concourse of action was actually psychic in nature, psychically instigated and followed through with the usual reactionary muscular motions expressing these motions as acts of necessity in the deployment of their everyday life.

It was thoroughly explained, the motivating forces of all of these extrusionary reactions in the field of muscular coordinates were inspired, energized, powered by psychic forces arising in the psychic anatomy by the interchange or oscillation of energies from the exterior plane of life, biased and again rectified in the brain cells after being sorted and re-biased in the psychic anatomy for suitable reactionary expression into the conscious plane of life.

The movement of small objects on a table then assumes a more proportionate place in our introspection as it more properly deserves a secondary purpose—

one in which only the agnostics or the atheists of this world can be shocked, so to speak, into accepting something beyond the limited periphery of their material lives. The preparation for life in a Higher World is not predicated upon the attainment of a large dimension of terrestrial circumference such as might be measured in the balance written in your bankbook or how much influence you politically control over your fellowman. Rather, it is in that extra-terrestrial dimension which is now called by the earth-man as paranormal, merely a term which relegates such expression beyond the circumference of the daily material life.

As I have stated, my entire life has been oriented in this paranormal field and all acts in my daily life were, at least to some degree, biased by higher and more intelligent life forces than were commonly expressed by the average earthman. In stating my experiences and the logic, science, et cetera of my position, I might even be accused of boasting but again, as I once previously did, I will paraphrase Webster, "If this be boasting, then I will make the most of it."

To go back in the last thirty years of my life, I could easily compose a biography in which I could factually state hundreds of thousands of such extraterrestrial phenomena which would be even much more astounding than moving small objects around a table. As a matter of fact, within the last few years in the Unariun Mission, there is within the circumference of this Mission, as it embraces students from all over the world, the manifestation by individuals of certain paranormal manifestations which are beyond the ken of ordinary humans. In this dictation of these Unarius teachings, there has been impinged a certain reference level which automatically tunes the reader into the Higher World and all Unarius students without exception who read the various liturgies which I have dictated almost immediately become transcended. We have

12

in our files many thousands of handwritten testimonials from students who repeatedly assert that in reading they become drowsy, begin to see pinpoints of light radiation. Yes, even those who converse about the liturgy over the phone often become drowsy in the process.

One student in particular relates of a certain stranger who is a board member of a certain library, in speaking about our books to be placed in that library, that this person became drowsy and sleepy and had to be repeatedly called in order to be kept from falling totally asleep.

It is quite clear and evident that there is a tremendous power behind the Unariun movement and all assertions have been made in our literature as to our affiliations with a Higher World, and the millions of advanced Superbeings who inhabit that world are diligently working with us, projecting psychokinetically, mind energies polarized through us—and I am speaking of Ruth and myself—to the minds of various Unariun students. This is not boasting; it is an assertion of fact which should be made upon the premise that these individuals can be given the necessary constituents and the impetus to survive beyond their material life. For without this, their Unarius, they would indeed be in a hopeless position incarcerated in what is known in the Higher Worlds as one of the hellholes —the lost world.

And to further reinstate my own position in the field of expressionary energies called psychokinesis or into other such terms as teleportation, telekinesis, and such —by whatever definition the various protagonists of these expressions have labeled the movements or appearances of manifestations of psychic energy, such as it may be, this is the way of life for me and has become the way of life for my most avid helper, Ruth. She has most aptly demonstrated the apparent fact that she has lived with me in other lifetimes as I have appeared upon the Earth, and has also conditioned herself and has been given extensive preparation and education in the Higher Worlds between her Earth lives; otherwise, she would be totally incapable of being the polarity which she is, and again to repeat, a most proper proof—an inviolate proof—and one of the many proofs which can be given as to the power and efficacy of our Unarius Mission.

Were it not for this Unarius Mission as it so expresses itself in all dimensions, all factions and in all levels of our heterogeneous earth society, then indeed would mankind be lost. Today there is an overwhelming, so it may seem, preponderance of negative expressions throughout the world. To pinpoint or to enumerate these different expressionary elements is unnecessary and time-consuming; a daily newspaper would suffice to most properly fill in any person as to the state of what is apparently an immoral decadency going on at the present time. Truly in this sense then, the biblical prophecy, for such as it is worth, "The Battle of Armageddon" is in full force.

Individually then, whether a person is a protagonist or an antagonist, such factors and elements which would relate him to a more constructive evolutionary concourse must be most avidly striven for. The world and all of its numerous temptations are indeed obstructionary forces in the choice of an evolutionary pathway as it concerns the individual—biased as he is by the preponderance of former lifetime experiences in other lifetimes which relate him in his life experience to the earth world. The proposition of obtaining immortality by the extension and development of the psychic anatomy and its deployment as an expressionary, as well as an integrated element in higher energy worlds, is indeed beyond the comprehension and the dedicated will of the average individual, even though such an individual may have been in many ways, alerted

14

to the possibility of the continuity of life.

The mystical elements which surround the individual on this earth planet and which are not immediately justified within the mental horizon of his reactionary plane of thought must assume mystical or extraterrestrial forces. These he has personified as numerous godlike personages, those which have lived in the cultures of the past and have intimidated or influenced his way of life. Even into the present time and generation, these gods in one form or another, still exist either as temporal elements in his everyday superstitions or they may be manifested as the supreme god-image, in which he can relegate and apparently regulate to some extent, the pressures within the subconscious portion of his psychic anatomy. He must assume the constant convenience of this god-image and within the narrow confines of this configuration he attempts to placate or to rebuild a deflated ego by constantly intimidating this god-image, trying to bring him down to the level of his own life and vicariously, through this deflation of his god-image, assume a more normal proportion in his ego. That he can, in his prayers, attempt to intimidate, coerce, falsely promise and urge this god-image and then believe his prayers have been answered is in itself a complete justification regardless of the very obvious fact that circumstances do not bear out his erroneous conclusions.

Compared to this system of easy compromise and the package-deal of religion as it presents itself, the conquest of self upon the more proper frontiers of personal psychology is a herculean task beyond the circumference of the human mind. Again most propitiously do the higher civilizations of the Higher Worlds enter into the justification of this temporal world and begin to help him over the first barrier—the conquest of self. The most important conquest man will ever make is in the admission that within the circumference of his own mind and in the incorporation of the admissions and usages, the fears and insecurities, etc., which he has accepted as his normal dimension of life, that he has become his worst enemy. Moreover, he has not considered, nor does he possess knowledge of the forces involved, their origins or their final culmination as extrusionary elements in his daily life.

It is quite natural then that there is much in the average individual life which must temporize him and give him a sense that there is sort of a mystical aura, a heavenly supposition or world which is constantly in effect. Also, he must epitomize evil as a personality which he has given a satanic image and has propagated very extensively the reactionary propaganda of good and evil, again belying and portraying his abysmal lack of knowledge of the forces which involve his daily life.

How well it would be then, rather than as curiosity seekers, if a person was so interested in his destiny, in the concourse of his evolution the promise of a higher life, that he could assume a more rational approach, that he could realize in his everyday life there was ample and abundant proof that all that he was in the world, even the heavens which surrounded his world had certain basic origins which were extraterrestrial in nature. Even the astronomer or the astrophysicist is today, completely engulfed in the erroneous extension of his third-dimensional physical sciences as they concern galaxies and universes, or the interspersion of distances, the propagation of energy throughout the universes; moreover, he is constantly changing his views, constantly being forced into a different position and an admission of his past error by new discoveries.

Such instruments as telescopes which float serenely through space some four hundred miles above the earth and beyond the reach of our atmospheric turbulences have exposed and relayed to the astronomer more facts about his galaxy and universe than he had previously supposed. Distances have been stretched like a rubber-band, far beyond the limited dimension of his light year—and again bespeaks the abysmal ignorance of the third-dimensional mind which must constantly relegate the expansion of consciousness and confine it into the bullpen of his terrestrial world.

We who are the Unariuns, we who are the lifesavers and who watch over these terrestrial earths—hundreds of millions of them that are revolving around their respective suns throughout the many galaxies, the many universes in the interdimensional cosmogony—know that these are only one small fraction of the very apparent Infinite. They are only one small surface plane of expression of this Infinite—a way in which, within the limited bands of certain spectrums of energy manifestations, the Infinite Intelligence, the Infinite Mind, expresses Itself in some small way.

Yes, the billions who inhabit this earth world, just as the billions who inhabit other earth worlds, are all small units—participles of energy which are oscillating with certain energy configurations, united with past energy configurations impounded within the timeless dimension of their psychic anatomy and there, within the reaction, the composite formation of harmonics have compounded the basic constituents of their earth life. Yet, they have the unmitigated and senseless bigotry to say in their own way and by the constant deployment of their sciences and religions, their philosophies and creeds, to compound the entire expression of life within the circumference of their third-dimensional world!

Yes, indeed, I have been at this day and hour somewhat irked, I might say, by the constant and never-ending deployment, the exhibitionism of certain individuals, of certain groups who assume a vast and totally unsupported position in the alchemy of their so-called investigation of the psychic world. In particular, one man, a house painter or a painter of houses, who fell upon his head from a ladder and in the subsequent three weeks of unconsciousness, formed certain alliances with subastral worlds, and who (and to this present day) upon regaining his consciousness, is obsessed by these astral forces who have deployed themselves through the consciousness of his mind into certain types of exhibitionism, and he has, like the jackdaw of Aesop, assumed the glory, the false mantle, the cloak, or put feathers on his tail that belonged most properly to other worlds and with other expressions.

I could enumerate a group, and fortunately a minority group of those completely ignorant of the forces, the construction of the interdimensional cosmos, who sit in circles within totally dark rooms to develop an alter-ego, powered and motivated by their own subconscious into psychokinetically raising or levitating a six-ounce aluminum trumpet and there to falsely attempt to describe a spiritual world which is in reality, the maze of subconscious tunnels of their own subconscious.

I could enumerate numerous other expressions of life in which certain individuals or groups have clustered together, such as the fundamentalists, the evangelical groups, the Pentecostals, those which I say are well within the fringe-line of lunacy. Because of the tremendous psychic pressures bearing in upon them, their failure to either justify, explain or to readapt themselves in any of the common defense mechanisms, they have resorted to a crystalline subterfuge, and within the citadel of a closed mind, have relegated the entire world through the distorted lens of this crystalline structure. Their Bible becomes their way of life, their false god, the prerogative of all they do and they verbally have renounced themselves completely to this false god and to the position which they have given to a man who was formerly, completely dedicated to the overthrow of this false god; a man who now assumes the position of the son of this false god, or is even incorporated in the god-image as himself! Such is the unmitigated, unreasoning holocaust of thought which composes and comprises this citadel, the crystalline structure of this warped and distorted psychism, a psychotic, completely bigoted conspiracy against logic and reason which gives a fanatical glare to the eye of all those who have absconded within its depths.

No, there is nothing to compare with ignorance and its destructive edge which cuts into logic and reason, destroys all the constructive factors of life and puts the personal exponent of such a diatribe within a spinning orbit where, within, the centrifugal forces, will extract from him the last vestiges of sanity and reason and make him a candidate for the lowest brothel of hell.

Getting back to more reasonable and more logical factors of life to what is termed extrasensory perception, psychokinesis, parapsychology, teleportation, whatever names may occur to you or that you have coined within the framework of your own mind, these are but elements of energy manifestations which, in your recognition, is your first admission that there is something beyond the periphery of your third-dimensional world. By what manner, way or means you interpret these forces, these energies, these manifestations, may well determine whether or not you will assume a constructive forward motion which will lead you into a higher dimension. Or conversely, that you will distort, malign or otherwise profane the manifestations of interdimensional energies which will plunge you downward in an ever-spinning cycle which will, by your own determination, completely dissolve you into the aftermath of irrelevant dissolution.

If this be Heaven and Hell or if this be Pentecostal, then again thanks to Webster, make the most of it. I do not preach Heaven and Hell as a fundamentalist or as a coercionary element. Like the statements and stories, all true, which I can tell of my past experiences, these statements, be they arbitrary, must remain as they are —facts or plain fact—which must, in your own reactionary thinking, implement you to make the correct decisions, inspire you to carry forth this most necessary extension of your development—to expedite the forward motion of your evolution. The courage that comes from knowing you are right, delivered to you in small doses by your daily efforts as you begin to inseminate some of the logic and reason, may come to you from beyond the horizon.

Many years ago, I incorporated within the books which have been published under my name, statements that there were countless millions of planets revolving within our galaxy around their respective suns. At that time, such a statement would have aroused a most antagonistic attitude in many of the scientific echelons of our society. It would have been tantamount to complete sociological exorcism from certain evangelical religious groups which would have swarmed down upon me like the bats from Hell had they known of my whereabouts and read my statements. Yet, I remain as of today, aloof; I am, as I have been in the past, completely protected from the encroachments of these predators or from the threat of either physical or any other kind of damage; yes, even death, which they might inflict upon me if they knew who I am and where I was and what I have been teaching, lo these many years. This is the effect this Mission has had upon the citadels of Hell as have existed in this world for almost two thousand years.

There is nothing in the religious atmosphere of our present-day Christianity which would propagate or which would otherwise further a logical scientific course. Just as it was in the Middle Ages, this atmosphere is far thicker and more poisonous than any

20

which floats above our cities. This religious smog stifled the cultures, the arts, the sciences throughout the Middle Ages. Fortunately, as of today this smog is dissipating. The hierarchy of the Holy Roman Empire, as it has existed for almost two thousand years, is well into its first stages of dissolution. There is quarreling among the bishopric and the priesthood. There is open rebellion against the papacy, and the little man who sits in the Vatican is almost alone trying to uphold what he believes to be the past glory of the Roman Church. He has conceded and made very definite concessions on everything except "The Pill", and today Vatican roulette (the rhythm method) is the sole means of birth control advocated by this little man, despite the fact we have a population explosion, the over-whelming evidence of how terribly sinful, if we can call it that, to bring an unwanted child into the world and to attempt to bring him up and turn him loose in a world which has already gone beyond the boundaries of being able to support such a life. This child will be placed in competition far beyond the mental and phy-sical means at his disposal, and it is quite logical and natural that he will resort to numerous subterfuges, such as thievery, drugs and other abuses whereby he can hope to extend his life on earth.

How horrendous is this crime of unwanted birth and how horrendous is anyone's position which defends the constant propagation of human life upon an earthplane where it is totally inadequate in its way or means to support such life.

No, I do not condone such factors as abortion, yet abortion is most necessary in a case where, like can-cer, the disease is already apparent and must be dealt with in the most expedient manner possible. A long time ago the peoples of this world and particularly the Western peoples involved with Christianity should have overthrown the yoke of their religion. They should have probed with the tentacles of their mind into the unknown frontiers forbidden to them by their religion. They should have educated themselves into the problematical statistics of this fragile planet and its ability, environmentally speaking, to support a limited number of people. And again, that all of these people who came into this world should have been given all of the advantages which could come from a selective genetical control, that malformed bodies or retarded minds would not come into this world to become burdens upon their society—an atrocious example of the unreasoning, willful desires of man.

Instead, we would have had a healthy society, genetically cleansed and purified from strains of insanity, mental retardation, epileptic tendencies, physical deformities and a host of other very apparent derelictions which now encumber and burden our society, that fill our hospitals, our prisons and our asylums with countless thousands of derelicts which are the byproducts of this insane propagation.

As the Bible says, "Go forth into the world and be fruitful and multiply." Yet we see today many who have overdone this statement to its nth degree, an unreasoning attempt, so it would seem, to fill the world with their own spawn, senselessly to bring a life into the world to battle the monstrosities which confront these poor souls on every hand. Today we are reaping the winds of these indiscretions, of these insanities. There are millions of teenagers, young adolescents, yes, even children, who have resorted into the hellhole of drug usage, sex abuses, even murder in order to attempt to escape the ever-fearful monstrosity of their social structure which surrounds them on every side.

How perverted then is a society which has propagated itself beyond the dimension of logic or reason. Yes, two thousand or three thousand years ago, to some small desert tribe of nomads, being fruitful was one of the necessities of life; and most logically, if the tribe was to survive, they must multiply. Today we have many women who are living on relief rolls; the last count was perhaps well over several million, who, without husbands, have brought into the world as many as twenty children, and the welfare agencies of this country have paid them to do this—children who must go through this world in a society which has automatically ostracized them from the beginning! Genetically, they have been limited in their mental abilities and perspectives. Physically, they may be of a color which is racially not acceptable to the Caucasian element of this country, and there are many other factors which level a pointing finger of guilt against a society, a government, a religion which fosters and propagates such senseless and useless exploitation of life.

Sadly though, as a philosopher, as a traveler through time and space, as a man from a Higher World, I can only look upon these things and within the dimension of my philosophy, I can only reason that for the most part these should be elements for which, within their own pressures, their own evils, and their own extruded necessities, there must be levitation and rectification. If any of these people who inhabit this world today and who know nothing of the interdimensional cosmos, the vast worlds beyond this world, the scientific laws which govern and make possible this world, were to know of these things, then, of course, they would not be the people they are; yet, most necessarily, the beginnings of your evolution demanded a constant and never-ending regeneration and interplay of life's experiences.

The microcosm can furnish us specific examples of the beginnings of this evolution. At the lowest point on the scale of planetary life are the protozoans—tiny one-celled animals which could well be the beginnings of life upon this planet. From this very minute speck of protoplasm in a single cell must be the first extrusion of Infinite Mind, for within these one-celled creatures can we find all the elements which make life on this planet possible, and even only as one cell, yet these tiny creatures manifest life very much as humans do in a higher state of evolution. Yes, and even beyond that, for these tiny creatures have learned to live that way for hundreds of years; they may live for hours, days, or weeks in temperatures above the boiling point or below the freezing point. They have existed on this planet for two billion years where man can only recount his existence or trace it back some two million years.

There are creatures on this Earth, all of which are familiar to us, which can be frozen solid and live for months in a frozen state—even creatures with blood, just as you and I—yet they can be thawed out and assume their normal concourse of life. We are surrounded on all sides by the life cycles of these insects and animals which spend half of their life in a state of hibernation where they are subjected to temperatures for weeks and months as much as forty or fifty degrees below zero.

Where does all of this intelligence come from—the adaptability to environmental conditions? Intelligence it is; a small caterpillar which becomes a beautiful butterfly in its own way exhibits intelligence far beyond the scope of our most advanced savant. The metamorphosis of life as we see it on every side is a mute but loud testimonial of the constant, never-ending, abundant inflow of intelligent, interdimensional energy which flows into this world, into every creature, yes, and even into the rocks which make our mountains and hills and which fill our stream-beds with flowing water. And while the people are busily engaged in the rape of this planet to plunder its resources, to devitalize its oxygen, atmosphere, to pollute its streambeds and water sour-

24

ces, to kill all the creatures—to make them extinct in this world by the very poison of his existence so that man is, as of today, plunging ahead in one of his many insanities; over-population, pollution, social suicide, drug addiction, the exploitation of sexual promiscuity and intimacies, publicly displayed on our stages and motion picture screens.

Yes indeed, the people today are degenerate and even the most sacred precinct of our society—those who have held themselves aloof and have considered themselves virtuous, law-abiding citizens—are all tarred with the same brush. By accepting these degenerate manifestations, in this acceptance they have condoned them and they have made them relevant to their society and their time. They have helped those others, the exponents and the propagators, to loose the wolves of hell upon this world.

To those then who listen to my voice, let them be warned and let them be armed with new courage—warned as to the dangers in the pursuance of the material, physical life; a life which supports them only in a first initial phase of their evolutionary cycle. And should they fail to recognize their trajectory through time and space in the interdimensional cosmos, then most surely will they perish. For just as all energy, all intelligence, wisdom, everything must come from this interdimensional cosmos, so each person must always be mindful that he is receptive, eager and willing; that he is purposely inclined and motivated toward the positive bias which comes from this energy within the interdimensional cosmos.

And again, should he fail to always keep this positive bias, then indeed will the supporting energies of his life be shut off from him. Not that anyone will do this, but that he himself turns the valve when he turns his face away from the progressive infinity.

In summing it all up then, one fact is important:

the inhabitants of this Earth, whatever their calling may be, their sex or their way of life, are completely in ignorance of all the facts which I have stated in these articles, the only exception being the Unariun student who, in possession of these facts, is now on the threshold of understanding and will, in the thousands of years ahead of him in this future, and if he pursues this constructive course of learning, eventually develop a psychic anatomy or more properly, he will develop into a psychic anatomy which will be well beyond the limitations of an earth world and its third-dimensional reactionary fields. In other words, he will be a spiritual being who will live a life in conscious attunement with the Infinite.

Mental telepathy, teleportation and all other so described faculties will be a part of his life and will take the place of sight, hearing, taste, smell and feeling—a mind so developed that it may be able to exist simultaneously in a number of places at the same instant —all done by proper attunement—for in the fourth-dimensional world there is no time or space. How different than your present earth life where everything is time and space—two words which are synonymous and have the same meaning.

Even the vocabulary with which I speak limits me to the degree where these word forms will autosuggestively cause certain oscillations to occur in your brain and psychic anatomy and which, in turn, will be reattuned to past similar oscillations which have been part of your life experience.

The net connotation recreates the necessary pictures which you call consciousness, similar in certain respects to life in a Higher World, but with crutches. The word forms of speech, the limitations of eyesight which must oscillate to a narrow band of frequencies, or the other of the five senses are all autosuggestively sorted by the subconscious—some information to be

26

discarded because it is ego deflationary, other information may be blown up and distorted by the same ego selectivity. This is all part of what you are. You made it that way, unknowingly perhaps or in ignorance, but with all this error and lack of knowledge, etc., there is always an incumbency, sickness, mental and physical derelictions of all kinds; unhappiness, despair and death—the complete gamut of human ignorance.

Learn then, for in learning there is salvation—a way and a means to end the circumstance of ignorance. No one else can do it for you and there are no gods to snatch you up into Heaven. The prerogative has already been indelibly written the moment you began your earth life in that long-ago. The moment you began to be consciously selective with factors and in certain areas of your life, selectivity was the beginning of good and evil and these two became the parents of all your emotions.

What then of the future? Shall it be more of the same, or shall we take the first necessary step: select the proper pathway and learn to live above and beyond the shadowy hinterlands of a reactionary earth-world?

Conditioned Reflexes

One of the first and central figures in our modern present-day psychology was a Russian psychologist and physician named Ivan Petrovich Pavlov (1849-1936). It was Pavlov who first discovered and developed what is no doubt the most basic underlying principle of this psychology—a basic tenet called conditioned reflexes. With a group of dogs, Pavlov began his famous experiment. Just before feeding the dogs, he would ring a certain little hand bell, then begin the feeding. After a few days time, Pavlov noticed that after he rang the bell the dogs began to exhibit certain reactions. They would begin to bark and howl and their saliva glands were very strongly activated. In time, Pavlov also noted that any time during the day he rang that bell, the saliva glands were activated; however, if any other bell was used, there was no reaction! It was this reaction Pavlov called a conditioned reflex.

Now, as of today and just as it has always been, all people live just like Pavlov's dogs, on conditioned reflexes; and as a matter of fact, there is not one single act in the daily life of any individual which is not either directly concerned with or is actually one or a number of conditioned reflexes! However, with the average person, there may be thousands of these conditioned reflexes or even millions. In fact, they form what is more commonly referred to as the subconscious mind. These conditioned reflexes are basic constituents in what is called life and what makes life possible as a normal continuity.

These conditioned reflexes can also cause people to do many strange things. Inversely manifested as a conditioned reflex, the fear of death causes people to dance on top of flagpoles, to sky-dive and drive race cars.

The fear of drowning can inversely make a person a channel swimmer or a scuba diver.

Sex, in all of its manifestations, is a conditioned reflex; inversely, it can help to create in certain people homosexuality. Inversely, too, certain conditioned reflexes cause many kinds of masochism, sexual gratification through physical pain and suffering or flagellation. A conditioned reflex causes either our foot to move on the gas pedal or the brakes as the traffic lights change, and like Pavlov's dogs, we drool when we pass a hamburger stand and smell the aroma of cooking meat.

Now, after some thinking on the subject, you can see that this subject composition is indeed a very complex and intricate proposition. Actually, billions of oscillating wave forms are involved, some harmonically attuned and others adversely. All of these little wave forms are part of the psychic anatomy and in many areas oscillate harmonically with it. In some cases and with certain conditioned reflexes, past lifetimes are very actively concerned in this oscillating condition.

An allergy, like hives from strawberries, is actually a former bloody episode reactivated by the red, juicy strawberry. The conditioned reflex instigates a certain chemical reaction in the body which appears as little bumps called hives. Actually, this reaction and all other similar allergic reactions were subdivided into such consonants as a guilt complex. In reality, the total complex of conditioned reflexes could hardly be divided even though such contemporaries as Freud defined what he called the primary complex as sex.

The subdivision of this conditioned reflex complex is like carrying coals to Newcastle; or we might find an analogy in the four blind men who tried to describe an elephant after each one felt a different portion of the elephant's anatomy.

In any human, this conditioned reflex complex not only incorporates the present life but all other preceding lifetimes, yes, even back and beyond the time where any practical revelations might be attained by a clairvoyant diagnosis an extension of present-day psychosomatics.

So you see, there isn't really anything too difficult in understanding your own personal psychology, provided of course, you can do so objectively and not make your analysis under the insidious and unnoticed influence of a number of conditioned reflexes.

It is also well to remember Pavlov's dogs in your daily concourse of life and as you go about your life. Are all of the things you do the result of conditioned reflexes or are you more constructively-minded, and can you try to find a more intelligent continuity, a reasonable purpose, or any other factors which would help to keep your face pointed in that forward, upward direction on the path of your personal evolution?

A conditioned reflex is, of course, highly useful, even a way of life to a jungle beast. Even mankind on this planet earth has not yet escaped the boundaries of this conditioned reflex life.

In a more ultimate and progressive position in life, such conditioned reflexes are quite senseless and useless. Consciousness is maintained as an integrated factor through attunement—attunement which can and does harmonically relate consciousness to an infinitely intelligent infinity. Also, such subversive influences as the fear of death and a host of other earthly fears are no longer present, for in oscillating infinitely there is infinite security.

Therefore, waste no time; begin immediately to separate yourself from the world and Pavlov's dogs. True, you no longer have a tail to wag but the motivations of your earth life are still, in many respects, just as strong as they are with the animals who have tails to wag.

And when your life is no longer an activated continuity of conditioned reflexes, then mark that place with a headstone with this epitaph engraved, "Here lies my old self—my old life. Rest in peace!"

Oh, Sweet Mystery of Life

(On Lesbianism, Homosexuality, etc.)

During the past several years, considerable emphasis has been expressed on certain segments of human society which is called homosexual, heterosexual, lesbianism, etc., and apparently, as the emphasis has grown, so has the mystery of the why of these different sexual deviations.

The mystery can be very easily solved in the context of our modern electrical physics and anyone who understands the basic laws which underlie and control electrical energy can understand not only sexual deviations but also any and all of the other so-called mysteries now currently confronting human society.

Long ago, Einstein proved that all mass is energy—complex electrical units called atoms, and he also proved the existence of adjacent dimensions which he called the fourth, fifth, sixth, etc.

Like all other things on this earth, human beings are actually electrical energy. There are countless billions of atoms which comprise the body compounded as molecules, cells, etc. This body is controlled and regenerated by a second body called the psychic anatomy which has, in the past, been referred to as the soul. This psychic anatomy is more properly a fourth-dimensional body; that is, it is composed of billions of small or larger wave forms of energy which revolve endlessly within themselves and again, according to Einstein, have merged time with space. Their starting and stopping place is within the circumference of their oscillating motions.

This psychic anatomy has been developed in its entire context from a number of lifetimes, a true understanding of reincarnation. Starting as a very primitive savage, any human can and does, through scores or hundreds of lifetimes, develop this psychic anatomy as a conductive process in the concourse of everyday life. The daily life experience of any human is a two-way oscillating process between the psychic anatomy, the conscious mind, the control and reproduction of cells and other life processes, etc.

During the course of this development of the psychic anatomy from life to life, it may gradually become polarized in either one or the other sexual gender; the degree of polarization varies in every human. Modern psychology says every human male or female is ten to forty percent of the opposite gender, now easily understood as a polarization derived from previous lifetimes.

At the moment of conception a disincarnate psychic anatomy, a human spirit (in a spirit world) attaches itself harmonically to the newly-forming fetus. This attachment is made possible by a certain harmonic compatibility which exists with the psychic anatomies of the parents; however, the newly attached psychic anatomy rarely has the determinant qualities necessary to determine the physical sex of the fetus and the future child. This physical sex determination is usually arrived at in the familiar genetical equation—the pairing off of their respective chromosomes and gene structures. That is why the newborn infant may physically be a male but the psychic anatomy which engenders all life within the body may be female.

Now again as consciousness in life is a two-way oscillating condition, the child is constantly in this manner, making basic computer-like derivations in the present from past lifetime experiences lived in other lives as a female. And although the child is physically male, he (or she) will, of course, be attracted to other males—hence, a homosexual, and conversely, the same is true in lesbianism. The amount of mix-up in sexual

33

attitudes will depend very largely upon the amount of sexual polarity development which was attained in other previous lifetimes. Heterosexuality is also one of the many variations found in this situation.

The proposition of reincarnation from life to life and the embodiment of all human traits and characteristics in the psychic anatomy will also explain many other mysteries of life—mental retardation, genius, aptitudes in various arts and sciences, certain familiarities expressed by certain people to certain other people, countries or places—and there have been thousands of authentically recorded cases which undeniably link a respective person with a past lifetime. Thus, properly established, this reincarnation concept also explains why certain people become murderers, thieves and other types of deviations, cerebral palsy, muscular distrophy and other so-called genetical defects more properly related to other lifetime experiences, psychic shocks, etc., and a host of other derelictions and incurable diseases. Even cancer can be traced back to previous lifetime experiences which involved psychic shocks which left their indelible oscillating-impression in the psychic anatomy to be regenerated as an "incurable" disease in the present. This principle will also explain the historical rise and fall of civilizations.

Most properly then, the entire earth, the solar system and the physical universe is an extension or plane surface of expression from the fourth, fifth and sixth-dimensional universes. As Jesus said, "In my Father's house are many mansions." And so again, all things must be properly reduced to their expressionary values, oscillating wave forms of energy instigated and propagated in a regenerative process from an adjacent and higher dimension.

Atomic Science from Eros

You have heard it said that God can be likened to a Universal Intelligence that is all-pervading, omnipotent and omnipresent. This is quite true in the generally accepted understanding. However, God is the expression of Infinity and, in such an expression, must manifest Himself, not only in Infinity but in every finite way. This is done on the generally accepted equation of the atom. The scientist of today knows of about 101 basic atomic structures which he calls elements.* This he has placed in an atomic scale, ranging from the lightest to the heaviest. He has theorized that this lightness or heaviness is determined by certain minute particles known as electrons or, as they are sometimes called in their relationship of positive or negative charges, neutrons or protons—the latter being the generally accepted idea of what composes the nucleus or core of this atom.

Now, strangely enough, the scientist has never seen an atom nor any of the tiny particles of which it is supposed to be composed. It is also rather strange that he has succeeded in building up a whole new science about this hypothesis. The scientist is not, however, quite correct in assuming that an atom is composed of solid particles revolving in orbits around a nucleus. What might appear to be a solid electron or neutron would be, if it could be examined, simply an aggregate mass of tiny cycular wave forms. These wave forms are, of course, held together in a frequency pattern by a flux of energy which is actually energy expressed in another dimension which stems from the central vortex of the atom, which has erroneously been called the nucleus.

*The amount has since risen to about 110 in 1977.

35

This central vortex is actually, in a sense of the word, a tiny hole through which this free-moving intelligent energy from an outside dimension enters into the atom. This energy is actually the controlling God force of the atom and in expressing this intelligence into the atom, determines not only its characteristic, elemental make-up or atomic weight, but is also the dominating characteristics which enter into molecular structures which, in turn, can become cells and living tissue in the body.

Each cell can be said to have, not only its predetermined cell-structure life intelligence, but carries also the numerous intelligences which are a part of the original elemental atomic structures. Therefore, in the final analysis, any element can be said to be that particular element—not because of supposed particles revolving in orbits, but rather, intelligence expressed through the central vortex and remanifested and individualized as its characteristic elemental substance.

An atom exists simply because of the continuity of the life force of God which flows into it. Any disruption which may alter this flow or which would cause frequency changes in the flux densities which hold the wave forms together will seriously impair or destroy the original superimposed intelligence. Such atoms, composing cell tissue in the body will, upon entering into this disrupted continuity, become cancerous or they may reflect other and diverse conditions. One of the factors entering into the disruption of the intelligent life force of the atom comes through the interrelated concepts and facets of man's life, which may be referred to as negation. No cures within a diseased body can take place until this negative process is temporarily stopped and reversed.

Under an intense positive condition of mind, a person can, temporarily, elevate his consciousness to a point which is above the low level of negation in such a condition; a temporary or permanent alignment can take place within the atomic structure of the body which will reinstate the continuity of the life-giving intelligence. The dominant factors of such spiritual levitation can be found in the emotional stresses which are sometimes induced by intense pain and suffering, and with the desire and need to be well and happy, will, when combined with the strong conviction which is called faith, or the belief in the Supreme Creative Principle of life, and are all factors which enter into spiritual healing—induce cancellation of the negative block.

A more logical course to pursue, however, is one in which the logic and reasoning of the individual knows of this life-giving continuity which is continually pouring into every atom of his body. He will therefore assume a more logical course in his evolution, and live a more progressive spiritual life.

Do Saucers Fly In Our Gravitational Field?

Steinmetz says that saucers are neutral and work outside the field of gravitation or physical laws. A dimension encompasses a field of atomic structures which obey certain physical laws. The difference of dimensional characteristics is expressed in the way atomic structures are subjected to physical laws. Each dimension has its own set of physical laws.

The universe can be likened to a venturi tube. The large end of the funnel represents infinity to where space and time is compressed down to the center axis which is somewhere near the point of mass of atomic structures. Then it re-expands into sub-infinity or the largeness becomes the smallness with the expanding perimeter of the tube so that space and time expand into a counter-direction.

In other words, the microscopic world represents the point where expansion takes place into the sub-infinite dimensions. It expands smaller and smaller as it drops or raises in dimension. Energy is always reciprocating from time into space, and space into time, or from infinity into sub-infinity.

Light, for instance: a huge circle of light is a bright, white, hot steel band that represents 186,000 miles per second. Within that band are all the known atomic structures or elements, and this band forms the ring or the exact center of the venturi tube. At that point only, do atoms or energy travel at 186,000 miles per second. Beyond this point there is a constant expansion of the speed of light or energy. Multiply two and one half times the square root of any given point of the speed of light, at the point of expansion. As it approaches infinity it increases speed. The point of terminal velocity of the speed of energy when it reaches infinity means the complete elimination of time and space. Einstein says he was working on this when he left the planet Earth.

Time is only the relationship of energy in a certain dimension.

Beyond the place of ego consciousness, beyond the place of the physical body, need be the pure realm of consciousness. Many reflect the first plane of relative mastership, others reflect the second plane. There are seven realms of God's kingdom in which all spiritual forces unfold and are accounted for. Only the very highest thinkers of earth are in the first, second and third plane of mastership.

As water seeks its own level and the lodestone attracts its own element, man in his Spiritual Consciousness revolves into his own consciousness within cycles of the fourth dimension. These things of earth may be called time and space or the passing of the old one. You will find great groups, affected by cosmic laws, will represent fragments of the last generation, and start a new generation. It is a passing of the old and the coming of all new, for the bells of Heaven have struck; and while they are still ringing, their thunder will be felt until the eons of all time.

What is the Sun?

To the earth scientist the sun is only a hard core or nucleus of energy which expresses frequency in an earth or material spectrum; however, the sun is actually larger than our entire solar system. If we refer back to our concept of the atom, here is an allegorical equation. The atom has the hard core or nucleus which is the central vortex, while around in space surrounding this nucleus are vibrations or circular tracts of energy wave forms which carry positive and negative charges.

Our solar system functions just the same way. It is actually a blown-up atom on a tremendously large scale. The various planets are revolving around the nucleus or sun, on orbits which are wave form patterns. The planets, themselves, although they may appear solid, are only so because they are a product of concept. Actually, each planet, in turn, represents a hard core, or nucleus of energy. Surrounding each planet and out into space are the unseen, invisible fluxes which you have called magnetic forces. This is a misnomer. These so-called magnetic structures are actually connecting spectra of energy which connect the whole structure of your solar system with the radiant energies which surround it in free space.

Thus you see, from our perspective, we view your whole planetary system as a tremendously enlarged atom; as one of such similarly related component parts which form, in either case, the positive and negative charges or, as the planets themselves, whichever the case may be.

I hope your earth scientists are able to lift their vision sufficiently to see this. If you consult your encyclopedia, you will see that all planets in your solar system are revolving around the sun in a counter clockwise rotation and on a flat plane. Likewise, you will see such pictures of spiral nebulae, such as you call the universe, are also pictured in a flat plane— something like a large disc with many radiating curved lines like a pinwheel. If you consult your history books, you will read where once, man believed the earth was flat and pushed around the sun by an Angel. This you know now is a fallacy. So, likewise, in the future, you will recognize that the flat plane appearance has also been an illusion. Your solar system, just as your universe, is only a small fraction of the vast parabolas of space; and while your concept seems to relate you in this astronomical aspect, as flat plane surfaces, yet you are as the small boy standing in the middle of a vast plain, and in looking about you, you may think it is flat, but it is actually only a small, remote fraction of the total surface of your earth planet.

So, when the day comes when you travel in free space, you will find definite barriers or lines of demarcation which are beyond the speed of light. Such barriers or lines are actually curved planes or surfaces which are oscillating in their particular frequency which relates them, in the law of harmonic relationship, to all other dimensions.

More on Interdimensional Science—the Sun

We can relate the Infinite Cosmos as being a great ball or an infinite sphere of infinite proportions composed somewhat like the molecular interlinkage of the soap bubble as it is seen to appear under a microscope, and so far as planets, dimensions or atoms are concerned, these things appear on the subsurface or on the extreme exterior surface—thinking of infinity as this great sphere—atoms, themselves, appearing in direct proportions. Just as with planets such as the earth, or even the solar system or the universe itself, they all compose the surface or the skin of this great infinite globe or ball. That is not exactly a true picture but that is the one way the human mind can conceive it, because the mind has to have certain definite parallels or planes in order to equate or equalize the concepts within the mind. We have to have certain points of anchorage, certain ballistics involved in order to juggle the concept within the mind; otherwise, one would become lost. So this sphere concept, in itself, could help many people to rationalize these interdimensional principles. It is very difficult for one to conceive such a thing as the tiny atom when one can put as many as 200,000 of them on the head of a pin and would not be able to see them with the naked eye; yet within themselves, they represent, as far as subinfinity is concerned, the same principle from the interior surface as does anything else. There is seen only the surface appearance of all things.

For instance, the music coming from out the radio is only the appearance of a number of sound waves which have actually started as an electronic impulse thousands of miles distant. In other words, the business of separating space, the points of origin, etc., so far as the human mind is concerned, are all basically primitive developments of consciousness. Ultimately, we have to resolve those things within our own consciousness to the point where exterior consciousness is dissolved and we can see interior consciousness to the point where it becomes all-expansive and all-inclusive. That, too, means that man is functioning from the inner of the great infinite globe instead of the exterior surface where all things are contained in dimensional relationships of the immediate perspective from the past relationships. When we are (conscious) on the interior of this great infinite globe means that we are looking outwardly in all directions at one time or seeing things infinitely.

In relating these various principles and concepts, we relate a true picture to the scientist as to how the great worlds and planetary systems are formed from out the great vortexes in other dimensions—not simply by collecting cosmic dust together; actually, it is physically impossible. There is not enough of this dust precipitation in the entire cosmic universe for such. What they call dust would have to be automatically subdivided. This is very infantile and childish. The worlds and the sun were created in one particular way: they have become the point of a great and certain particular kind of a vortex of energy which has a great variety of forces within itself; that is, negative and positive forms of energy that can be likened to centripetal or centrifugal forces that stem down into the center of the vortex and which, in turn, because of the tremendous forces involved, compress energy, so to say, into atomic forms. They collect or formulate into worlds or suns.

The scientist will find, when he gets out into so-called space, say 150,000 to 200,000 miles away from the earth, that the earth looks very much like the sun. It will have a highly charged field of force around it that is ionized, which will make the surface of the

43

earth practically invisible. One will not be able to see the surface of the earth any more than one can see the surface of Venus, because ionization is taking place with certain types of gases and certain kinds of radioactive particles that present a sort of luminosity just the same as it does around the planet Venus. The scientist has already become aware of the fact that there is a very highly charged layer up there somewhere. Anywhere from 400 to 1,000 miles out, the radioactivity is extremely intense, and that is only an indication of the things to come when he gets even farther out than that. So far as the atmosphere of the earth is concerned or the immediate vicinity of the earth, the atmosphere is comparatively free; it is almost as free as a vacuum—the same as it is in outer space when it comes to various kinds of energies. You can almost visualize it as some sort of a terrific pressure which holds or keeps the atmosphere of the earth close to its surface from the outside, in a sense of the word—pressure as it might exist in the terms of contrariwise frequency relationship.

Question: Then they could shoot their rockets out there and would not realize these facts, would they not?

Answer: No, they would not because first, there is a very necessary requisite; we first must have within our minds the possibility for them to exist or to be there, and until the scientist gets beyond this hidebound, classical, third-dimensional interpretation of everything, he is not going to get very far, even if he does get out into space. He will still have the same conflicts and problems when he does get out there, and he will never lose them until he arrives, like some of the higher forms of mankind who live in higher elevations of life throughout the infinite universe, where he can realize that the atomic forms can be changed in their vibrational rates.

By changing the vibrating rate of an atom means

44

that we are altering its respective field of force, which is gravity. There is a direct relationship between the field of force, an atom, and that of gravity; the two are synonymous in a general electromagnetic configuration. In other words, so far as the universe is concerned, the earth is merely a blown up enlargement of an atom, that is all. It is not really dense like they think it is. Density is only a comparative sense of equivalents that we have arrived at through hundreds of thousands of years of life in any particular plane of introspection.

You see, so far as all of these electromagnetic lines are concerned in the infinite universe, the lines of force around the earth can be similar in all respects to the lines of force around the two poles in the magnet, the north and the south pole. An electromagnetic line of force is not simply like a piece of string or that we draw a straight line, or a wire that we curve around the globe or earth, but such a line of force as we find it in any cosmic universe or any atom always presents two different polarities; it will have a positive and a negative polarity as far as a line of force is concerned. It can be pictured as something that is divided.

Under ordinary conditions, the balance between these two polarities in a magnetic line of force is exactly equal—just as we find it in a stepped-up version of the two poles in the electromagnet. So far as the electromagnetic poles are concerned, there is a direct interchange of energy from one pole to the other, and this particular interchange of energy is carried on to the magnetic lines of force which contain the positive and negative equivalents of each pole which, when they come into conjunction or relationship to the contrariwise polarity patterns of other lines of force from the other poles, produce a certain interchange of energy which is dynamically balanced.

Now we have the same situation existing to some

extent in the fields of force which involve the common alternating motor, the rotor coils of the armature, and the static coils which are on the frame of the motor. We find that by alternately charging them either positively or negatively in relationship to each other, that we can induce a pulling or a rotating force on the armature of that motor. That is because under these conditions we have changed the relationship of polarity or of positive and negative through the lines of force which are in effect, or in motion, at any particular given time within the structure of the motor.

The same is true with the magnet. If we take another very powerful magnet and put it in contact with the first magnet, we will find that the north and the north poles repel each other and the south and the south poles repel each other. There must be polarity interchange of energy before they attract, just as they did from one pole to the other through the lines of force. Now we have two different sets of poles and two different magnets which are expressing the same law in a different relationship. It is all possible because we have this dynamically balanced positive and negative relationship in every line of force.

It is the same situation with the sun and the earth. The energy which man believes he gets from the sun does not come from the sun at all; it is immediately around us at all times, just as it is with the sun. In our relationship to the sun through these magnetic lines of force, there is always a completely dynamically balanced condition which, like the motor, changes by the rotation of the earth—changes in its respect so that the polarities are shut off when we turn away from the face of the sun, so that we do not induce any more of the energy transference into the various different spectra which we associate with heat, light, etc.; because all of the interchange of energy which takes place in the process from the sun to the earth is done through the magnetic lines of force. It takes place continuously, not only in the immediate vicinity of the earth but it takes place simultaneously on the surface of the sun at the same time—or within or through the very core of the sun, more correctly to say. This is done just as it is in the structures of the two poles of the horseshoe magnet. In that sense of the word, we have completely eliminated time and space, because it is an instantaneous exchange of energy in our relationship to polarity patterns of lines of force, in respect to the lines of force on and about the sun. These lines of force are either balanced or again are unbalanced so that there is a certain transference of energy from one dimension into another.

Now in the electric motor we know that it or any motor gets hot after it is in use for awhile; it has a temperature rise. That is because hysteresis in the core varies, or the very frame, the material that composes the armature of the motor, has succeeded in changing (through atomic structures and from the lines of force around each atom—and because of the same condition of polarity transference) pure electronic energy into heat energy. The same principle is active and paramount in the force fields or hysteresis which the scientist calls heat from the sun. It is this interchange of frequency and polarity patterns which results in so-called heat.

The Brain—An Electronic Computer

(The following article was printed in the Los Angeles Times, January 28, 1969, which does show the scientists are making some measure of progress; however, the brain waves they are capable of measuring are but a subharmonic and not the true, original oscillation from the subconscious or the mental consciousness of the person.)

Expert Blames Strife on "Seeing Eye to Ear"

United Nations (AP)—"When diplomats don't see eye to eye, a prominent brain specialist says, it is sometimes because they have different types of brain rhythm. For example, he says, if one is a visual thinker and the other an abstract thinker, they may be unable to reach an imaginative compromise because they're approaching the problem "eye to ear".

The scientist suggests that some future world crises might be averted if diplomats had their brain rhythm-type stamped on their passports so that incompatibles would not be assigned to negotiate with each other.

Father of Ideas:

These ideas are advanced by Dr. W. Grey Walter in the Unesco journal, "Impact of Science on Society". Walter is director of the physiology department of the Burden Neurological Institute and a professor at the University of Ais-Marseille, France.

He says the world's population can be divided into three groups—nonvisualists, pure visualists and mixed visualists—which can be distinguished by the presence or absence of alpha rhythms, or external electric echoes of brain activity.

Walter says the antagonism between visual thinkers and abstract thinkers can cause an irrational rup-
ture of communications among scientists, politicians,
administrators, diplomats and even married couples,
destroying all chances of effective dialog. The two
antagonists think they are speaking the same language
but are not. Their mental accents, so to say, separate
them as surely as verbal accents in a class-conscious
society."

* * *

In our most recent discussions on the subject, hypnosis and other allied subjects pertinent and relevant
to brain function were discussed and it was again
firmly re-established that such adjunctive factors and
other presently existing exploratory devices and other
such expressions as are concerned with brain function
are actually electrophysical and not confined strictly
in the physical dimension as is now so totally conceived by scientists and doctors of this time; however
there are also other relevant factors which are, like
hypnosis and certain reactive mind functions, equally
important and should be discussed at this time. In
fact, there has been a whole new dimension opened
up to bring medical science up to the present time in
our comparative analysis with the Unariun texts. We
will therefore explore and discuss in simplest terms
possible what is happening in the world of science
and medicine today.

Quite recently, certain doctors in hospitals and
clinics have developed a treatment which they believe
is valuable in the cure of Parkinson's disease—a certain condition which causes a trembling or palsy of the
extremities. By merely drilling or cutting a hole in the

top of the skull and inserting a long hollow probe down into the hypothalamus, they then circulate liquid nitrogen which has a temperature of some 200 degrees below zero Fahrenheit. A certain portion of this hypothalamus is frozen and there is an immediate cessation of the trembling palsy-like symptoms of the patients; the doctors believing that such results are a cure. There has been no explanation as yet into any other far-reaching effects of what such a process might involve.

Also equally relevant are certain types of lobotomies —brain operations which actually sever certain portions of the brain, the belief being that they will cure certain criminal tendencies or that they may correct certain types of insanities. Again on this subject, it is quite openly apparent that the man of medicine or the scientist does not know anything about the psychic anatomy and is conducting his research and operative techniques purely within the physical dimension. There is currently available to everyone through medical books and other types of journals, a total and complete synthesis of all currently available knowledge as it has been so compiled by the medical scientific professions, the structure of the brain and its many billions of cells, the different portions of the brain, the cortexal layers and the underlying thalamus and even into the terminating hypothalamus. All of these structural compounds have been so illustrated and documented that even the small child has this information available to him.

But again, the most important part of this whole consensus of knowledge is missing and that missing portion is, of course, the true human, the psychic anatomy—the energy body—a fourth-dimensional adjunctive body living in complete control and harmony with the physical body, and through certain kinds of inductive relationships, the process of life, thinking, consciousness, etc., is carried on through an extremely complex principle of electrical impulses which I have defined as sine waves, vortexal patterns within the psychic anatomy, the different planes of transmission, etc., and each brain cell does, in itself, represent an individual transmitter and receiver in this conductive and receiving process.

Now so far as the operation which is done is one which is basically developed from the science of cryogenics or super-cold, this is a very simple elemental process of destroying part of the brain. The doctor does not know that in the process of life in some way, due to certain life experiences, shocks, etc., certain spurious harmonics were set up within the brain wave patterns which relate certain information through this inductive process into the control of the vital motive centers of the body. All humans have certain planes of reference, I shall call them, wherein these electro-inductive processes are carried on much the same as we would find a tuned wave emitting from a transmitter.

All humans carry different wave frequencies, just as do the transmitters carry different vibrating impulses wherein such electronic circuitry as is contained in a television set, for example, can function normally according to these predetermined frequencies. When the probe is inserted into the hypothalamus and it literally destroys part or most of the hypothalamus, it merely interrupts these certain harmonic patterns. It has not, in any sense of the word, corrected the originating cause which is basically a series of impulses stemming from the psychic anatomy which generated spurious harmonic frequencies and thus produced the trembling of the limbs. The hypothalamus is the connecting link between such brain functions and certain physical reactive processes which are expressed by the body and in any normal capacity with any human, these types of harmonic frequencies represent these base plane references of which I have spoken.

This principle is equally true with organ transplant, such as heart, kidney, etc. All humans have these base plane references and are tuned differently either to a small or to a larger degree. In the final synthesis, all these compound electronic impulses stemming from the psychic anatomy into the physical, represent, individually speaking, certain different textures, I shall call them, in this total synthesis. Now in the defense mechanism of the body, the leucocytes, for example, as they have been born and bred, so to speak, through evolution and in the normal human anatomy, are tuned to these frequencies and they recognize them in every one of the many and almost countless billions of cells in the human anatomy; and to each individual leukocyte these are friendly signals. The leukocyte will defend any one or all of these cell structures to the death because they are tuned sympathetically to it and it recognizes these impulses.

However, if we introduce an organ into the body which does not have the same correlationship of tuned frequencies, the leukocyte immediately recognizes the differences and attacks the cell structure because this is exactly the function which it was developed to do through evolution. Any foreign substances such as germ cells or bacteria which enter into the human anatomy are immediately attacked by the leucocytes because they do not represent these vibrating impulses. A heart transplant, for example, functions exactly the same way, except instead of a germ organism, we have a heart organism and the doctor who made the transplant must, from that moment on, introduce drugs into the system of the transplant patient which will destroy the leucocytes and keep them down to a level where they cannot damage the newly introduced organ.

In time, it is quite possible of course, that this new heart or kidney, whichever the case may be, may to some extent, due to the reconstruction processes, be sort of indoctrinated or re-acclimated so that it will at least partially vibrate to these different vibrating structures of the normal human psychic anatomy which is in command of that physical body. However, the problem here and the ratio of incidences of failures or successes are astronomically against such transplants which, of course, accounts for the almost total failure of any transplant patient—or victim, whichever you prefer, to live beyond a certain predetermined time. The longest living kidney transplant at the present happens to be two years for only one person. A heart transplant has lived now beyond the time of one year. (Since this period he, too, has died.) Here again we are involved in the semantics of what constitutes the value of life, what people will place upon an extra added year or two of living in this material earth world and to their general lack of knowledge of what lies beyond this third dimension, all of which I have presented in the books and texts of the Unariun curriculum.

Now getting back to the proposition of a lobotomy or the severing of a certain portion of the brain which to the doctor or neurosurgeon may hopefully represent control of certain types of insanity: now, as I have said, this lobotomy operation is not new; it was performed by the Egyptians one or two thousand years B.C., and certain very primitive aboriginal tribes also developed their own type of cranial surgery, such as scraping or cutting out the bone, making a hole, the purpose of which was ostensibly to let out a demon which caused a headache. Today this same type of surgery has, hopefully, a much more therapeutic or corrective value.

In 1848, a Swiss doctor performed the first lobotomy; the success of this operation, however, was not particularly promising. In 1947, a certain criminal named Millard Wright, at his own request, had a lobotomy performed upon him. As a burglar and a sexual pervert, he was finally turned loose into the world and while he had previously committed his crimes without compassion or remorse, the difference was that now he went back to his old criminal activities but with a conscience and this conscience bothered him so much that he finally committed suicide. However, he did write a book on his experiences which can be obtained at the present time. The name of the book is "The Dark Side of the House". (Dial Press)

Lobotomies are being presently experimentally performed on certain types of criminals for the express purpose of trying to make them, in a sense, forget these criminal propensities; and by isolating a certain portion of the brain by simply cutting or severing it from the rest of the brain, the surgeon or doctor has tried to correct this condition. Again, this is a very crude and primitive approach and quite obviously points out the glaring fact that all scientists, doctors, biologists, etc., engaged in such exploratory or therapeutic practices upon the races of mankind as of today, know absolutely nothing about the true causative agents in any of these human derelictions and illnesses. They have absolutely no knowledge of the psychic anatomy or of the electrophysical process involved in this life process. The same proposition is quite true in the shock treatment therapy which has been quite extensively used in the different psychiatric wards and hospitals of the country, the idea here being simply to try to interrupt certain types of brain wave patterns as they were graphically illustrated on the encephalograph.

Now it's quite easy to see that the introduction of a considerable jolt of electricity into the brain is going to do some damage. It's going to disrupt certain oscillating patterns and wave forms. If this constant electrical process is continued and these jolts are continuously superimposed, then permanent damage will result. While the brain cells themselves do not contain, nerves, nor are they interconnected by nerve structures, there is a placenta-like nerve involvement throughout the brain wherein the different structures or portions of the brain are so interconnected. One of these main nerve connections is called the vagus nerve—the one which conducts as a main trunk line the nerve impulses into the physical body; the sense of sight, feel, hearing, etc. There is also, between these different brain cell structures, the cortexal layers and the thalamus, a fibrous-like material and surrounding the entire brain is a plasma.

Brain tumors of numerous kinds and from numerous causes can also manifest themselves within any portion of one of these brain lobes. The correct diagnosis, the placement or the exact position of the tumor and any operative procedures or techniques can be developed from some rather ingenious developments which have recently been brought about. This development involves a radioactive isotope which is introduced into the venous system. There, this radioactive substance goes into the brain and by an electronic instrument which moves with a stylus probe across the skull, a graph or chart is made and which, like a geiger counter will, through different densities of spots, locate where the tumor is, because the theory being, the tumor absorbs more of the radioactive substance than do the surrounding brain cells and by using this geiger counter instrument and its stylus probe to move across the cranium, the brain tumor can be quite accurately located and is far superior to the former process of draining the cranial fluid, introducing nitrogen gas and taking X-ray pictures.

Now, of course, brain surgery for tumors can be and is quite productive in a sense that some lives are saved, but again the semantics which are involved, and quite obviously the doctors do not know the originating cause of this brain tumor which could have been a bullet in a former lifetime or a blow on the head with a club or a stone ax. Any one of a thousand different causations could have, in some previous life, remanifest as a tumor in the present because the malfunction has not been corrected in the psychic anatomy. And this is really what Unarius is all about—to present, not only individually to a student the pertinent facts which are involved in the personal evolution wherein a true corrective therapy can be instituted, but also on a grand scale as it totally involves humanity. This therapeutic knowledge and subsequent practice could be instigated to the degree that the now currently unknown and incurable diseases would all quickly yield to that magic which is involved in the simple process of knowledge, the application of feedback, correction of the different malignant anomalies which are in the psychic anatomy and thus free this particular person from any future redevelopments and subsequent pain, and even death from these psychic anomalies and malfunctions.

It might be well to mention, too, that any of the many other different mental aberrations now classified in psychology or psychiatry or materia medica can also very easily and logically be explained. Take the proposition of the retarded child, the epileptic—and an epileptic is one in which we have quite a similar proposition as is found in Parkinson's disease—there is a buildup in the psychic anatomy and in the brain cell structures, a certain spurious harmonic pattern which, when it is built up to a certain point, discharges and practically, for a time being, paralyzes all normal brain functions. The person then is said to be having an epileptic seizure. It is quite possible to prevent such seizures by merely changing certain wave form patterns and by discharging certain other harmonics which are being regenerated in the psychic anatomy, a simple process of analysis and corrective therapy along these well-established concepts which I have presented.

There is, of course, much more which could be discussed in relationship to these different types of mental aberrations and the position which materia medica or the medical profession and science, as a whole, takes on this proposition of life, a tremendous and highly complex proposition which is not physical or biological but which is basically electrical. It should be defined and understood as such. The cell structures in the body compounded of molecules should always be visualized as atoms; and as atoms they are electrical constituents and vibrate or oscillate according to well-known and predetermined laws of harmonics, all interconnected in what I have described as electromagnetic fields of force, with each other as molecules; and as molecules, with each other as cells, and with each other as cells combining to make organs, and as a total combination of organs, the human anatomy. The same is quite true with any other animate object upon the face of this planet; the human being, however, remaining as the most highly developed and highly complex of all such anatomies.

And so at this point we might well pause to speculate: the witch doctor in the thatched hut of a jungle village scraping away at the skull of a long-suffering patient is indeed a far cry from the comparatively highly skilled neurosurgeon in a modern operating room of some great city hospital. Yet, there are similarities; neither the witch doctor nor the neurosurgeon know the true originating causes of what they are trying to correct. Neither do these individuals recognize nor do they have any knowledge of the inner dimensions once called the Kingdom Within or the Many Mansions.

Life as a whole, and as it is so represented on such a planet as the earth, is merely a prehensile extension of the total effigy of Infinite Creation as it so manifests in all its multiplicities. It is never duplicated, but always with some either obvious or indefinable differences which, individually, relate all such consonance back into the basic principles and elements of creation itself—the ever-resurgent, regenerating and re-creating facsimile of Infinite Creation; creation as it is so presented in the vast interdimensional cosmos and interpreted individually on the planet earth as an ego —an individual ego—most necessarily developed in all its reactive factors as the supporting effigy of life itself. For life on such a planet as this earth is one of a constant conflict and a never-ending succession of alertness; an embattlement with the hostile environment. And in this planetary environment does life present what seems to be obvious conflicts and differences, yet are ever soluble when they can be comprehensively understood on the basis of evolutionary reincarnation, again one of the most necessary adjunctive prehensile supplementations of Infinite Creation.

So man becomes, while within himself all-important, a proud, boastful creature who, figuratively pounding upon his chest as he displays himself to the world, yet always must he be so identified with those whom he is trying to impress with his superiority. For this superiority lives in the redundance of those who recognize these so-called fancied superiorities, either as they are inclinated within his own texture of the ego, or as they are sublimated by outside, exterior, surface manifestations. And what then of the future? Could the future be different than it is so presented by any one of the pages of the past, or even in the differences as they manifest in the present. For the neurosurgeon could have indeed been the reincarnate jungle witch doctor, just as is the atomic physicist who has reconstructed the nuclear holocaust within the dimension of our own time, only reconstituting the psychic effigy of the world he helped destroy in ancient Atlantis.

So, the synonyms are constantly and never-ceasingly being displayed, only properly understood as evolution or reincarnation, the proposition of life so assiduously being searched for, to be placed as an element which can be dealt with as butter and cheese, yet always the ever and never-quite-placed element of understanding which eludes the biochemist, the biologist, the astrophysicist, the doctor, or any one of those who have, either in scientific or in philosophical trends, searched for the enigma of life; yet so simply presented in the constant and never-changing facade of life as it is so presented ever and about us. The cause, the answer and the constant deployment of these creative principles are some of the most redundant factors of our lives, yet are never comprehensively understood or even suspected that they are there. For always must this inescapable life factor be so placed within comprehension as a cell, a molecule or whatever it is that the nomenclature of that science so invents to substitute a comprehensive understanding against the insanity of his biological world.

So let them indulge in their cranial surgeries, their lobotomies, their transplants; despite the affluences and incomprehensible extensions of man's inquisitive seekings, there are always checks and balances—built-in checks and balances against such inordinate and incomprehensible extrusions of evolution. For man himself does, in the final consensus of all such insanities, destroy not only the desire to propagate and instigate such insanities but these insanities in themselves are self-destructive. Only within the context of a universal interdimensional cosmos can we find the true answer to what life is, its origins and to whatever terminus we, individually, may expect in our evolution; a terminus which is always and ever present according to how we define and confine our own mental stature within the structure of our understanding, to how we

let the ego structure build itself into gargantuan proportions and completely contradictory to such a com-
prehnsive understanding. For the ego is, in itself, a
great monster—an ever-present monster—that while it
may, to some degree, be justifiable as an implemen-
tation for life upon the planet earth, yet this ego must
always be comprehensively understood and rebuilt as
evolution so dictates; and as evolution so dictates, so
shall our environments change. And with the changing
of our environment is a commensurate understanding
and comprehension of all that which is involved.

To the doctor, the neurosurgeon who performs a
lobotomy, perhaps he has indoctrinated himself in his
own ego structure that he is performing the most ultimate in the consensus of human understanding, yet
infinitely small and abysmally ignorant when it is compared to the entire facade of Infinite Creation. So let
the moral lesson remain; we as instrumentations of
Infinite Intelligence must always be completely ductile
to the proposition of infinite evolutionary progression.
We must ever change—change in our environmental
attitudes and our environments—change within ourselves as to our attitudes toward all things, change in
our comprehensions, yet always remaining steadfast to
those principles from which Infinite Creation was so
compounded.

More on Mind Function

(A Discussion to Ruth)

Using the chart which was drawn in the lessons on mental function could be most helpful in conjunction with the following:

Up until now, we have only discussed the very relative, or very primary reactions. It has all been a comparatively simple realization of what actually takes place in the mind in the process of thinking. There is so much more to it that we have to understand if we are going to explain all of the processes of memory: what it means to induct a thought or to reconstruct a thought and what it means to start the memory process.

Now for one thing, the scientist of today knows he can take a little fine wire-like probe with a little electricity on it and he can touch certain portions of the brain, one of the outside layers of the brain they call the cortex. Now with this little bit of current, the person who is undergoing the test has instant flashbacks and memories of instances that happened in his past lifetime; he may see the time he got married; when he was a little boy going to school, and so on and so forth. Any number of these incidents seem to flash in memory when the operating doctor places this little electric probe in different portions of the cortex in the front part of the brain, the frontal lobes, so this is all a great mystery to him because he doesn't know exactly what happens. The reason is because he doesn't possess the picture, the whole complete picture of what is actually functioning and what is in operation at the time because he doesn't know anything about the psychic anatomy, except he realizes, of course, in some way through his subconscious, but he doesn't know just what it is.

For instance, another one of the mysteries he doesn't know about is how we have life and death; why a person will be born, grows up, starts to deteriorate, grows into old age and finally dies.

There is a very logical and simple explanation for that too, because it is simply a cycle. We have to remember that every time a person dies, all of the elements which remain in the subconscious at that time of death are discharged. All that remains of that person is what has been polarized in the mental part of the psychic anatomy from out of that subconscious. Therefore, when a person is reborn again to this world, he does so without that subconscious part of his psychic anatomy; so he starts to construct that part of the psychic anatomy on this basic life cycle that he previously had. It's like building a new house on an old foundation, we shall say.

The life cycle as it was engendered, for instance, from realizations of many, many past lifetimes and many associations, regenerated this life cycle so that it included about three score and ten years of life a man is theoretically supposed to live, so on this cycle he begins to rebuild the subconscious. Therefore, throughout that lifetime, he will be able to remember everything that goes into that subconscious, providing it has a certain greatness or intensity that it can construct some part of a vortex of energy in that subconscious part of the psychic anatomy and, in turn, will of course polarize a certain facsimile or certain picture in the vortex of the mental part of the psychic anatomy. That remains with him forever because in the mental part of the psychic anatomy, we find what is called or referred to as the akashic record. In other words, anybody who is clairvoyantly trained can tune in to the mental part of the psychic anatomy and see these pictures. The reason they remain there forever is because they are oscillating with the superconscious.

Now we have to obtain the overall picture. This psychic anatomy can be pictured as something like a pulsating or a breathing ball of radiant energy and the various different parts of it, such as the subconscious part, the mental part and finally, highest of all, the superconscious vortex. When we obtain that little picture, we will see that all of the past lifetimes are breathing in and out, we shall say, from the mental consciousness. Now we will carry our picture on a little further and find out just exactly how this energy functions. We should remember that energy can also breathe or oscillate. Now for it to oscillate, it means it has to go through the phase reversal, 180 degrees, as a wave form, whether it is contained in a cycle or whether it goes as a singular wave form, along a wire or radio impulse through the air. It is like putting one foot forward, then bringing the other one up—it's left and right, left and right—that is, positive to negative, negative to positive. That is the 180-degree reversal. Now any transposition of energy, I don't care what it is, has to maintain some relationship to that.

Even a storage battery has to do that because one pole of a storage battery is positive, the other one is negative at the same time. They call that direct current but there is the same submission to principle there in the storage battery as there is in anything else. However, we are considering only alternating current impulses throughout this psychic anatomy in conjunction with the brain cells.

Now we get up to another point in our analysis here. We have to remember that every one of these brain cells—we call them transducers, and that's exactly what they are because they have a certain quality in the brain cell that permits the flow of, shall we say, one-half of the cycle to flow forward but it doesn't permit the other half of the cycle to flow backward quite so easily. In other words, there is a certain resistance in one direction with each one of these brain cells. Now as far as their own electromagnetic fields are concerned, they are so aligned, just as they would be in a magnet so that they can transduce current through these various layers, such as the cortex and the subcortex, and so on in the brain. We have to have this complete rectification of the energy impulses which perform exactly the same function as the screen of the television tube; in other words, in this relationship of energy as it is expressed back and forth in rectified units between vortical layers, this means there is a separation and integration of energy wave forms which creates the original impulse as it came into the brain. That means therefore, that now so far as the brain and psychic anatomy are concerned, they are breathing in and out simultaneously or oscillating simultaneously in a complete three-dimensional way. That is, there has to be three dimensions of these oscillations take place simultaneously, or oscillating simultaneously in a complete three-dimensional way.

Of course, one of them is a dimensional relationship oscillation of all these various brain cells in their cortical layers functioning as rectifying units to completely integrate the whole compound or complex structure of the wave forms, which were an exact facsimile of the original wave forms which came into the eyes or the ears or the nose or the mouth, or wherever the sense organ was in the human body, to complete an exact facsimile of this same experience in a reverse fashion. Now, that is memory.

In order for a person, we shall say, to reconstruct memory, we have to remember these oscillations are always sustained throughout this tri-dimensional anatomy, this tri-dimensional configuration, that is, from the different portions of the psychic anatomy into the brain and so on. Now any time a person wishes to recall a picture, it has to be done, as we will say, either from a conscious, suggestive position or an autosuggestive position. In any case, there always has to be a certain catalytic energy, we shall call it, which performs the necessary function to properly align these various complex wave structures which contain thousands of memory conscious forms within themselves which come out of the psychic anatomy. They, in turn, become the ones which are actually sorted by the various brain cells to form the complete picture. The reason they do that is because we always have some autosuggestive form which immediately confronts us either from the physical world or of such physical manifestations.

Now, if we sit and think, so far as the various functions of the brain cells are concerned we are, intercepting as it were, as a part of our realization process, any one or a number of these various configurations. That is all done autosuggestively, and one train leads to the next, etc. We always find there is a direct association with frequency relationships as they are compatible one to another before the picture can be formed. It is quite difficult for any person, an ordinary, reactionary person, we shall say, to reach right up out of the blue and get a thought without having one or a number of external factors which stimulate certain energy wave forms which, in turn, realign the various wave forms which are coming into the brain areas and which are oscillating in the psychic anatomy to that point where the brain cells now become conscious; that is, they are all functioning in unison with this same set of oscillating wave forms so that the integration process can take place and the complete picture is refabricated. So isn't it a wonderful thing?

So now we see that when the operator, the doctor or the scientist puts a small pulse of energy on any one of the cortical layers in these various frontal lobes of the brain, what he actually does is to externally supply this autosuggestive force in the form of a small potential of energy. In other words, he is merely intercepting some already existing wave forms in those brain structures which are breathing in and out of the psychic anatomy and they, in turn, are temporarily realigned within themselves so that they form a past picture. And wherever and in whatever place the operator places the probe on the brain merely means, at that particular given moment and in that particular place, there is, we shall say, a reproduction in some sort of a small facsimile of the picture which is stemming out of the psychic anatomy but which is not yet coordinated in a rectifying process with the various other brain cells in the different layers.

Now when he places that little electricity there, that automatically aligns these up with the other different brain cells so that the picture is again rectified and integrated as an exact facsimile. You can easily visualize, if you carry these things further, what automatically takes place all the time within the psychic anatomy. This is a pulse, we say a beat, which is composed of hundreds of thousands or even millions of energy wave forms which, when they are properly integrated and rectified in the brain cells, can form pictures. Any one, or a group of them, can form a part or the whole complete picture of some past incident in a past lifetime and when they are integrated with the mental part of the psychic anatomy, the past lifetimes can come in too. That is what we call reading the akashic record because we are intercepting the waves which are radiating, we will say, in the fourth dimension from the part of the psychic anatomy we have called the mental structures.

Now all of these things, of course, so far as the psychic anatomy is concerned, are fourth-dimensional energy wave forms and they are not synonymous, in a sense of the word, with the third-dimensional type because they are cyclic in motion. The third-dimensional type means they travel from one point to another as a pulse or 180-degree phase and that is what takes place in the brain. Now that is why the scientist can measure certain brain impulses. He can obtain the pattern or a picture on his encephalograph because he is seeing an outside portion of the brain which has been rectified by the brain cells.

Now we have shown in a very simple manner in our lesson course diagram, what we call sine wave A, B and C, so far as the psychic anatomy is concerned. We call those fundamental frequencies which can be compared to the pulse of the human body or the breath of the human body; that is, the psychic anatomy is breathing in and out; it is pulsating on these basic carrier frequencies. They are, shall we say, the links that tie them together. It is on these various carriers, we shall say, that the new subconscious in the new life begins to be developed because the carrier from the mental part of the psychic anatomy begins to reconstruct the subconscious in conjunction with the various experience quotients of energy which come into the newly forming subconscious from the outside world. They are, we shall say, comparatively temporary in nature; that is, they can fade simply because they can become discharged in the sense of the word that they have to depend to a large degree upon any supporting force or any supporting energy which comes into them from the psychic anatomy.

Now the psychic anatomy is more closely attuned to the superconscious, which means that the superconsciousness is actually a combination of a large number of dimensions; that is, it has an alignment with a large number of dimensions. It is composed of facsimiles of energy quotients from a large number of dimensions;

therefore, it has contact we shall say, in this broad term of reference with a certain amount of power or force which is stemming into it constantly in a regenerative wave form fashion. This gives the superconscious tremendous power—power in the sense of the word that it is a positive potential and so much stronger than any other comparative potentials in the psychic anatomy. So when it beats in various different impulses, very positive, powerful entities of consciousness come in contact with various other portions of the psychic anatomy; it will automatically transform them, or we shall say, performs in some sense of the word the same capacity as the brain cells do; it polarizes it and reconstructs out of the harmonics, an exact facsimile in another dimension of what has happened in the subconscious.

Now, this begins to all add up and make sense, doesn't it? As I said, in the lessons, the diagram we have, while it is necessarily simple for students to understand, yet we can take that up and construct a complete and valid hypothesis in any kind of a mind function, which is a great mystery to the scientist of this time and day. It is very true because we have just gone into what is memory processes, which is merely a rectification process whereby the brain cells are taking various reflective quotients of energy from the psychic anatomy and rectifying them within their various layers in such a manner and fashion that they again reproduce an exact facsimile of the whole operation which took place as an inductive experience factor. When the energy came in, it did the same thing in reverse to what is now taking place in consciousness as memory. It is an exact facsimile in every sense of the word. That is the reason consciousness begins to be realized at that moment because these various energy pulses produce just exactly the same image. We won't say exactly the same image but it amounts to the same thing as an image because it is the exact facsimile of the original experience as a series of incoming signals of energy except that now, in memory, we have reversed the process.

Now, is the picture quite clear with you, dear?—"I should say, much more so!"—It is a very wonderful process when you begin to realize that life is much more than can be fully realized from the surface. We can't evaluate any process of life from the surface. If we do, we only get fouled up and get a lot of enigmas and a lot of paradoxes and a lot of things that can't be answered.

Now what happens at the moment of death? That merely means that so far as the physical anatomy is concerned, these various sine wave frequencies which are stemming out of the psychic anatomy are broken off; they are disengaged. Because out of the psychic anatomy, and especially so far as the subconscious is concerned, there is another regrouping, we shall call them, of wave forms which contain the exact configuration of every atom in our body in relationship to its molecular and finally, its cell structure. That is true of the blood; it is true of all the bone marrow, it is true of everything there is in the system because all of these various configurations as atomic constituents in the human body are exact configurations in the psychic body, except that there they are in energy forms or facsimiles. Now they are revolving in the energy formations in the various vortexes in the psychic anatomy. They, in turn, have their own particular fundamental frequencies or sine waves which they are radiating into the physical anatomy and which are stemming into this physical anatomy as intelligent governing forces in the element of reconstructing and maintaining the metabolism of the human body.

Now, the old yogi knows about the chakras—the various centers in which the psychic anatomy makes the strongest contact with the physical anatomy or places like the solar plexus, the palms of the hands and the soles of the feet, the end and the beginning of the spinal column, and so on and so forth, and that is merely another system in which we will say there are inductions which take place according to certain polarities. Each one of these centers represents a part of a polarity system of induction so far as the psychic anatomy is concerned. And again, we find that same pulse—the breathing in and out of the psychic anatomy into the physical through these various centers—and in this breathing they carry various other component parts of these energy pictures which go to make up the reproductive process of the human body which the doctor calls metabolism.

Now when we understand these things very thoroughly, as they should be understood, as manifestations of the workings of these various formations as they are concerned either with the physical body or the psychic anatomy, then we have the true picture. We have exactly what we need to supply the answers to everything in our analysis or in reconstructing our hypothesis which will give us an intelligent view of exactly what life is.

Now at the moment of death, of course there is the severance, we shall say, in the linkage of these sine waves from the physical anatomy and also the mental part of the brain to the psychic anatomy. However, the psychic anatomy does not cease to exist. The subconscious will persist, we shall say, because it is in a dimension which is not quite as spiritual in nature (we shall say for lack of a better word) as the mental part of the psychic anatomy. In other words, it is a sort of an in-between world in the physical and third dimension and the fourth dimension, and therefore is more influenced by what the scientist calls time. So therefore, not having this supporting source of energy coming into it like it should have, like the mental part has, it will gradually fade. It will be gradually dissipated so that usually, by the time the person comes back into the world as a new creature, he has no memory of his past lifetime; unless, of course, he has that ability to mentally interject pictures from the mental part of the psychic anatomy into his conscious mind to form the picture of his past lifetimes.

Now that can happen under extreme conditions—what we call psychisms—where in moments of intense emotional stress these normally reactive wave forms are temporarily altered, which are breathing in and out of the psychic anatomy so that the biases into the brain cells are temporarily changed and the pulses swing around in the wrong direction. Then the person can see the image of the past temporarily. That is what happens at the moment of death sometimes because, in that particular moment, all of a sudden the complete cyclic movement of the whole psychic anatomy in conjunction with the physical, and especially with the brain, is temporarily reversed and he can instantly see into the mental part of his psychic anatomy, all that has ever happened to him.

And this also explains very reasonably why it is that many people are earthbound—what they call earthbound. It merely means that the purveyance or the persistence factor of the subconscious, before it completely fades, gives this person, in the spiritual world, the only thing he knows of in his immediate relationship. He actually relives his life so far as he is attuned to the new world, his spiritual world, through his fast-fading subconscious. In years' time it will eventually completely fade.

Now we can also explain how it is that we can find ghosts which haunt castles. That is a very interesting bit of diversified information we can explain very easily on these grounds. So far as the subconscious part of

71

the psychic anatomy is concerned after this person dies, if this person starts reconstructing, we shall say, a new subconscious psychic anatomy in the spiritual world from spiritual elements which he can do if he lives this thing strongly enough—he is going to construct in facsimile, the same kind of a situation that he had while he was living in the physical body. In other words, he has constructed a new subconscious psychic anatomy which enables him to rattle windows, move doors and to sound like footsteps on the stairs, because he possesses a certain physical quality, although it is almost invisible in the sense that we have to have certain lack of light to enable us to see this apparition which is really the form of the new psychic anatomy.

So we can explain all these things that people call ghosts, and various other mysteries of life are very simply, very intelligently and very scientifically analyzed; you can very easily form within your own mind the picture of what actually happens and what takes place. Therefore, we have completely debunked all of these occultisms, these superstitions and these various supernatural phenomena about which people are so impressed and the reason they are is because they are completely ignorant about how it happened.

Now you can easily understand what a poltergeist is. In other words, that is an obsessive entity that sometimes comes in and plagues people to death. We heard, for instance, about this poltergeist in New York throwing things around the room; people had to duck and it went on for months and years. Well, if we understood how we reconstructed what we call an apparition, a poltergeist is just the same thing. He has endowed this thing with the new subconscious psychic anatomy part of him with all the personal elements of his old self which were mean, nasty and hateful and he is really making things miserable for the people around him. He can actually see into the physical world. He sees well enough and he possesses enough physical strength, we shall say, in the psychic anatomy to pick up objects and throw them. On the same basis, we can easily understand how we can cast off evil spirits, exorcise, we shall say, and to right so-called psychic conditions which are puzzling people and which are not explainable in any other way except when we begin to rationalize or to build up and intelligently construct a hypothesis as we understand it in energy configurations.

You have now, and we have given you here on the tape, more than the scientist here on earth could possibly hope to achieve in the next thousand years because before he achieves what you have found out here on the tape, he has to achieve a whole and complete new dimension of prospective within his mind. He has to tear down this invisible barrier between this world and the next; he has to reconstruct his whole hypothesis, at least as far as energy is concerned, into a new set of evaluations in which he can visualize a vortex of energy—something which is complete in itself—we will call it a whole world which is complete in itself. Now he has the picture in the physical form all about him and there really isn't any reason why he shouldn't. The earth is such a thing; the earth is a whole entity. Actually, the earth as a physical mass is nonexistent. He is puzzled as to why it came together. He thinks it came together physically but it didn't come together physically. It was already together and merely made its appearance as a form of transference of energy from one dimension to another in atomic constituents. It was actually, we shall say, materialized into these atomic constituents from these great invisible worlds because of the vortical action which exists in these great invisible worlds. Within the center of this vortex, energy was transformed and retransformed into various different constituents of energy according to these positive and negative impelling forces which we have likened to centripetal and centrifugal forces, so that the end result was a group, a mass or core of atoms which formed the physical world. It didn't come out of nowhere, like cosmic dust, like he thinks about or like he thinks has happened, because that is very childish. We can't possibly imagine that a space so filled with such an incalculably fine condition would regenerate such a huge mass in the solar system, for instance. It isn't logical; besides, where did the dust come from?

Now one way or another, he is going to defeat himself in his hypothesis until he arrives at that conclusion—that all of his physical world, whatever he can see physically, comes from other dimensions. It was, in a sense, materialized in this world or inducted into this world and assumed material dimensional forms simply as the direct result of these various processes in centrifugal and centripetal action within the vortexes themselves, because all of the energy which composes our world actually existed at one time as part of energy configurations in this great vortex. That is a much more logical conclusion than the one he has and in which he is so vague about. The same is true of the sun. Because the sun only represents a positive polarity in this great vortex, so far as the apex or the interior of this vortex is concerned, the sun is only regenerating because of the intense energy pressures, we shall say, in the processes of integration and reintegration within the core of this vortex. The sun, in turn, manifests and remanifests a certain positive polarity in the third dimension, which means that this great energy pressure within the vortex is being released outwardly into this dimension in the form of energy which the scientist calls heat and light. It is very simple.

Now we can compare our world as actually being a sun in relationship with other particular different dimensions of which the world is a part. The earth could very easily be a sun to these dimensions; in the same way the electromagnetic field of the earth could shine to adjacent worlds the same as the sun shines in this world, because what the sun is called—heat and light—is only electromagnetic fields of the sun being transformed into these various earthlike constituents of energy from the processes that are happening in the great magnetic belts, in the great radiation belts around the earth in conjunction with the sun. It isn't heat or light at all; it is part of the magnetic flux in this generating form in this great vortical pattern.

So you see, what the scientist is confronted with is the ultimatum that he must eventually completely tear down all of his physical science and reconstruct a new science out of these unknown dimensions and this is not a radical theory; it has already been partly envisioned by men like Oppenheimer in 1956, when he made the statement that we have passed the point of diminished returns, and anything valuable or valid in the future will have to be reconstructed from an entirely different mathematical system. So I am not alone. I can visualize these things because I know where the source is. I know it is very foolish to try to equate infinity in a few surface appearances.

The scientist will eventually have to destroy the illusion of heat and light and various other elemental factors in the physical dimension. He will have to destroy them because they are still going to give intent and purpose to a false science. They will have to realize they are only just as much of an illusion as the atom itself is, because the atom is a great illusion so far as it is universally accepted by science as mass; because he knows very well every atom is a solar system of energy. It is actually nonexistent as mass, but he refuses to give up his old science which is built out of this mass equation. Now isn't it stupid?

Understanding the magnetic fluxes, we will call them, the magnetic field is basically part of the concept we have just previously discussed. In other words, we find in a horseshoe magnet what we call a north pole and a south pole, and the reason it is a north pole and a south pole is because all of the molecules which form the metal of the horseshoe magnet are aligned so that their electromagnetic fields are focused on the ends of this particular pole. Now that, of course, forms another alignment with the north magnetic pole of the earth and with the south magnetic pole of the earth. It doesn't make any difference which way you turn that magnet as the north-pole always is aligned in the same relationship to the earth as it formerly was. You can whirl it around your head and it doesn't change its polarity at all because the existence of these polarities are not in this dimension. Therefore, they are not affected by either time or space and have no relationship so far as mass is concerned in their polarity position.

Now that is quite hard to visualize, however, you can prove this very easily for yourself and you can do it this way. Take an ordinary little ten-cent horseshoe magnet and a needle and you face yourself toward the North; then you hold the horseshoe magnet so that the poles are upright, then you drop the needle on the poles of the magnet. Now if you withdraw the needle, it will be magnetized; but before you withdraw the needle you make a small red mark or put a piece of tape on that pole of the magnet which is closest to the north pole, which is farthest away from you because you are holding the magnet upright so the poles point straight up in a vertical position. Now if you put this needle on a little piece of wood that is floating in a basin of water, the south pole of that needle will automatically point toward the north. And it won't make any difference which way you turn that needle; it will always turn around and point right back to the North. Now if the

76

needle still stays in the same position as it did when you took it off the magnet, then you can say that you have marked the south pole of your magnet.

Now you do the same process with two magnets. When you have the correct south and north pole markers on your magnet, you will see that when you put them together—the ends of these two magnets together—if you put the north and south poles together opposite each other, there is a very strong attraction; it requires quite a little pulling to pull them apart. If you reverse them, you see it takes a little pushing to keep them together. Now that is the principle of attraction and repulsion and it is the principle with which the scientist has constructed all of the motors and generators which he uses in the scientific world. It is also the principle which he uses in many other different pieces of electronic apparatus because it is a very strong force.

Now you will discover with your magnets, as I just said, that no matter which way you turn them around it doesn't change their polarity. Now that seems very peculiar (doesn't it?) when you realize that their polarity—the power of that magnet—is actually a related factor to the magnetic field of the earth? The earth, in turn, is a small magnet which is so related in exactly the same way with the sun. The sun, in turn, is another factor which is so related with every other particular stellar object in the whole universe. The universe, in turn, becomes another magnet which is so linked with every other universe in the whole cosmogony or the macrocosm, whichever you want to call it.

So now we begin to obtain an overall picture, we shall say; so far as our visible world is concerned, but these things are held together by very strong magnetic fluxes, very strong lines of magnetic force. These magnetic lines of force are not third-dimensional in nature and we haven't any instruments to measure them, for

77

one thing. The only thing we can use to determine them are certain reactive components such as iron or steel and it is extremely difficult to measure them because of the function in that borderline region between the third and the fourth dimension. They are actually, so far as we are concerned, a part of the fourth dimension because they are positively biased, we shall say, from the fourth dimension; in other words, they stem from the fourth dimension because all those magnetic lines of force are all the same magnetic lines of force that we find in the great vortexes. They are, in other words, harmonic regenerations of wave structures which hold the great vortexes together—great or small vortexes. It doesn't make any difference whether it is a vortex that comes out in the middle as an atom or whether it is a vortex that comes out in the middle as an earth, or whether it is a vortex which comes out in the middle as a sun or even a universe. The regeneration within this great vortex generates these magnetic lines of force or flux as a direct by-product or harmonic of all its internal functions. It is one of the harmonics which is regenerating into the third dimension. The reason that you can't change polarities is because you can't change the vortex. You would have to change the structures in the vortex before you could change the polarities in your horseshoe magnet.

Now we have given you a little of the advanced science on what holds the universe together and how man functions in so many other different planes of life —the spiritual worlds, or worlds where men have learned to use flying saucers and various other different things that people term supernatural phenomena, but there isn't such a thing as supernatural phenomena. In fact, there isn't any such thing as phenomena, as phenomena merely means that we have not yet directly applied logic, reason or understanding to what we can see. When we really begin to become scientifically minded, we have a very logical, a lucid and clear explanation of even the most confounding of all mysteries, the mystery of life itself and we can actually construct a cell which has life. In fact, we can construct a human being which has life. Of course the human being will have to evolve; if we so construct this human being, he would naturally have to evolve, we shall say, into a number of progressive evolutions before he would possess the power, as we call it, of individual consciousness. But we could still give the body life, and we might even eventually in our science give him all of the intelligence of which a normal human being possesses, because if a thing holds true in one case it always holds true in all cases.

To construct a cell which has life, merely means that we take some sort of a third-dimensional plasma which is a proteid combination of various proteid elements which has atomic structures or molecular structures, which can be compared as very similar to that of the brain cells. In other words, in physical function, the various cells of the human body act, in a sense of the word, as little transducers. They are relating in their own way, in their own consciousness as a product of their own frequency relationship their own particular reactive component which the scientist calls life.

Now, to construct a cell we will take some of this plasma, we will say which contains molecules constructed of various atoms, and these molecules have the faculty of rectifying—rectification being a process of integration. In conjunction with this plasmic fluid, we construct a synthetic number of wave forms. Each wave form has a certain intelligence impressed on it so that it has a certain function. We create the necessary frequencies in which these wave forms can function as a fourth-dimensional entity. When it is brought in contact with the plasmic fluid and it merges and becomes activated with it, we have a living cell because then the living cell is producing, on the outside third dimension, exactly what we have put into the fourth-dimensional entity of its consciousness or its psychic anatomy. We have merely constructed a psychic anatomy in all of the functions which we wish this cell to possess. And it will reflect or breathe in and out just as our own psychic anatomy does, into the plasmic fluid of the cell and the cell, in turn, will rectify these various oscillations of being breathed in and out of it. It will rectify them so that it will form a complete picture as a reactive component of function in the third dimension.

Now when the doctor or scientist learns of these vital concepts, he will no longer need to go to the great lengths and breadths in his present experiments to gain this knowledge. He will not need to hypnotize his patients to try (unsuccessfully) to solve their problems, and he will come to learn, as will the psychiatrists and those who work with the mentally ill in the asylums, etc., that their present-day practices are little more than archaic and quite ineffective. They must begin to learn, first of all, just what the creature they call man is—that he is, in fact, first, last and in all ways, an electronic mechanism. Not until he begins to treat his patients as such can he hope for any better results than the very low percentage he now experiences.

We, the Unariuns, do trust the scientists of today will soon alert themselves to these creative, regenerative principles of life.

Experts Fear World Famine in Near Future

Los Angeles Times — Part VII - Dec. 8, 1968

By Robert Musel — UPI Staff Writer

This could be the epitaph of the human race: "They loved children."

More warnings have been uttered by scientists on the perils of overpopulation than on any subject in modern times except perhaps nuclear weapons. Yet nearly 120 million babies squalled their way into an already crowded world in the past year alone.

Some were wanted, some unwanted, but mostly they were cherished, once they arrived (at the rate of 225 a minute), in the manner of the species.

And they added to a problem that some fear could, at its most extreme, beset a future American President with the dilemma of deciding which nations among those dependent on his country for bulk grains should eat and which would have to face starvation.

Subtract the number of global deaths last year and the population of our planet soared in 12 months by a stunning 70 million people.

Shocking Increase

It went up by a number equal to the combined inhabitants of Great Britain, Sweden, Norway and Denmark, or by as many people as now live in all of Mexico and Canada. Or, to put it another geographical way, by a mass equal to the entire population of North and South Vietnam, Cambodia, Malaysia and Taiwan.

Nearly everywhere it was a case of the rich nations getting richer—and the poor getting the children.

Rarely have scientists been as agreed about anything as they are that this must stop. The living space of the world is limited. The resources of the world are limited. If mankind does not control its fearsome fecundity it will drown in its own flesh.

This may sound like the synopsis of a horror film, but some experts are talking of the 1970s or 1980s as "the time of the famines", the last chance for the race to decide whether it will limit and save itself or whether it will plunge towards oblivion in a tragedy beyond the imaginings of science fiction.

Malnutrition Deaths

In a presidential message on population last July, President Nixon reported estimates that every day 10,000 people—most of them children—die from diseases allied to malnutrition. He spoke almost exactly a year after the hotly debated decision of Pope Paul IV to continue for Catholics the ban on the pill and other methods of contraception.

Scientists are divided into a minority of optimists and a majority of pessimists on population. The optimists believe that, regardless of the damage to the environment, "the green revolution"—prolific new species of rice and wheat—will stave off hunger until family planning takes hold and brings the birth rate down.

The pessimists are worried that the day is coming when the state will have to step in with radical solutions. Some suggestions for that dark day, compiled by the Population Council, include higher taxes on bigger families, seeding water with infertility substances, permitting the marriage of homosexuals, obtaining licenses to have children, compulsory sterilization of men with three or more living children.

Opposing Attitudes

One optimist is Dr. Jonas Salk of polio vaccine fame who argues that every living organism has an intuitive response to extreme crowding: it slows down the rate of conception. Among the pessimists are William and Paul Paddock whose widely discussed book, "Famine 1975", cites that year as the deadline for salvation of whole nations.

The Paddocks do not believe the underdeveloped world can either curb its exploding population or feed it and that sometime in the next decade the United States, unable to grow enough food for everybody, will have to make the historic and awesome decision of how to selectively distribute its surplus. They predict some improvident nations will have to be abandoned.

The Department of Agriculture concedes that a time might come when food production would not be able to stay ahead of the present rate of population increase, but it doesn't see this happening before 1984—the year of George Orwell's vision of the death of democracy. This estimate gives the world a little more breathing space, a little more time to contemplate such depressing statistics as the rise in illiteracy.

Illiterates Increase

A recent United Nations study said the number of illiterates jumped almost 60 million to 800 million in the past decade because the high birth rates simply overwhelmed the educational programs of the underdeveloped countries. More than 1 million Arabs and 4 million Africans passed beyond school age each year without having learned to read or write—and these figures are considered very conservative.

Another pessimist, Dr. Paul Ehrlich, praises the Paddock book as one of the most important of our age. His own contribution, "The Population Bomb"—the title is self explanatory—says mankind is in a race between intelligent control of population and oblivion. "What do you call people who use the rhythm method?" he asks, and gives the answer: "Parents."

There can be few in the literate world unaware that a vast and growing problem exists. Four American Presidents have spoken of it. On Human Rights Day in 1967, 30 heads of state, including President Lyndon B. Johnson, addressed a memorandum to the United Nations blaming overpopulation for damaging living standards; for poor housing, for inadequate food; for deterioration in health, sanitation and transportation, and for frustrating desires of men to lead better lives.

Creates Commission

In adding his voice last July, Mr. Nixon predicted that the present population of the United States (203 million) would leap to 300 million in the next 30 years. Warning that immediate action was necessary to save the world's environment and food supply, he announced the setting up of a commission on population growth and the American future.

Only the optimists believed his words would have much effect. The pessimists pointed out that he had stressed the freedom of the individual to select the size of his own family.

"There is no reason to expect that the millions of decisions about family size made by couples in their own interest will automatically control population for the benefit of society," said Prof. Kingsley Davis of the University of California. "On the contrary, there are good reasons to think they will not do so."

What brought humanity to this pass? Sex, of course. Mankind is the only animal who indulges in year-round sex—a wise move by nature to keep couples together during the long infancy and adolescence of the human child.

Rate of Increase

"In 1830 there were 1 billion people on the planet earth," Nixon said in his message. "By 1930 there were 2 billion and by 1960 there were 3 billion. Today the world population is 3½ billion.

"These statistics illustrate the dramatically increasing rate of population growth. It took many thousands of years to produce the first billion people; the next billion took a century; the third came after 30 years; the fourth will be produced in just 15."

Estimating more than 7 billion people in the year 2000, the President said that due to high birth rates and sharply lowered death rates, populations in many countries in Latin America, Asia and Africa are growing at a rate 10 times as fast as a century ago and some might triple in the next 30 years.

"Malnutrition, hunger, poverty and desperation are a way of life for more people than were alive 50 years ago," commented William H. Draper Jr., national chairman of the Population Crisis Committee.

Dr. Ehrlich believes the worst is yet to come. U.S. population now grows at the at least manageable figure of 1% a year, meaning it would take 70 years to double. (Population growth is calculated like compound interest.)

Ominous U.S. Future

"The U.S. low birth rate will soon be replaced by higher rates as more post-World War II baby boom children move into the reproductive years," Dr. Ehrlich cautioned, adding: "Roughly 40% of the population of the underdeveloped countries (in Asia, Africa and Latin America) is made up of people under 15. When they move into the reproductive years in the 1970s we are going to see the greatest baby boom of all time."

"They are the reasons for the ominous predictions about the year 2000. They are the fuse of the population bomb."

Population growth is not simply due to the birth of more babies. It is also the result of the continuing conquest of such diseases as malaria, yellow fever, smallpox and cholera, which cut the death rate in some undeveloped countries an average of 24%. As the National Academy of Sciences put it: "Either the birth rate of the world must come down or the death rate must go back up."

There are conflicting opinions on the urgency of the American population situation. Prof. E. F. Watts of the University of California, who thinks it possible that global pollution caused by too many people might bring back the ice age by screening out the sun, believes the United States already has twice its best number of people. By the year 2000, he says, it will have only 84% of the land needed to produce food for its 331 million people (his estimate).

Big U.S. Consumption

Lewis C. Frank Jr., of the Information Center on Population, says that in some ways U.S. population growth is more serious for the world than the explosions elsewhere because we already use over half the world's non-replaceable raw materials to support only 6% of the world's people.

"Our growth makes new demands on these resources and further imperils the world we bequeath to our children," he said.

An American mother may see her child as a bundle of joy. But the impoverished nations, wondering how to conserve their resources for their own people, are beginning to see him as a monster super-consumer who, during his life span of 70 or 50 years, will need, directly or indirectly, 26 million gallons of water, 21,000 gallons of gasoline, 10,000 pounds of meat, 28,000 pounds of milk and cream, $6,300 worth of clothing, $7,000 worth of furniture and $5,000 to $8,000 in school-building materials.

They may not always be willing to give it to him. When Africa, Asia and Latin America demand a fairer share of world resources from the developed countries of North America and Europe, there could ensue a perilous period for the world.

Use of Abortion

In Britain, a secret committee of senior civil servants has been meeting for over a year to consider how to limit population if it became necessary—one recommendation was for better use of abortion. Prof. Franc Novak of Yugoslavia told an International Planned Parenthood Federation congress in Budapest that a worldwide "abortion epidemic" has been under way—one a second, 30 million a year. The Hungarian and Romanian birth rates dropped so drastically when abortion was made freely available that the governments had to restrict it again in recent years.

Population-limiting programs are not always easy, even when government sponsored, due to religious or traditional objections or ignorance. India started the first of its kind in 1951 but despite 6 million sterilizations, 3 million contraceptive loops and an educational campaign, its population went up by 100 million in the past decade (to 537 million).

The birth control pill causes problems in poorer lands. It cannot be given to undernourished women. The theory baffles simple people. Workers have found men in India who were taking the pills so there would be no break in continuity while their wives were away seeing mother.

Trouble in China

China is hampered in its efforts to contain its colossal 740 million people by family tradition and the fact that in an agricultural economy children become assets at the age of 7 (while in industrial nations they are liabilities till they mature). This is the so-called "demographic trap" many poor countries are in—the high birth rate keeps them from advancing to the industrialization which would lower the birth rate.

Not all nations want to reduce their birth rates and some are trying hard to increase it. Former President Charles de Gaulle dreamed of a nation of 100 million people by the year 2000 but the practical French, aware the high cost in living means a drop in living standards with every additional child are not cooperating. The population is sticking stubbornly at 50 million and a new "make more babies" campaign is now being launched.

While you were reading this article, 2,250 babies were born.

*   *   *   *   *

The above transcript taken from the Los Angeles Times, as of Dec. 8, 1969, is but one of many dire prophetic predictions which clearly indicate that mankind on the planet Earth is rapidly rushing toward the precipice of extinction.

From all fronts economists, ecologists, sociologists,

scientists, etc., are making grave assertions, backed up by facts that not only is there danger of extinction from famine, we are also poisoning our environment. Carbon dioxide precipitation is changing the Earth's climate. Carbon monoxide, nitrous oxides, etc., poison the air we breathe. Fresh water streams and lakes are polluted by sewage and DDT. Even the oceans are becoming polluted.

Religions too, are falling apart as witnessed by the present Catholic revolution. Indeed, all facets of life are seriously affected by overwhelming materialism: riots, drug addictions and sexual malpractice. The solution to you individually as a Unariun student to all this, lies within the covers of your books and lessons. If you are to survive and gain immortality in a higher world, then preparation is a "must". This world like many others must be left to its own evolution; a beginning and an end to those who do not pursue the evolutionary pathway.

Astrology vs. Harmonic Regeneration
(This article was given in 1970.)

On a number of occasions I have been asked if I believe in astrology, or certain students may have implied a belief in astrology and that I should therefore establish some criteria of judgment. Briefly, then, as a direct answer: no, I do not believe in astrology per se, as it is now, or even as it was historically practiced. Astrologists are not scientists and they cannot therefore delineate solar mechanics as involving a large number of known and unknown electromagnetic fields which are not only integral factors of our solar system, but must be considered as part of the intergalactic and inter-universal electromagnetic fields. The total comprehension involved is extremely complex and far beyond the reach of any earth mind—even our most advanced scientists who specialize in astrophysics, calculus, etc.

The first consideration, therefore, is at least some comprehension as to what these complex electromagnetic fields consist of, how they work, and so on. In the second Lesson Course is a primary presentation of the interdimensional vortexes which give rise to stars, suns, planets, atoms, even molecules. The tremendously compressed energies form the core or nucleus of the vortex which, under cyclic law, regenerates into atomic forms which become, in part, the elements familiar to the earth scientists. These vortexes revolve around within themselves and also assume circular orbits similar to our present-day known astronomical concept of the solar system. These solar systems, planetwise speaking, can be considered as eddies. Likewise, the galaxy and the universe assume their own basic patterns in their revolutions and actual photographs of these galaxies, such as Andromeda, are familiar to everyone.

Now this vast intercosmic interplay infinitely fills the space around our little planet. There are unheard of and unknown electromagnetic fields of great intensity, any or all of which could be as influential as the more common denominators known to the astrologer. In totality, these entire interdimensional mechanics should be considered steady state, that is, any time differentials, as we might interpret these cyclic motions, would occur at extremely regular intervals. Present-day astronomers can predict thousands of years in advance, the exact positions of all nine planets (plus moon configurations) at any given time, which directly proves the steady state condition which exists in the interdimensional cosmos.

Some of these known and unknown cyclic movements occur at tremendous speeds. It is believed certain heavenly objects travel in speeds measured close to the velocity of light (186,000 miles per second). There are unknown cyclic movements in this interdimensional cosmos which travel millions of times the speed of light but speaking closer to home, the earth travels around the sun at about 64,000 miles per hour. Now if you will think for a moment— even during the matter of a fraction of a second, the earth travels hundreds of miles. Any person being born under a certain sign, astrologically speaking, has his (or her) horoscope read or forecast on the basis of the year, month, day and the hour, but no astrologer computes in the matter of seconds. Within an hour, the earth could have moved through and bisected billions of electromagnetic lines of force. Also, it must be rationalized that there is absolutely no valid reason why any of these electromagnetic lines of force could, at some future day in that person's life, influence the life and the events of that person.

Moreover, the astrologer is incorrect in the first

premise of astrology. The day and hour of birth should not be used, but rather the moment of conception. The ancient Chinese astrologer always computed from that point—conception. As I said, there is no indication whatsoever, in any energy wave form transmissions, and such, which are occurring at any split second of time that could influence, in a personal way, the future life of any person, or that certain future events could be predicted on the basis of a birthday, time and hour.

Universally speaking, all peoples of the earth, regardless of their birth date, are synchronously affected, to some small degree, by the universal interplay of oscillating energies, electromagnetic force fields, etcetera. The affectation, however, is more psychic than physical. Such affectations must therefore be influential or inclement vibrations regenerated in the psychic anatomy, according to all basic harmonic patterns involved. In one aspect then, the astrologer is correct in recognizing certain influences derived in what is called solar mechanics. He is incorrect, however, in stating that the planets exert these influences or that his astrology can predict the nature of these influences. Rather, the vast and tremendous electromagnetic fields of which a planet is the nucleus, are the influential factors, also, that such influences do not determine or predict success or failure as implied upon some future event to take place in some individual's life, according to his birthday.

The astrologer does not have the mentality or the training to properly intercept and interpret the vast conglomeration of interdimensional wave forms which are the composite of our interdimensional cosmos.

The total of these countless billions of oscillations also affect and create all manners and forms of life on the planet earth, just as they do any other planet and its life forms, or even the sun itself. The reason is simple: there would be no suns, no solar systems, no galaxies or universes unless there were these interdimensional energy force field oscillations, because they are the sustaining impulse energies of every atom which is the core of a vortex; and even the means of these affectations are, however, steady state. They have existed eternally and will continue to do so eternally because we cannot, third-dimensionally speaking, extract a third-dimensional time differential which would be comprehensive to us. Therefore, infinity is forever eternal, so far as our consciousness is concerned.

So you see, there are billions of very pertinent factors which influence life on any earth planet, including our own; factors which are totally unknown to either the astrologer or the most advanced scientists. So far as you are personally concerned, those certain inclement factors which you have impounded in your psychic anatomy from previous lifetimes have a much greater influence in your present everyday life. In fact, everything you do in your present life is predicated upon what you were and what you were doing hundreds or even thousands of years ago. Your present life is a reorientation and an expansion of this past life, substantiated and made possible by all the numerous aspects of life around you which, as symbolic forms, cause the necessary reactive components to be instigated, thus perpetuating your libido, or life drive.

Just in case you have heard reports of a certain astrologer which seem to be accurate predictions, the subject here is as broad as it is long. In scientific nomenclature, there is a mandate: to prove a certain scientific fact, as an experiment it must be performed successfully ninety-nine times out of a hundred attempts. No astrologer or other so-called seer can successfully repeat any prediction or predictions simply because of the vast interplay of the interdimensional energy fields which I have described—that the total of all which concerns such predictions is moving at incredible speeds. How then can any predictions be made, especially with a mind untrained to recognize all factors which create the future?

Therefore we can and must attribute all such seemingly accurate predictions as coincidence, or that the astrologer made a personal prediction to some person for the obvious reason that this person sought out the astrologer to have a prediction made, the astrologer being astute enough to gather certain remarks and inferences made by the seeker which betrayed the secret aspirations and desires for which that person, the seeker, was too weak and too undetermined to make the necessary effort to realize and fulfill these ambitions and aspirations without a conviction from another source—a conviction which the astrologer could make on the basis of the aforementioned inferences.

You might ask: do I believe that it is possible to predict the future? Yes, indeed I do; not by any means such as astrology which is purely a gimmick. Astrology is a vestigial remnant of a science taught by an ancient civilization from another world, more than 100,000 years ago, just as I have explained to you. In fact, I was one of the teachers of that ancient time.

The proposition of foretelling the future must be done by a highly-trained mind; a mind which has advanced far beyond the capacity of any human earth mind which is, or has ever lived, on this planet—with but very few exceptions and these exceptions have been and are the Unariun Emissaries who have related a certain Mission, which I have discussed in other liturgies.

My own personal life record would reveal the almost countless, accurate, future predictions made under any and all circumstances. The total involvement concerned in these predictions, and all factors concerned, are far too vast and complex to be discussed in this particular article and will be dealt with fully at a later day.

It should, however, be suggested at this time, that so far as the present-day prophets, astrologers and seers, etc., are concerned, they like others who have preceded them, can and do maintain a haphazard, intuitive intercourse with a number of astral worlds which are, in certain respects, linked to our earth world in the totality of a number of vibratory planes. It is within these dimensional factors that so many of these so-called paranormal, intuitive, spiritualistic activities take place. Even flying saucers are an adjunctive transmission in these interconnecting astral planes. Again, the totality of this concept is extremely complex and involves the entire mystical nature of mankind.

It is therefore clearly evident that no human who has in his evolution, coming up from the remote beginnings of an earth world life to his present status, is by any stretch of the imagination, sufficiently developed in his intellectual capacity to bisect and analyze the interdimensional cosmos or any of its attendant third-dimensional earth world manifestations. The interpretations of these manifestations, as they are somehow and in some very small way, recognized collectively or individually by homosapiens, have resolved themselves, in his limited mental capacity, into such attendant mysticisms as astrology, numerology, religion and other paranormal bisections, and a subsequent aberrated attempt has been made to acclimatize these aspects into his earth world environment.

The proposition of predicting the future can be sublimated into other factors such as autosuggestion; or through an objective conviction, sufficient mental and physical energy can be projected into attaining the fulfillment of this conviction which could be termed psychokinesis.

In the interdimensional cosmos, the future of any

person, any object, any planet, solar system or galaxy has already been predicted, and it has been predicted in an infinite number of ways. The fulfillment of any materialization in this future is always determined in the law, order and harmony constantly in force in the interplay of this interdimensional cosmos. Only in man do we find a deviation from any directional fulfillment. The power of reason, or what is called reason by man, as the mental ability to connect and interconnect certain incidental factors in his life for whatever purposes he may desire, always ultimately, in the achievement of his objectivisms, changes his future; yet in principle and in the constant steady state expansion of law, order and harmony, nothing is violated.

Only man, individually or collectively, has become subjected to an infinite number of futures, any and all of which are exactly synonymous and similar in all aspects and become dissimilar only as a matter of personal interpretation, for this future is the infinite interplay of interdimensional cosmic energies any or all of which, in the idiom of their oscillating components, interpret a specific meaning to the net conglomeration of all previously incepted information contained in the net oscillating configurations of the past.

Therefore, the past and the future are the same. The present is the moment where, in a specific time differential, any person can combine and recombine the past in the present and thus obtain a new differential interpretation which is the future. Thus, do not be waylaid or deviated from your true constructive course of evolution by the false prophets of this world and they assume many forms: politicos, religionists, astrologers and seers, each one a clamoring voice in the wilderness of human derelictions and deviations; weak voices, loud voices, vainly crying to mask the insecurities of their own lives; voices made strong by the weaknesses which are a part of their lives, and the louder they howl, the greater are their weaknesses! Only in the pursuit of knowledge and formulating it into the constructive vessel of your life can you rise above this maelstrom of human dereliction and depravity.

The lust for life in a material world becomes an anachronism which ends in death—a death perpetuated and shrouded by an impenetrable veil of ignorance. Become wise therefore; the flower of wisdom becomes the fruit which will sustain you in the immortality of your future.

Yes, we should also ask by what manner and means does any astrologer determine whether a certain planet is benign or malignant in its influences; or that any conjunctions or oppositions would create a specified condition according to a birth date? The anthropology of astrology and its origins, etc., are as vague as are any of the legends which give rise to our religions. Even the origins, if they could be determined, could be a subject of doubt and misgivings because, as is indicated in present-day astrology, such origins would have had to originate from such untrained and insufficient minds as are exhibited at this present time.

When the Masters of the ancient civilization tried to teach creation and solar mechanics to the primitive aborigines which they found about the planet earth, these primitives were most confounded and could not understand, except that they recognized the certain influential factors which, through the succeeding ages of time, were abrogated into the numerous mysticisms, religions, astrologies and numerologies.

Akhenaton, too, who served as a Unariun transport, met with great difficulty and eventual failure in his efforts to teach the Egyptians solar mechanics and influential differentials.

This is the concourse of human history. The limited mentality of homosapiens on this earth has always abrogated the efforts of interplanetary dwellers to teach them a better way of life. Within the narrow defiles of the human earth mind, any truth, great or small, is squeezed down into a narrow distorted form, wherein the earthman can suit his limited mental capacities and resolve his contorted configurations into whatever palliative he desires, or suits his purpose.

Necromancy or fortune-telling, whether it is by means of astrology, religion, spiritualism, palmistry, tea leaves or coffee grounds—and there are thousands of forms —is, in itself, the net sum and total of all man's mystical world wherein he hopes to assuage the ever-present fears and insecurities or even waylay the grim specter of death in some fancied future resurrection. None of this is reasonable or logical, nor is it sustained by any of the cardinal principles and laws of the interdimensional cosmos which, in the context of evolutionary fulfillments, did create the heavens and the earth as man sees them.

Logically then, the solution to this great universal enigma which is man's earth life, is to seek out and find the creation. Learn of the interdimensional cosmos through countless evolutions; travel through some of the many mansions. Immortality is not a selective event dictated by some fancied god, but is an attainment and an achievement in logic and reason.

Abstract Form of Consciousness

The embryo of life existence of the individual soul begins with the life spark of Infinite Intelligence which expands into a great fourth-dimensional ring or cycle which is called the Life Cycle or soul progression of this individual soul. This Life Cycle is composed of an infinite number of pulsations of frequencies or energies, each assuming a different wave form, but which are in harmonic relationship to each other. While being infinite in number, in nature and variety, therefore they can reflect in their own consciousness, the part of themselves into the third dimension, and which in turn assumes the mass proportion of the atomic structures known as elements.

These elemental substances are therefore grouped into the visible form of the earth body. The linkage of the earth body to the life cycle is complete through the superstructure called the psychic body. The psychic body is, in itself, a self-contained reservoir, retaining in static form the life experiences of the physical consciousness.

In the development of what is called the Superconscious Mind, is the sum and total of all the energies which have been expressed through experience in the psychic body and retained in an etheric or cyclic form. This Superconscious Mind and, body will, in turn, graduate through many evolutions of life cycles which are in harmonic relationship to the fundamental embryonic life cycle.

In the final conclusion, it may be termed a Superconscious Being of Infinite Dimension and of Infinite Mind who reflects outwardly from within himself, the individual personification of the great creative force called God.

The Life Cycle

The all-pervading, all-permeating, all-existing intelligent God resides or lives or expresses Himself in an infinite way through many, many dimensions. Jesus spoke of it thusly, "In my Father's house there are many mansions." Mansions, of course, are the relative planes and the dimensions of existence. Therefore, in the creation of man, it can be said that God, as He is of infinite nature and intelligence, must express Himself in an infinite number of ways. This, then, begins to assume a definite or a tangible or a personal expression. We will say that God is creating Himself as an individual in an infinite number of ways by the creation of each human being.

As it is quite necessary, if we think a moment, in this infinite nature of God, that God must also combine all of the elements of infinity into the nature of the personal expression or the human being; therefore comes the necessity for the living or the learning or the realization into all realms and dimensions of consciousness as an individual. God begins the creation of man something like this: we can say that, in His Infinite Mind, man so begins as a basic fundamental life cycle. This is, in itself, a cycle which will remain throughout eternity with the individual. Within this cycle or place are an infinite number of tiny or larger wave forms. These wave forms are, in themselves, frequencies or intensities which can convey—and as they are unchanged through time or eternity—and will continually reflect or convey in the proper sense of content, the intelligence which was placed within them.

Now we begin to understand that here God has placed in this life cycle, all of His Infinite Intelligence, all of the things in the nature of which God is. But it is still in a form which is not personalized, nor can it be expressed in a personal fashion upon a lower plane of consciousness. So therefore, this intelligence must, by necessity, and as it is Infinite in nature, again reflect or assume another form. This second form, or the projection of all of the things of which it contains, is called the psychic body. We can visualize it as something similar to the screen in the motion picture theater, and that the projector with the film which portrays the picture is the life cycle.

The screen, or psychic body, therefore contains a reflected concept of all that is within the original basic life cycle. This psychic body or, as it is sometimes called, the thought body or the thought form body, is even expressed in the terms of the psychiatrist as the subconscious mind. It is, in itself, by necessity, a by-product of not only the intelligence of the life cycle but in the expression of the thing in which it is—the life within itself—becomes outwardly the objective mind or the conscious mind of the individual. It can also take unto itself such manifold experiences as the individual is going through during his various periods of life of this particular time of his evolution.

It has been explained previously that the existence and the experience of all things in this earth or on other worlds takes place in the mental consciousness; even though they may express themselves or move about as material forms, happenings or experiences, yet essentially, they are mental in nature. And as mental in nature, they regenerate themselves in a cycular pattern within this psychic body.

Now, it is easy to see that the psychic body can become the receptacle of not only the intelligence of God from the life cycle, but can also retain the intelligence or the experience, or even the inferior or the negative experiences of the individual, but the psychic body does even more than this. Through the life cycle

101

and into the psychic body is the creative life force of God Himself. This, in turn, recreates into idea or form, the structure and the elements of the human body. This human body or the physical form is the idea body. It is simply a vehicle in which the consciousness lives or dwells within this relative plane. It can be likened, if you will, to the suit and the helmet the deep sea diver wears when he descends to the ocean floor, so that through the lifetime of the individual, he is merely manipulating a mechanism or an organism which is essential to his life upon this plane.

He has the lungs to breathe the gas; he has the necessary intestinal mechanism to assimilate the various atomic structures known as foods within this dimension and to regenerate the necessary heat for the body metabolism. This all, in the sum and total, is merely the expression of the divine will and consciousness which comes from the individual life cycle.

Now we can begin to see that, as it has truly been said, man is created of God. In the Bible it speaks that God gathered together the dust of the earth and created man. This is merely a parable and one in which only a childlike mind would be able to tolerate, but our own consensus and evaluation of what man really is, would, by necessity, be more than just that. The earth in itself, of course in its evolution, does become the elemental substances of the body, but first we have to have the creative intelligence behind all of this in order for the body to do this. This creative intelligence is God and manifests from the life cycle.

In going about your life, if the individual knew of the pertinent facts, knew that he or she, with each act, each daily thought, each consciousness in the expression of life about himself or herself was being permanently engraved, if we could liken it to that, within the psychic body, this, in its countless evolutions of the lives of the individual throughout this earth and many other earths, becomes the sum and total of all that he is, becomes the sum and total of his individual expression. He can therefore, by the same token of all this, become very godlike. He can assume all the propensities from the individual expression of such a God.

Jesus of Nazareth was able to express in some ways, the godlike nature of man, and the creative intelligence behind this way of life. With his many miracles which He worked while on this earth plane, He was merely setting up the actual working counterpart of this divine intelligence. In a large sense, Jesus merely set aside the element of time and space and reverted into the fourth dimension, into the original or the place of conception of all things. Therefore, in this particular dimension, as the life force was continually creating and recreating itself, also that all things had been created or were created with the infinite nature of God, all things were not only possible but they are; so Jesus merely brought into the conscious expression a part of God which was already there but which could not be seen with the finite mind.

Remember, therefore, that your act of consciousness of this day or the deed of this hour will be something which can be a basic block on which to build your future, or it can become a stumbling block. It can become something which you may have to spend, not only one lifetime but many lifetimes to eradicate, or to eliminate some great negative cycle in the consciousness of the psychic body of the individual.

And so, dear student, do not feel for one moment that because you have read your Unarius texts a time or two that you have conceived all that these works behold for you. Not so. The Science of Unarius is infinite in nature and you can spend a lifetime or several lifetimes to conceive these principles. And I say to you in all sincerity, you shall never come to any point in your evolution where you cannot gain a greater measure of understanding, of inner awareness and a greater oneness and closer relationship with the all-creative Infinite Consciousness. It is in this way that the Infinite lives in man and that man does become godlike in nature.

Discussion on Cyclic Motion

Basically, and to refresh your memory, there is no such thing as a solid. The conveyance of any idea, form or consciousness is always done with a sine wave or a combination of sine waves, or other sine waves which are superimposed on sine waves. Now in this third-dimensional world, all of these sine waves have a beginning and end; in other words, there is time. The element of time separates the beginning and end, and the most ultimate consonant of time is the speed of light: 186,000 miles per second. In the fourth dimension, as was postulated by Einstein, time was an integrated factor; in other words, as we have drawn these things up for you, then concept, idea, form or continuity as a conveyance of any information, intelligence or counter-intelligence must, of course, be cyclic in motion. That is, the sine wave, like the mythical hoop snake, has taken its tail in its mouth and it becomes a complete circle, and in this circle there is more or less of a complex matrix of sine wave frequencies.

Now each one of these sine wave frequencies has, within itself, its own vibrating consonant; that is, its attunement. Within the cycle itself, each one of these separate entities of sine wave frequencies which is conveying information, is harmonically linked or joined to all other frequencies within the cycle, and extending this same precept outwardly through the same basic relationship of harmonics, this whole cyclic motion, which is the conveyance of form or consciousness, is then relinked infinitely throughout infinity. Within the cycle itself, as it is so harmonically attuned with the thousands or hundreds of thousands of sine wave frequencies, these too are beating positively and negatively as they are joined, shall we say, or as they so bisect themselves in this frequency oscillation.

These conjunctions form minor polarities, and minor polarities can, on the same basis of frequency relationship, re-establish themselves as major polarities within the cycle. If we, in triangulation, bisect any portion or three or four portions and make contacts with this cyclic motion, we can establish there certain differences in the phase relationships of these cycles. That is, by bisecting these cycles or separating them, we have introduced time into their consonant expression. We have, in effect, given them a beginning and an end and so, therefore, we now have a difference of phase relationship within the cycle as it is so expressed into the third dimension. This is immediately proven as we have so established these things in the Unariun science, by what has recently been conveyed in the Los Angeles Times as of August 4, 1964 wherein an article gave certain details about certain discoveries in science. To wit: that the old Newtonian law of the complete forward motion, or that it must conversely revert into a complete rearward motion within itself, was invalid. In other words, the scientists have now found and have evidence, in proof, that no forward motion of energy can completely reverse itself and travel exactly in the opposite direction. In other words, if the apple which had fallen on Newton's head had burst into, say, a thousand pieces and suddenly reversed itself and gone up backwards into the tree, all of the little pieces would not have fitted together, nor would the apple have gone back in the same line or in the same place in the tree.

Now we can easily see how this is so if we remember the triangulation of a basic cycle. If we remember that the entire incident of the apple falling on Newton's head was contained in a cyclic motion in the fourth dimension, and as it was so separated (at the time of Newton) into the third dimension—and with the introduction of time which started when Newton sat down under the tree and the apple dropped on his head— then we have a differential of time which was introduced into that expressionary cycle as it had so existed or pulsed in the fourth dimension.

In this differential of time, however, had we so introduced or bisected, in triangulation, any other particular point of junctions or separations within the cycle, then it is quite possible that Newton would have discovered this law of gravity in an entirely different fashion. It could have been a different apple tree in a different place, or it could have even been a pear tree. It could have been a stone falling from a hillside or it could have been that it was not Newton but some other individual who discovered that law. Basically, the whole concept, as it was contained in this episode and so portrayed in the life of Newton, was expressed in the cyclic motion in infinity itself. The difference or the differential in interpretation, as it so manifests itself in the third dimension, is wherever this cycle is so separated into this third dimension by the introduction of the time consonant.

Now why am I taking all the trouble to explain all of this to you? And perhaps you may not understand it, even partially. The reason is very clear. It is because, instead of Newton and an apple, we have, for instance, our dear sister who wrote. As of today, just as I have told you previously, after she had reached a certain plateau in one of these previous lifetimes many thousands of years ago, she was, up to that point, triangulating her cycle of life in a progressive fashion, and according to the time consonant which she reflected into this third-dimensional world, this cycle was forward or positively inclined into infinity. However, as she so reached a certain plateau, suddenly, for some reason or another (and the reasons are not too important at this moment), this particular differential was suspended or stopped; instead, a new differential or a new point of triangulation was introduced and she began to reflect into her conscious life, or the third dimension, the retrogressive motion of consciousness which, as it so oscillated into this cycle of life, linked her in a reverse fashion back into the past. And while the appearances of the past did not manifest themselves as they had formerly occurred in this backward like manner, yet the basic differences, as they are so conceived or postulated in infinity, again remanifested themselves. In other words, there was a negative or retrogressive motion backwards.

Now this will also explain to you how it is possible that the Infinite Intelligence or God, as it is sometimes called, is both good and evil. It is simply because of a certain, we shall call it, duality of the nature of infinity; that is, it always presents to the third-dimensional world, and with the integration of the time consonant, a forward motion which is progressive and positively linked to infinity and which always links all cycles to this forward motion in a constructive fashion; that all things which come to any individual thusly linked to the future in a positive progression, such creative things will come to him that they will always be positively inclined into his life. That is, he will prosper; not necessarily in the manner of great wealth but he will prosper in the manner in which his intellect is developed and his personality, his character is strengthened and he becomes a better person.

Conversely, if he is negatively linked to the past, then there is a declination of the cyclic movement and he again reinterprets successively the experience quotients into the present life as he so inclines himself in this backward motion. This, of course, in a sense, is something like unraveling a sweater. He won't manifest the negative oscillating quality of that retrogressive motion necessarily as it was superimposed in consciousness in the past. As a specific experience, as it so became a part of consciousness, it was, in the past, a progressive, forward, cyclic motion and has, in the present, now become a retrogressive motion or negatively declined motion of consciousness.

Now as I have said before, there are always differences when the triangulation process occurs. In other words, in the third dimension and in bisecting the net frequencies which are contained in all cyclic motions, these again are interpreted into the third dimensional world in differences of phase relationships. If you remember the taped message on the "Electronic Man" and the explanation of phase relationships in that lesson, while that was tailored in more or less of a straight-line proposition which was more easily understood, at this time we are reducing the differential factors of time consonant factors into the third dimension which will explain to you quite adequately, after you have grasped this science, how it is possible for such things to occur as have happened to our dear sister.

By the same token, the inference is quite clear. It could easily happen to you as a student. In fact, it has, and at this moment and with the help of the Unariun Brotherhood, you are attempting to reverse this rear ward or backward cyclic declination to again re-establish yourself into a progressive, forward motion into infinity where life is always constructively inclined into your personality, your character, or your make-up for you must remember, you will never reflect anything more than what is contained in infinity itself. Indeed, the proposition of becoming an advanced personality is embodied in this concept; that we are reflecting or oscillating, at least to a very high degree, the net sum and total, as far as principle is concerned at least, what infinity is—and a constructive infinity at that—as it must also be positively inclined at all times. In other words, no matter how far you are along this pathway,

109

how advanced you may become, you are still infinitesimally small compared to the net total and whole
of infinity. This, in itself, proves the concept of infinity
and nothing would add to nothing if these things were
not so.

Therefore, if you see such things as angelic beauty in
the countenance of a person, or you become seemingly
bewitched by the strong energy projections from such a
person, it is well to question these things before you let
them form any particular part of your psychic anatomy
or that they may influence thought processes or conduct in your daily life. That person may be expressing
in a reverse fashion and negatively linked to the past
what she or he was ten thousand years ago, and as
a negatively declined person, this negative declination
will become a part of your life if you incept it into your
personality.

The scientists are so sorely troubled, we shall say,
in trying to differentiate the cyclic differences in motion
in time as they are either progressively inclined or they
are declined so that they re-manifest themselves
partially, or one way or another, in out-of-phase relationship with the true course which they formerly
took. In other words, if they had drawn a straight line
of motion, say for example, to the north and they had
suddenly reversed their motion, they would not be
traveling back exactly south. This difference in phase
relationship, as it was expressed in the fourth-dimensional cycle, which was the true embodiment and which
caused, we shall say, the straight line to the north to
travel, then we can see that due to this phase differential, as it is contained in the fourth-dimensional
cycle, will make the line which is traveling theoretically
south, travel southwest or southeast. That is a rather
crude picturization of what the scientists are trying to
solve in relationship to Newton's original, basic law of
physics. You will understand it much better and more

completely when you have grasped what I have just discussed with you, and if you have not grasped it at this moment, do not despair. Even the most brilliant scientist of today would be flabbergasted and floored if he attempted to solve this. I have tried to present it to you in a very simple way, and to me at least, it is in understandable form.

If you draw a circle and you place on this circle a triangle, which happens to be a mystical symbol of a past religion which came out of the Lemurian civilization, (it is still used as an esoterical or mystical symbol in many religions of the world today and is a part of the Jewish Kabala), it means that at any point on a circle with this triangle, and by turning the triangle within the circle, we can bisect this circle at any three given points simultaneously.

When we carry this concept into energy wave forms which are revolving within this circle, it is very easy to see that we can contact this circle at three different points simultaneously and that by the simple process of rotating the triangle, we always come out with three different compositions of form which are contained within the circle. Now this triangulation has been called other things; it has been called the holy trinity, the Father, the son and the holy spirit, which means merely that somehow science was corrupted into a religious symbol. In simple terms, one point of this triangle represents the present, one point represents the past, and the third point represents the future. The relationship of the present, past and future is always determined by whatever points they are contacting. A particular or a specific point upon this circle or within this circle, as I have said—and I will repeat—is contained the entire intelligence or information or the entity of intelligence which is expressing itself fourth-dimensionally. So therefore, at any given moment of your life you are engaged in that triangulation process. Through con-

111

sciousness, you are constantly rotating this triangle back and forth within the circle of your life. According to your consciousness or your present, you are constantly relating the past to your present at different points of your evolution.

Conversely, you are also relating the present to your future. So you see that it is very important to understand energy, how information can exist on a sine wave and how the sine wave can be a fourth-dimensional proposition—a cyclic form which expresses itself simultaneously without time in this fourth dimension because it is all self-contained. There is the cycle of life, which is again subdivided into an infinite number of cycles or cyclic wave forms which become your experiences in daily life. These are all harmonically linked to the net sum and total of infinity. By the same abstraction, these experiences can, by beating harmonically with this infinite, become any one or a variety of experiences that you can possibly conceive, and far beyond the point of conception. It is this principle which makes all people different. Each person's path of evolution is different even though the principles which make it possible are absolute in all respects. To describe the evolution of one person is to describe the evolution of another, yet we must always go within the wave forms which are contained in these cyclic motions where we find differences within these people's lives.

Now these concepts are indeed far advanced in our time. They're given to you by a Spaceman who has come to your world to explain these things fundamentally to you. He has lived many lives among you in the past and in different relationships to you. He has expressed himself, living through the human body as a matter of form and principle, and to make the whole proposition much more conducive to those who would accept what he has come to teach, he has adopted the manner and form through the physical body which is customarily associated with all earth people. This he is doing in the present and this he has done in the past. Whether he will do so in the future, remains for his part at least, a choice; but for the present, we must remember that such a person who has come to the earth, such a developed spiritual entity who is reflecting through the human body or the personality of self into the earth world does not in any sense of the word reflect the same basic values into experience as does the ordinary earthman who is coming up through the progressive cycle of evolution. To the more advanced intellect, he is looking down, for the moment of convenience or, to serve a purpose, he must look backwards. In a sense of the word, he must triangulate his own consciousness into the past where he once lived as an earthman and, as such, then he can, through the wave forms contained in this cycle, express himself outwardly into the third-dimensional world in the manner customarily associated with that time.

So you see, many of the mysteries of life can be very easily cleared up when we begin to understand energy, as there is nothing more or less. Infinity is composed of energy and energy in many, many different forms. Some are more understandable as they are on our third-dimensional plane, but as you progress into the future, you will have to do so by the necessity of your understanding infinity as a proposition whereby all things are manifest as energy wave forms and in cyclic motions. The Higher Worlds are composed wholly and entirely by the transpositions of energies in these cyclic motions. If you wish to live in one of these Higher Worlds, then it is imperative that you conceive these principles, for you could do so only by virtue of the fact that you understood how to do so. You would have to incept or "soak in", we shall say, the energy which must come to you in the form of understanding principle,

113

relationship, integration, and also of regeneration. That is your life. The metabolism of the spiritual body is composed as an oscillating proposition with infinity. It does not depend, shall we say, upon the so-called molecular interactions or the so-called chemical reactions which are postulated in medical science or in the biological science, for the proposition of life itself is more specifically contained within the dimension and the circumference of a cyclic motion which is part of infinity.

(Science received via mental transmission at various times from the higher minds on the Spiritual Planets, such as Einstein, Spinoza, Steinmetz, Sister Kenny, et cetera.)

Inspiration from Albert Einstein (1955)

There is one equation in which I'd like to make a correction: in this fourth dimension equation that space was curved due to the fact that the curvature of the earth, combined with the gravitational and magnetic fields of force that extend out into space, give the illusion of a parabolic curve. This makes triangulation of distant stars because of the angles of incidence or reference from straight base lines where, as they enter this magnetic field around the earth, cause them to travel in a slightly parabolic arc. Therefore, the analogy of triangulation was not correct because of the starting points. The astronomer is taking the outside lines of measurements—the only true angle of incidence they could have.

Light is affected by magnetic fields of force, as earth's, which act as a buffer. There is as much as a fifteen percent error in the present estimates regarding light. Light travels at about 210,000 miles per second instead of the customarily estimated 186,300 miles per second. Light travels much swifter in a vacuum than it does in air. Scientists of today have not succeeded in producing a tube one hundred miles long, not even ten miles, which would give him an estimate or an approximation. Even electronic timing devices would be as much as ten percent in error because of the interpretation of the electric impulses into an electronic signal needed to make the necessary mark to define the speed. The scientist knows sound travels slower at sea levels than at high altitudes. Sound, because of its comparably slower speed, is easier to measure. With light at more than 200,000 miles per second, the problem is much more difficult; however, there is a definite relationship—the resistance of air against light.

This is a secondary factor entering in from distances of stars, as light approaching the earth is curved slightly toward the center of the earth, which is the path of least resistance—much the same manner in which light is focused by a lens. The magnetic lines of force from north and south magnetic poles also cause their distortions of light entering the earth's atmosphere. These distortions are compounded by their constant movement around the north and south axis of the earth. The modern astronomer with his system of triangulation is sometimes in considerable error. Moreover, these errors are constantly repeated in respect to the position of the star which is being measured, inasmuch as points of triangulation are dependent with the exact timing of the earth in its rotations.

These errors can be further multiplied if the exact position of the earth in its orbit of the ellipse around the sun is not definitely established. Positioning of the earth in this orbit is extremely difficult because of the vastness of the distances involved compared to the size of the earth and the instruments used for measuring. There are also several secondary motions which the earth goes through as it revolves around the sun. This is a concentric, wobble-like motion and is more stabilized according to frequency, but varies slightly in pitch or in wave length. In all, the earth has about five different motions. These are all factors which must be taken into consideration before a definite relationship of distance with various suns and stars of the universe can be established.

The universe itself is constantly expanding. Light, in traveling through such space, assumes an affinity with such an expanding condition because in free space the factor of terminal velocities has been removed to an unknown point.

The inertia of light is relative to the density of the earth's atmosphere through which it passes. Therefore, the speed of light, as has been determined upon the surface of the earth through atmospheric conditions, is not the same speed of light which travels through free space. In free space, light has no restrictive inertia which has been built up through atmospheric pressures, but instead, travels in a vastly accelerated speed in which it takes on an expanded condition which is similar to the dimension through which it is traveling.

The astronomer of today knows little or nothing about this vastly accelerated speed of light, traveling on the free arc of space; and in such space, time can be said to be a subdominant or nonexisting factor in such speed, for light travels in such space in an entirely different rate or frequency in which space itself becomes active, inasmuch as the light now fills the place formerly occupied by space. Atomic structures within the surface of the earth and moving in their own field of molecular relationship, generate outwardly, static electricity; therefore, the earth can be said to be a highly statically charged mass of energy which causes any loose or floating particles, including air molecules of various kinds, to be attracted to the surface. The surface atoms and molecules, in turn, are attracted even more strongly to the deeper atomic structures, the rate of attraction increasing according to its square root, the base line which is its original outgoing wave form. In a general sense, the earth can be said to be attracting itself into itself.

From Einstein

So you see, when I came over here this time, it was like other times too. When I see these things now, I say it is very wonderful. Now I see them like they are; they are real things—not like little figures which I used to put on the paper—and I would say all these things are so because they are so and so. And like Ming-tse says, there are lots of so and so's running around, and I do not wish to become another so and so. So we have to put these things down so everybody can understand them. When you see how it is that you look through the large end of the telescope to the small end, things get small, and when you look up through the little end, you see everything gets big. As I said a long time ago, when we point out these venturi tubes, it is just like turning the telescope around each time from the large end to the small and vice versa. That is the way all those things exist, you see.

So we always have to learn to visualize things, not as you might see merely movement, or these things appear or disappear, or you say you wiggle your little toe, and so on and so forth, but you are transferring a certain relationship of energy from an infinite number of dimensions in that one particular movement of wiggling your little toe. It means you are wiggling the whole infinite universe, and in a sense of the word, that is true because everything is linked and re-linked. Only the religionist or the scientist has a big butcher knife and he cuts all these things into little pieces. The man at the altar says this is Satan and this is Heaven; this is hell and this is something else. The scientist says, where does this go if it is not reactive to such and such and so and so—and here we go again with all the so and so's. There are too many people running around with a butcher knife. They seem to like to cut every-thing to pieces and it shouldn't be cut to pieces; it should be left whole, because there's nothing without something. It all has to be something with something else. That is what the man (Mal Var) from Venus told you a long time ago in the book. When the man presses the key on the telegraph, he is actually activating energy which comes from the Infinite.

The principle exists that you constantly oscillate energy through the nerves of your body from the impulses which link you to the psychic body. These things are all configurations of energy which come from various different polarity patterns, different things in the psychic body and they, in turn, are linked to the superconsciousness, and so on. That is the way, because the psychic body is another great big atom in comparison with smaller atoms which are pulsating, gyrating globs of energy which contain an infinite number of formations and pulsations of energy.

Well, I'll say I am a little so and so—a little wiggle which was made back here when somebody stabbed me with a knife—or here I'm a little wiggle and I went to College back in England a hundred years ago, and I'm a little wiggle when I drowned out here in the ocean. We are all wiggles, all similar little wiggles—the same in some ways, but some have something the other little wiggles don't have. Each little wiggle can al-ways say to itself, "I am so and so." Always from these little things, they have a little voice, and the little voice is what you call the harmonic structure. It's the little things the scientist is very vague about; he likes to call them magnetism. Magnetism is the voice in the atom of all the energy forms; the voices which call to each other and bring each other together in these little harmonic structures. They are the arms which link each other together and hold on tight. All these things too, you see, are expressing their own intelligence and something else which is saying to it that it must be so—the Infinite becoming finite in all things—and it is that way.

As Ernest says, it is pressure. Well, pressure is the term used by the physicists. In the sense of the word, if you think of something you are generating an electrical pressure, and that pressure has to travel somewhere all during your life. When you think about wiggling your little toe, you generate pressure of energy; an EMF which goes down the nerves to the little toe and says, "You wiggle," and it wiggles. So that is the way we have to put things to people who are not educated along the lines of physics and electronics, and they don't have the faculties to tune in to where all of these things are, where they exist in perfect form and consciousness.

If everyone could look back far enough into his mind and get over the barriers of his materialism, he could see all these things like Ernest sees them, and you, too, Sister Ruth, will do the same; you have been doing the same for over three years now. You have been seeing these things, not only here on earth, but you have been seeing them when you were asleep too. You have been seeing them so many times; that is the reason you can understand them so much more easily. Most people can't. They have become a part of you, just as all the other little wiggles are a part of you. It all has to be sublimation; in other words, linkages to harmonic structures, the little arms, fingers and voices of the energies which are the harmonics in the ear. Their frequency relationship locks themselves in. You will see it on the television—what they call the pulses of synchronization from the transmitter when they are so properly integrated with circuitry in the television set, which generates similar pulses. And when these pulses are beating with each other like, we'll say, two hearts that go bump, bump, bump together, well, you can't tear them apart. Nothing can jiggle them; they've locked. Why? Because like the gears in the machine, like the gears in your watch, they cannot be torn apart, because they are very fundamental in their structure and their relationship to each other. Always back of these things, they find more and more powerful things which are saying the same things—and when they go on out, they get even greater things which are saying that all these things are so. And now I'm beginning to say more so and so's again.

But I'll not stay long; I only wish to break the monotony a moment and say hello, and when the little machine is done, I'll go. You see, so many things I could explain to you from science, but your earth scientists are a bunch of dummkopfs, anyway. The very greatest of all their inventions they have stumbled upon, like bats running around in a bright room. You know bats are blind when they have too much light, but the scientist is blind too, when he has too much light. For instance, he invented the silicon cell, which is the cell of little tiny crystals. He goes out on the slag heaps of the great refineries and sees a lot of silicon, which is a by-product of the heat in the furnaces from smelting out copper. Beryllium and many other different by-products, very, very valuable to use, he finds on the slag heap, and he finds them accidentally, stumbling blindly.

Silicon is a transducer; in other words, it can, under a small, stimulating current, throw off a great stream of electrons even much more efficiently than a tungsten filament. So what does he do? He makes a silicon cell which, when it is activated by light, can transduce light into electricity. He takes silicon and he forms a certain junction with two or three other little things like "cat whiskers" and he puts a little "juice" on one end; it comes out as little electrons on the other. So now he has something much better than the vacuum tube. But it is all accident, stumbling around like bats in a very

121

bright daylight. You see when bats come out of the attic in the daylight they are blind; they cannot see; their eyes are too thick. They can only see at night because they have eyes that see at night. The old saying that a bat is blind is very foolish. The darker the night, the better he can see because his eyes are so constructed that way; and a bat also hears better than radar. He sends out tiny little squeaks; the squeaks echo back to him and he can tell when there are strings around the room.

So the man of science thinks he is smart, but he is a dummkopf. He has invented penicillin by mistake. He invented all of those many other things, all by mistake. So he is a dummkopf because he is not able to tune up to these things like Ernest does, and like somebody who comes along and leaves something for the posterity of mankind. To say this is so and this is not so, according to my slide rule—the little digits here on my pencil and paper and which must conform—all foolishness. I was an expert in mathematics in my time, and it is probably well, because it was my tongs, with which I could reach into the laboratories and shake them by the back of the neck. But we have to go beyond that if we are going to get somewhere, and we'll have to go beyond that because we cannot have a system of mathematics which will go "upstairs" simply because man cannot, in himself, think "upstairs". When he can do that, perhaps he will invent a system of mathematics to equate the Infinite.

Those things around him are like the many, many roads—like a bunch of rats running around in an old warehouse; they have many trails. So the scientist just picked the wrong trail, but someday he won't have to. There is one man who is quite a smart boy and his name is Oppenheimer. He says, "Well, you can look upstairs," and now he's starting to look up a little bit too. He woke up and he said, "Well, these figures are no good anymore," running around like mad, calling all the magazines. You know, I read these things through Ernest's mind, too; when I tune in by his "sending set", I can tune in to him. That Oppenheimer is a smart boy; he is the father of the atom bomb. Anyway, you know! He was getting things when he would go way out there in the big B-29 airplanes—the cosmic rays with mesons, which regenerated themselves into positrons and neutrons, and so forth. Ernest had it even two years before that, and he had it all on paper. Why? Because he could tune "upstairs" without the B-29. There has to be these things these days.

Someone always has to go ahead and dig the postholes to put the fence in. Someone is always going up the road and surveying for a new highway; someone has always got to go ahead. And they are the ones who suffer the most; they are the ones who get in the poison ivy. They are the ones who fall in the ditches and on the rocks, in the nettles and the things you know. The people who lag along behind do not know how many people have sweat, strived and toiled over that highway to make it look smooth and nice, and it took many, many years, perhaps. Everything good that is brought to man is by sweat, toil and blood and mostly, the blood is shed by those who are bringing these things to man.

I was fortunate in my own life. I was given a medal and they say I was a great man, but I felt very foolish because I knew it was not great at all; how absolutely weak all of the things were around and how much more we have to gain. The more we gained, the more I knew how weak we were; we were weak in the brain power. Now they are all wrapped up in their sputniks —and such foolishness. They have to have a lot of these beep-beeps going around, sending out all these beep-beeps. So what? The Russians have one with an eye in it, so we say, well, pretty soon we'll have one with an eye in it. And they'll tell us what they're doing in the United States; they'll look down our chimneys and see what we are doing in the houses. Yes, and then the Americans have to think up one with an eye in it that looks down the Russian's chimneys to see what they are doing. So what? Everybody has to be busybodies —a big bunch of noseys! Why don't they learn to live with themselves and live in conditions which are harmonious with each other, instead of being busybodies and saying, "Well, you have a bigger bomb than I have. If your bomb goes off, then what? You're a so and so for doing that," and so on and so forth.

The bomb is anything but cold, but there would be many necks which would be hot under the collar. Many of those necks would be red and many of those necks are too stiff to bend one way or the other. People should use a little more temperance in their way of life and be a little more philosophical towards their fellowman. They get out on the highways and they get so stiffnecked they kill themselves off, well, like cattle, and they run around like crazy nuts. They love to get to a camping ground and get all bit up with mosquitoes, then they have to rush back like a bunch of madmen so they can work themselves into another place. It's very, very stupid the way I look at it. They are all little children and maybe they are learning things. Maybe someday they will be able to get up to where things will be a little better for them, because they all have one thing in common anyway—big energies into the Infinite. After all, man is just one more of the countless dimensions of expression.

Philosophy — Einstein (1958)

You see, one great trouble with humanity (and I wrote two books on philosophy which I consider much more important than the scientific works I gave, so I can be qualified somewhat as a philosopher), and the greatest mistake people make today is that they are shirking their own personal, moral responsibility toward the Creator. Each person, if he understood what his moral responsibility was, would certainly not do the things which he is doing; he could not do them because, to most people, living in the material world means merely the pacification of their carnal appetites. Man will find an infinite number of expressions for these voracious appetites in so many ways. He eats himself half sick and drinks himself into a stupor, and he fills his lungs full of foul vapors from the cigarettes. He lives all kinds of crazy and false patterns of life and even eats food which is saturated with poison because he is waging a war with the insect world, and to us over here, it is a wonder that he survives through the quantity of poison which he has maintained on that level. It is certainly not quality which he is expressing today.

When we look back into the past and see the great renaissance of intelligence, the artistic as well as the scientific achievements of the past ages in comparison with the world as it is today, it is a very barren and sterile place. But I could go on for hours and become a little German chatterbox. We say to you both, if you keep on going like you are, you will see that it is just kindergarten to what it will become in a little while. You can be assured of that because I know from where I am sitting here (psychically) tonight, beside Ernest, that the Earth is but one tiny little speck in God's Infinite Cosmos—a very tiny speck.

Even smaller yet is the sphere of intelligence in which the average person is revolving in his particular dimension of retrospection. They are like little insects; they only seem to have the will to live because they wish to become procreative, and to eat their way, it is to me like you see people as an intestinal tube, with teeth on one end and an anus on the other and they are literally eating their way through the world like human garbage disposals. So what are they living for? Well, there are some things which require a great amount of reasoning to justify, but I guess they all have their purposes. If you could picture, as we see it sometimes, they are as little earthworms that burrow their way through the earth by literally eating a hole before them. You see, human beings are much that way; they are only grown-up worms busily eating a hole as they go along, armed with teeth on one end of an intestinal tract.

You think they are very far from the worms? No! They have a long way to go, yet we all have a long way to go, and I am no exception because when I look up from where I am, I think too, maybe I am just like a little firefly which is on the bush along the side of the road. I have a very small and dim light indeed and a very long way to go. From where I sit, I can see upstairs into a long way and into the many, many things which, in some time in the future, when I have evolved, perhaps I will be in companionship with those things.

(Ruth asked him if he thought he would again return to earth to bring man future wisdom.) Ya, it is possible, perhaps, that I may wish to come back, but right now I am busy learning and studying; we are going about the Father's Business here in Unarius. And so we say, well, perhaps sometime when I feel the impulse or I shall say, there is an intelligent reason that we may gather together a coalition, and in the future there is a proper time and cycle to come down unto the Earth and man will be in a more receptive position to favor his evolution, then we can bring something in. But otherwise, it is like trying to shoot ducks with a blindfold on; you cannot do it. You just point your gun and pull the trigger and maybe a duck comes down and maybe it does not. And so that is the way with things; you must have a little insight into cycular patterns and find out.

Of course, like it was in the Middle Ages way back there, we had to have so many people come in to counteract the great black dragon which was strangling mankind in Europe—the black dragon with the robes. And so we all came in and we were saying that these things are so and these things are not so, and many people were killed because of it. And so we were so-and so's in those days too, sometimes.

Well, I shall run along now and leave you dear ones to whatever it is that you manifest from day to day, that we shall be close and we shall try to help make things a little happier for you. Auf Wiedersehen.

On Polio

Sister Kenny informs us that children cannot get polio unless they are in the right vibration (negative) for it. They become victims of polio because of all the negative things they see and hear on television programs; they have feelings of lack, inferiority and particularly, insecurity at times. Then, while in these negative vibrations, they are receptive to these viruses that are born in the astral realms of negation. Parents sometimes get polio also as they become fearful of getting it from the children.

There will be a new vaccine developed, first to be tried on rabbits, within the next few years. Any vaccine used today will need to be continued again every two or three years to be effective. After a few years, it will be found that a new strain of polio will develop. Polio virus is a very infinitely small body of extremely negative energies that are intelligent in their own particular way and cannot get into the body unless the right vibration of negation is set up for them. Tiny viruses are intelligent wave form energies of almost atomic size, sometimes on the order of tiny negative intelligences that are generated by evil forces of astral worlds which group together as atomic dust.

What the doctors call viruses are destructive wave forms and each one gathers unto himself his own kind. In the category of colds and flu, all come from or start with negative thoughts from minds of both etheric and physical realms and radiate into a certain respective pattern. Doctors and surgeons admit they do not know what causes the so-called popular colds and viruses or what they are; they are only aware of the effect or result.

If the thought form of murder is generated in this

physical world, it can be collected on certain layers or planes, and one attracts unto himself as the moth toward the light.

What the doctor of today calls leucocytes are intelligences in themselves of a much more expanded nature. They know how to attack germs that get into the bloodstream but will not attack viruses until they are alerted for such.

Every white corpuscle is a fluid mass of viruses, in a sense, with the intelligence to kill other germs by superimposing the wave forms of various structures. Leukemia is the result of the white leucocytes of the bloodstream which have lost their intelligence and have become murderous to cells with which they come in contact and are therefore cancerous in nature. They lose their relationship to the controlling force of the vibration from the life cycle. Any cancerous conditions such as leukemia are cancerous by nature because they have lost this intelligence of the life force.

Nerve tissues, to the average doctor, look like a stringy-like substance, but actually they are atomic structures which are linked together so they can carry the impulses from the brain or, in the condition of pain, such atomic nerve structures have within themselves the necessary intelligence to reverse the process and convey the message to the brain.

The doctor of today does not understand as yet the atomic structure of these brain tissues and that in these atomic structures are the composite wave forms which link them through the psychic body to the life cycle. Such linkage is also carried out in all structures of the body in a relative degree, the psychic body being the reflective agent from the life cycle. Each corpuscle, which is a minute particle of electricity, or the electron, has an element of iron within the molecules or substructures. This iron is magnetized, in a sense of the word, from the energies stemming from the psychic body. Each corpuscle then becomes, in a sense, a tiny magnet and attracts and holds or adheres unto itself, tiny molecules of oxygen as it passes through the lungs, or it can pick up waste products which are poured into the capillary tract through the process of osmosis. These corpuscles are, in a literal sense, electronic brooms or electric garbage collectors, maintaining as they do, a minute static charge of electricity.

When man learns of these vital concepts—principles far in advance of your present day medical sciences, he will learn also the great importance of maintaning more positive states of consciousness. He will learn (and know) how to help his offspring to live less fearful and insecure lives from feelings of inadequacy, etc., as well as the parents themselves must live more complacent lives. When the inhabitants of your earth eventually come to realize these most important positive states and come to live more closely to Spirit, you will find such conditions as polio become far less existent and eventually nonexistent. Negation is at the root of all such problems; knowledge and application of same —the cure. Man must seek and learn how to attain via consciousness the greatest amount of spiritual energy inflow from the Infinite, through living the progressive, regenerative way.

Amid the Pyramids

October 7, 1969—During the last hundred years or
so, peoples of the Western Hemisphere have been
tremendously interested and intrigued by the lore of
ancient Egypt, as it was unearthed and apparently
translated by the efforts of archeologists. By far, however, the most important aspects in this Egyptology have
not been recognized and, in particular, the significance
of certain connections which this Egyptology had, in
a historical sense, with the much older and long-ago
defunct civilization of Atlantis. In particular, the Egyptian pyramids, a subject of great mystery and intense
controversy, even to the exploration of the giant pyramid of Gizeh (Pyramid of Khufu or Cheops at Gizeh)
with cosmic ray apparatus in an attempt to divulge
certain supposed unknown inner chambers. Like almost all other earth world ethnic cultures, religions,
occultisms and even superstitions, the Egyptian pyramid is actually a vestigial remnant, a degenerate form
done in stone, of what was once actually a great electronic instrument, designed and constructed by master scientists from another world and placed on an
Atlantean plain for the purposes of generating un-
limited power derived from the interdimensional cosmos.

As it existed on the Atlantean plain some 15,000
B.C., it was constructed of metals, not stone. The geo-
metrical configuration of a pyramid was purposefully
placed in relationship to north and south magnetic
poles and with the four sides representing maximum
surface interception. On the metallic surface of this
pyramid were placed millions of small cells whose
purpose was to absorb cosmic energies and convert
them into electrical energy which could turn certain

kinds of electrical motors coupled to huge generators.

Our present-day modern cameras utilize a small cell of selenium which absorbs light and transmits it into electrical energy which opens and closes the diaphragm aperture of the camera, a parallel to the cells of the pyramid which covered its entire four surfaces, and as the pyramid was possibly a thousand feet high covering ninety-six acres of ground, the total number of cells involved when hooked together could generate tremendous power. (The great pyramid Khufu, or Cheops, at Gizeh was 482 feet high covering 13 acres.)

The story of Amon Ra who came to Atlantis about 15,000 B.C., arrived there in a spaceship, together with a number of scientists and technicians who proceeded to construct a pyramid on the Atlantean plain; a pyramid which was exactly similar to that constructed on the plains of Ancient Lemuria some 140,000 years before that time. The story of the construction of this pyramid was later, through succeeding generations of earth people and handed down as they were, degenerated into legends not entirely accurate and with considerable element of mysticism.

The typical "Tower of Babel" story in the Old Testament was derived from this legend, i.e., the ancient tribes-people believed the Lemurians were building a tower to heaven., etc.

Then it was Amon Ra and his technicians had constructed the Atlantean pyramid, the interior of which was devoted to different sections, rooms, etc., all integrated in the development and distribution of this enormous power which was generated in these generators in the subterranean vault beneath the floor. In the center of the pyramid and on the floor stood the switchboard—not like the switchboards in powerhouses today but rather, it was a metal box about 20 feet square which contained a robot or computer which, in its function in the conversion and distribution of this energy and the enormous power involved, generated an electromagnetic field around it of such intensity that the metal appeared to glow much like an overheated stove turns red. This glow gave the appearance that the box was actually pure crystalline energy. This box also performed another important function. From the top of the box was a round metallic sphere about 10 feet in diameter and from this ball, which was actually a positive pole, a flamelike protuberance of energy stood straight up toward the apex of the pyramid where, from a long rod, there hung another similar sphere of metal. The purpose for which this "flame" of energy existed was one of extreme technical importance, inasmuch as the net total oscillations of energy generated in the cells on the outside surface of the pyramid were, in this process with the "flame" converted into usable high-frequency energies which were beamed into the nearby homes and other buildings of the Atlantean city of Atlantis, eliminating the need for wires, transformers, poles, etc., with which we are familiar in our present-day towns and cities. Our modern radar ranges use this method of short-wave energy radiations to cook food.

Now it is easily understandable that in these ancient times, either Lemuria or Atlantis, when the ignorant, superstitious aboriginal natives of this planet saw or heard about this wonderful scientific technocracy, they could not understand it and it became a great mystery to them. The square box in the middle of the floor became a pure cube of energy; the flame, which stemmed from the top upward toward the overhanging metallic ball appeared motionless but was actually pulsating or oscillating thousands or billions of times per second, at speeds too incomprehensible to see or even understand by our present-day mathematics.

In the early part of this century, Tesla developed his famous Tesla Coil, the top of which, from a round spherical ball, great lightning-like streamers of energy many feet long extended to nearby objects. Was Tesla, through a psychic memory, attempting to reproduce the great technical wonder which he saw in the great Atlantean temple? And many thousands of years before, when the Ancient Egyptians built the pyramid of Gizeh, they covered the outside surface with a monolithic alabaster-like material of an unknown composition in an attempt to duplicate the white metallic surface of the Atlantean pyramid. Yet, the Egyptians, descendants of the aborigines who had survived the cataclysms, only vaguely, psychically remembered; supported, no doubt from legends of the old Atlantean temple which they tried to duplicate. Yet, with none of the science or technocracy and knowing little or nothing of electronics, they could only build their pyramid from stone blocks and cover it with a white alabaster.

Perhaps the science brought to Lemuria and Atlantis by the Lemurians will, in the near future, be duplicated on this earth. Already different countries throughout the world are building great power plants, deriving great power from the atom. Yet, this is very crude when compared to the science of the Atlantean pyramid which converted from the electromagnetic fields of the solar system and the interdimensional cosmos, a vast source of power which could be projected by ray-beams and reflected from tower to tower (like our present-day microwave system), tremendous energy which powered and lighted cities all over the world.

The future holds the promise that all of this and much more will return to the earth. The people of tomorrow will have undreamed of luxuries and conveniences, a way of life which will exceed even the most fantastic science fiction stories; yet will our present-day mankind be able to survive? Indeed not. The homogenous mixture of races presents a far too low state of mentality, a heterogenous society torn and twisted with strictures and rent by irreparable schisms. And it is quite safe to predict in that future, should it ever arrive, the breed of man who will occupy it will be vastly different than those presently now living—a comparison to the golden-skinned Atlanteans in their beautiful highly-scientific society which, through its egregious philosophy, permitted the dark-skinned ones to overpower and destroy the world. And is it not apparent that in this time history is beginning to repeat itself?

Historically speaking, anthropology has always very severely abrogated the way of life in the ancient civilizations which it has uncovered. There have been no apparent evidences of any other kind of a society or ecology which would suggest a certain scientific aspect of life lived by the Ancients. In some instances, however, this could be far from the truth. Scientific or electronic apparatus, as it might have been used in any ancient civilization would be most necessarily, comparatively fragile, the apparatus small in size and portable, and could have long ago disappeared, at least partly into pots, pans, jewelry or temple bells and such things. For example: one archeological report cites the uncovering of electrolytic batteries in an ancient pre-Babylonian city more than 4,000 B.C. Artisans at that time were electroplating jewelry with gold, just as it is done at the present time. The batteries actually generated electricity when the electrolyte was refreshed.

Also about 4,000 B.C., according to archeology, the ancient Minoan civilization thrived somewhere in the Mediterranean just off the Grecian peninsula. The Minoans are said to have been highly cultured; they wrought beautiful ceramics, pottery, jewelry and other artifacts, delicately engraved and colored; the interiors of their homes, the floors and walls of which exhibited beautiful murals. Descriptions of their houses said they were air-conditioned but from totally opened doors and windows, apparently without any means of covering or closing. Now this is quite preposterous; even a primitive savage living in a grass thatched hut can cover the door with a wild animal skin. The climate in the Mediterranean areas can become quite cold in winter; snow falls in Italy and Greece, and summers are unbearably hot. Although the Minoan houses were apparently all constructed of carved stone blocks and beamed ceilings, ways and means would certainly have been used to close door and window openings. Doors and door frames, and window glass and window frames could have long ago vanished in the hands of vandals or to people who wished to use wood for their own purposes. Glass, stained or otherwise, would also have been useful. Interiors of the houses could have been heated with large metal urns or braziers which burn palm or whale oil. And there is a possibility that this Minoan civilization or even more ancient civilizations could have enjoyed electrical and mechanical technocracy far in advance of our present time.

From the great central pyramid in Atlantis, power beams would be relayed from reflectors on mountain tops into the different homes where these power beams would be converted into light, heat or even to cool the house. The proposition here is relatively simple. A round glass globe or sphere about a foot in diameter and filled with certain rare gases would fluoresce and give off a soft white light, just as does our modern fluorescent light. Heating or cooling is also simple: air is made up of molecules of gases, each molecule composed of a number of atoms. Electrical energy of a certain frequency when radiated through air is converted into heat through hysteresis in the electromagnetic fields of the atoms.

The same proposition in reverse makes the air become cold, remembering of course, that all atmosphere on the earth is always converting this certain electromagnetic energy into heat. Speaking from the point of absolute zero, minus 495 degrees Fahrenheit —all air on the surface of the earth is comparatively warm, even at the poles. Cooling or heating the air at any given point means merely to decrease or increase the electromagnetic hysteresis.

In a Minoan house, for example, a small object a foot or so square sitting on the floor of any room could be both the heater and the cooler. It would, according to the dictates of a thermostat, radiate certain energies into the room which would either slow down hysteresis and make the air cooler or speed up hysteresis and make the air warmer; a far different process than our present-day crude, clumsy, inefficient and enormous heating and cooling systems which must always either heat air in a furnace or cool it by means of refrigeration and, with a fan, blow it into the room through a large duct.

Again, any of these small air-conditioning units would have most certainly disappeared many thousands of years ago. Superstitious people may have destroyed them thinking they were evil or converted them into jewelry or weapons or destroyed them in other ways. Only the stone skeletons of the houses remain which bear only a small fragment of testimony as to a great and wonderful way of life lived in one of these ancient cities of the Atlantean epoch.

Amon Ra: The literal translation of Amon Ra means sun-god. The superstitious natives, when they saw the glowing white spaceship, thought that the sun-god had come to earth, hence the name Amon Ra.

The technical description of the generator-oscillator banks and the generation of the "flame", while very complex, can be more easily understood with this simplified explanation: in the subterranean chamber beneath the floor stood the motor-generator combination mounted on a vertical shaft. This piece of machinery worked exactly similar to our present-day Pabst synchronous-hysteresis motor, that is, exactly in reverse to ordinary motors which have a rotor rotating inside fixed stationary field coils. In the Pabst motor, the rotor is stationary and the metal field terminals rotate around it, similar to a squirrel cage. The Atlantean motor-generator combination works as follows: a huge externally-powered, (A.C.) alternating current motor rotated the squirrel cage which was actually a large number of extremely powerful high-gauss, high-intensity magnets affixed to the metal frame which rotated around what would normally be the rotor which was made from a high-permeability, soft iron core. Wound around a large number of these poles were almost countless thousands of turns of insulated wire.

These coils were, in turn, connected up to different banks of cells on the outside skin surface of the pyramid. The sequence of this wiring was such, that when the magnets turned around the rotor, the cells and the magnetic currents so generated were in extremely rapid sequence which built up an extremely high-frequency oscillating voltage which discharged across the two balls which I described previously. The purpose of this gap was to stabilize these oscillations under resistive conditions in open air.

As every electrophysicist knows a certain fundamental law of electronics—increasing the frequency increases the voltage or power—that is why a laser beam can pierce a diamond with less energy than would light a small flashlight. The energy from a five foot long lightning bolt from a Tesla coil (500,000 cycles per second) was less than two millionths of an ampere and would cause only a mild tingling sensation. A lightning bolt traveling from a cloud to the earth contains only enough energy to light a hundred watt bulb for about thirty seconds.

Electronic scientists of today, however, are still a bit mixed up on the proposition of voltage versus frequency. They string ½ inch thick laminated cable across the countryside for hundreds of miles from tall steel towers and push electricity through these cables in far away cities at voltages in excess of 300,000 and at only 60 cycles per second alternating frequency, whereas a small pencil-thin power beam oscillating at hundreds of millions of times per second could be reflected from tower to tower across country; one beam carrying sufficient power to energize the largest city.

In 1925, out in Colorado, Tesla sent electrical beams through the earth and lighted up light bulbs five miles away. His experimental station still stands.*

Flying saucers or spaceships are energized and fly by exactly the same principle as used in the Atlantean oscillator-generator or the Pabst hysteresis-synchronous motor. Perhaps when certain pseudo elements of our scientific society stop denying the ever-apparent infinite cosmos and the countless billions of different types of civilizations living on countless billions of planets, they will begin to at least admit the possibility that space travel across the galaxy or the universe is not only feasible but has been going on for millions of years.

Enigmatically, many of these moss-backed, hard-nosed pseudo-scientists have, in some way, been advocating or participating in our present-day space effort. We have already accomplished the moon and Mars is the next tentative target by 1980.

*Since this writing, his station has been torn down.

139

Part Two

In our preceding chapter we discovered the Egyptian pyramids, Khufu or Cheops, etc., as well as pyramids in other parts of the world—Yucatan peninsula, Inca, Peru, etc.—were, in their odd shapes and seemingly meaningless geometry, actually a decadent remnant of several huge pyramids which existed in Atlantis and even in the more ancient Lemuria which were, in reality, highly-developed electronic generators designed and built by Master Scientists from another world. Our description of this pyramid as it existed in Atlantis is far from complete, however, so let us continue to explore this most amazing achievement.

Briefly, a huge rotating squirrel-cage-generator turned by a motor was linked up to an electronic computer which was housed in a twenty-foot square metal box on the floor just above the generator. This computer automatically made and broke connections with banks of power-collector cells on the outside pyramid-surface in such a sequential manner that a tremendous oscillating voltage was built up. On the ten-foot ball which stood atop the metal box, this oscillating electricity discharged more than six hundred feet straight up to a similar metal ball hanging down from the pyramid's apex on a long metal rod.

In our 1900's, a scientist named Steinmetz hurled thunderbolts from two large metal spheres one hundred feet apart in a manner which is somehow strangely similar to the process used in the Atlantean Pyramid 16,000 years ago. This discharge across the two metal balls served as a tank-circuit, as it is called, and again a similarity to our modern early-day wireless, a motor turning a rimless rotary wheel from which protruded a number of spokes, actually electrodes. As the wheel rotated about 2,000 rpm (rotations per minute), a sizzling white spark jumped from the spokes to another electrode placed about one-half inch away from the spokes. It was this spark-gap which created the necessary high-intensity voltage.

Now, on top of the Atlantean pyramid was a fifty-foot metal column, something like a thick flagpole, which terminated in a circular bank of what looked like the spokes on a wheel. About ten feet long and sixteen inches in diameter, these spokes protruded at a number of irregular intervals, each one carefully sighted like a rifle, to a near or distant receiver. These spokes were actually composed of an exotic mixture of metals and formed into a homogenous, crystalline aggregate under extreme pressure and magnetic hysteresis. Each rod or spoke then contained billions of tiny crystals; each one pointed, so to speak, toward the outside flat end of the rod. They absorbed energy and like a boy who'd eaten too much watermelon, they reached certain capacity and discharged their energy toward the outside end of the rod.

The net total of these charge and discharge oscillations were on the order of millions of megacycles per second and as they functioned from the end of the rod, a beam of pure coherent energy emerged—and at the rate of more than 186,000 miles per second straight to a receiver, a beam of enormous power. How similar to our present first versions of the laser: a six-inch synthetic ruby rod, one inch in diameter and containing many chromium molecules; these chromium molecules were charged with electricity from an outside source of condenser banks and other associated equipment which generated a high-frequency impulse. As the chromium molecule atoms reached their saturation point, they discharged their energies which began to oscillate ping-pong fashion from each end of the optically-ground and silvered ends of the rod. When

141

this oscillating energy reached a certain point, it discharged through the more lightly silvered end in a single straight coherent beam of great intensity and power.

Again, could these present-day scientists have been duplicating, from a psychic memory, that which they saw and helped destroy in Ancient Atlantis? The power beams which emerged from the Atlantis pyramid were intercepted by similar metallic rods of crystallized metal which, because they oscillated in a similar manner and frequency, presented no resistance to the enormous power of the beam. The beam then traveled straight through the rod or was broken up and separated into separate beams by a crystal prism, which again sent beams pulsating through crystalline rods and on a new tangent to another receiver.

In utilizing these power beams in a dwelling, a metal ball fitted on top of a metal rod, like a small flagpole, contained a crystal of certain prismatic configurations which directed the beam down through the hollow center of the rod to a disbursement instrument which energized the entire house by means of induction so that the round milky-white crystal globes would glow with light, motors turn, etc.

In the land of Egypt and all other lands where there were pyramids, the Egyptians tried to duplicate the round spoke-like wheel which glowed with a blue-white corona and which shot beams of intense light in different directions. The Egyptians topped their stone pyramid with a large ball-like contrivance covered with small plates of pure polished gold in a scale-like manner; and as the earth turned, shafts of light were reflected in all directions.

Several thousands of years later, these metal balls with scales of gold had disappeared, so had the alabaster white coating except for small sections near the top, in order to use the smaller surface stones in nearby cities for building purposes.

In the nineteenth century, Napoleon's cannon shot off the nose of the Sphinx, his artillery-men using the great monolith for target practice.

Atlantis was blown into oblivion by the very power that it generated, wrongly used in the hands of ignorant black people who sought to rule the world. Again in our present day, could the racial strife in America and other countries be a psychic remanifestation of the destruction of the world more than 12,000 years ago? Yes, history repeats itself; the modern Egyptians wore in their temples and palaces a metallic headdress and woven metal scarves interwoven with threads of gold which hung down over their shoulders just as they did in the Ancient Atlantis when, after the scientists had gone, the Atlanteans started to worship the flame in the temple pyramid. The metallic headdress plus a metallic robe was necessary to protect them from the strong electromagnetic field in the pyramid and somehow the metallic headdress has arrived in our present modern time in the form of a scarf worn by women in a Catholic church, or the uraeus worn by the priest. Such is the way of the primitive earthman.

While he can construct a continuous gas laser beam, shoot it through a telescope to the moon where it is reflected by a reflector planted by Apollo 11 astronauts, and received on earth where, in its pulse, this beam accurately measures the distance to less than a mile, yet this same man constantly abrogates and vilifies the creation all about him by reading superstitious legends from his so-called "holy Bible", as he rides his space-craft through space! Or that he constantly degenerates and vilifies his earth life, pollutes his environment and the creative principles of life which have created his planetary home and brought him up from his primitive past, despite his ever-destructive, degenerate proclivities!

143

Cycles and Civilizations

(This dissertation was included in a student's life reading, and it was felt it should be added herein.)

We will present a synopsis or trace and present various civilizations, a starting place of these cycles and of their appearance of so many countless thousands of people who have lived in these age-old civilizations, and have incarnated back and forth through these various epochs countless times. For convenience sake, we shall start with Atlantis. As every truth seeker knows or has heard something about this ancient civilization which was predated by the Lemurian civilization even many thousands of years previously; in this old Atlantis about 25,000 years ago there was a very wonderful and beautiful civilization which flourished on the continent somewhere in the mid-Atlantic ocean.

This civilization, which lasted for many thousands of years, was directed under spiritual leadership from a great temple in Atlantis. Stemming out into various corners of the world, there flourished numerous colonies which were also largely directed by this same priesthood. Some several thousands of years later, a race of dark-skinned people succeeded in stealing certain secrets of machinery which were atomically conceived in nature, and handed down from the Lemurian Masters, and with these secrets the dark-skinned ones actually succeeded in blowing Atlantis completely out of the ocean.

Along with this terrible destruction, there was naturally a great loss of life. Then too, before this cataclysm, many thousands of people who had, by being fore-warned, migrated to various other countries such as Egypt, India, Persia, and Central and South America. From these remnants sprang other civilizations. So it was that through the many epochs of time, various and countless millions of citizens who had resided in these ancient civilizations, and knowing of this great Spiritual Leadership and that wonderful way of life, began seeking to find themselves in some new age and time wherein these same spiritual concepts were further expressed, and also that they might gain more wisdom and advance themselves in their own spiritual evolution, which is always a strong and motivating, inward desire of every human being.

And you, dear student, doubtless, along with the countless multitudes from these past ages, began coming and going into these various civilizations of Egypt, ancient India, China, Chaldea, and into the more recent civilizations such as the Hellenic Age, about 500 B.C. when the episode wherein Jesus and his Mission were given to the world about 2000 years ago, and so on through the dark Middle Ages to the present time.

Thus, it is that here in this present moment you find yourself with the remnants and vestiges of the various karmic and psychic shocks which you have incurred through these past evolutions, which you are now try-ing to work out, that you have reestablished yourself in a more progressive position for the future Aquarian Age.

This Age, incidentally, is mentioned in several places in both the Old and New Testament, and in the opening chapter of Genesis, it is referred to as the Seventh Day of the Lord. In the Book of Revelations there is men-tion of the Millennium and the building of the New City of Jerusalem, which is the thousand-year preparatory cycle wherein all karmic structures in the psychic selves of these millions of truth seekers are literally cancelled out or die, and are replaced by more spiritual concepts which will enable these persons to live in this future age and time. The New City of Jerusalem is that long-envisioned new Spiritual Age of Universal Brotherhood of mankind on the Earth, and governmental leadership through spiritual means of some sort, which is not now manifest in such political systems as we so possess.

This future Age will also see the end of the wars and great fears and hatreds which these warlike attitudes of nations are now imposing upon the Earth. There will also be the elimination of the so-called incurable diseases which are the bane of existence to untold millions of peoples upon the face of the Earth presently. A new scientific technocracy will exist, which will so advance man in his learning and thinking that certain scientific-spiritual concepts which are being presently used in more highly-developed civilizations on other planets will actually become a part of life upon the earth.

These concepts, incidentally, are included in your lessons course book and your other textbooks of Unarius. You will see also, how other races of people on other planets use many of these highly-advanced spiritual and scientific concepts and adaptations in their way of life.

And so, you can therefore very easily see that being concerned with possibly a thousand or so lifetimes and living in such conditions and circumstances which were idiomatic of any one particular life, you did indeed incept as basic psychic structures, the numerous and different experiences, negative, positive or otherwise, through various lifetimes. Some interesting aspects of this pattern relate to sex, and everyone has come and gone either as male or female in these more primitive evolutions. That is simply because certain definite strong polarity patterns which would relegate the person to one sex or another had not as yet been sufficiently developed. Other factors such as frequency relationship, strong urges to incarnate back into the physical, and other various factors would all more or less be responsible for whatever gender the individual finds himself incarnated into.

Also some ancient lifetimes were concerned with religious cultisms which were serpents. This practice still goes on in our modern world in the more primitive areas of the Earth such as the jungles, in India and Africa. In the ancient times, snake cultisms were very highly developed and involved whole nations, such as ancient India. It was actually the snake worshippers who destroyed Atlantis. The parable of the Garden of Eden is an interpretation which relates to the weaning away from his old spiritual life to the more materialistic and sexual attitudes which were practiced by the snake cultists. Human sacrifice on the altar of a snake god was quite common as well as snake pits and religious fanatics who would cast themselves into the pits believing that this was a sure way to Heaven. Most students have, at one time or another, perished by the direct result of being bitten by some poisonous reptile in one or more of these primitive lifetimes.

Now the principle of evolution which concerns various lifetimes are all very basic in nature. That is, during the oscillating processes between consciousness and the inner reaches of the psychic body, such as the subconscious, this energy body is being constantly rebuilt in the natural process of living. The old wave forms which related to previous experiences are gradually being replaced in the evolutionary pattern of progress. In the natural course of events it is quite easy to see that any very strong impingements, such as we call a psychic shock, a violent murder, or some other destructive element which suddenly enters into a person's life, in turn, creates a very catastrophic negative vortex of energy in the psychic body. This negative energy later always causes disease either of mind, body or both, for this individual, unless it is in some way cancelled out or otherwise corrected. These elements are presently missing from all of our known medical science today, whether they relate to chiropractics, naturopathy or the more orthodox channel of materia medica.

Other elements which are sadly lacking in our present-day understanding and especially in psychiatry, are the various concepts which relate to obsessions. Anyone who reads the New Testament can easily see that while Jesus taught a very understandable way of life which linked man with numerous dimensions, that our modern psychiatry has completely eliminated all such concepts and relegated them to the common terminology of witchcraft, and in a sense of the word they are accusing Jesus of sorcery and witchcraft as he practiced casting out evil spirits and obsession from the people in and around the Holy Land.

Just as the more primitive aspects of medicine or various healing therapies in the more ancient times can be likened and compared to the more modern advanced and developed forms of these same therapies, so can that science practiced by Jesus (as related in the Bible) be compared to the witchcraft in the jungle. By the same token the modern man of medicine, in whatever field he finds himself, if he is so concerned with healing people, should always include the elements which link man, as a spiritual being, into different planes of relationship. For the external body is merely the result or the appearance of a large number of sequences or events, which we will call evolution, which have led man up to this particular point of development. By far a large part of this development takes place in the spiritual consciousness, the opposite

polarity of development being of course the materialistic dimension or the experience realm in which the
various elements of introspection are entered into by
way of such experiences, comparative values, equa-
tions—as some people say, learning the hard way. In
the final and ultimate result of all this various experience and the oscillations which relate in implanting
the experience quotient as wave forms in the psychic
body, a person ultimately resolves into a much more
highly advanced personality in a spiritual sense.

This is to say, the more insidious and negative part
of these experiences in their wave forms and harmonic
structures are replaced. However, the individual does
retain conscious memory in another dimension of consciousness which is concerned with the psychic body
which oscillates more directly with the superconsciousness. Thus, in the course of thousands of years
into the future, he may gradually develop into some
personality which is much more godlike in nature, and
infinitely more wise than he is in present circumstances. To view each patient as incurring such various
physical and mental illnesses and idiosyncrasies as
may appear on the surface, and while these symptoms
are purely superficial in nature, yet they all have very
strong linkage into the psychic centers, relating each
person in proper perspective and proportion into
previous lifetimes where these different negative experiences, malformations and shocks were implanted into
the psychic anatomy.

Yes, dear student, there is but one way these nega-
tions can be removed. This is through awareness, the
understanding of this science, the objectifying by the
individual of these past incurrences and by so conceiving, does one change the phase relationship of these
past oscillations. Then he incurs, instead, a more positive vortex within his psychic anatomy, placing him in
a completely new frequency within himself, whereby

healing takes place as a result.

And so to you who are on this particular pathway and have, each one of you, prepared well and long in this distant past for this, your so-called "Second Coming", your spiritual awakening that you too may become a way-shower and a helper in this great work necessary for mankind in the future, so it would indeed be a grave mistake not to fully capitalize on all these various wisdoms which you have learned in the past and to bring them into complete fruition in this time and age, at least to a point where you can, in your future lifetimes—and there are many yet ahead of you —become one of the leaders and wayshowers in that Aquarian Age—an Age when man will surely need all the help which can possibly be mustered up from the more advanced souls and personalities who have traveled this pathway of Truth, who have perfected themselves and their intellects to the point where they have become an oscillating pole with the great Infinite Source.

Therefore, for the future, we can only strongly advise you to study the energy concepts contained in the lessons and books. Realize that life is simply a constant successive series of oscillations from polarity to polarity, as all forms of consciousness are thus contained in the dynamic oscillations, movement of energy from one pole to another, and extending our concepts into the structure of this psychic body, then into more universal and abstract concepts, all relating to interdimensional relationship. Then we will indeed have started on that spiraling pathway which leads us up into the starry skies. We can never occupy a higher spiritual plane until we have so prepared ourselves for it, that we are compatible with it. Do not be concerned that you do not remember consciously astral flights or your sleep teachings, or that you are living in the planes of consciousness wherein you are again

150

learning or that you are teaching. It makes small difference if the conscious mind is not connected in the memory sense with these experiences, for we will assure you that you are indeed under the protectorate of these great, Perfected, Infinite Minds of the Unariun Brotherhood. So for the future, may the Infinite Light always guide your footsteps as you walk with us this Illumined Pathway into the starry reaches of that never-ending Infinite Source.

INTERDIMENSIONAL

SOLAR

MECHANICS

Of Atoms and Astronauts

The Moon Flight (Viewed Psychically)

The Apollo (#15) space flight to the moon has just been completed and marks the fourth successful attempt by mankind to explore the surface of our sister planet. These space trips to the moon, together with others which have been made in more recent years, have brought to light some very important facts regarding the health and well-being of astronauts or men when they go beyond the periphery of the Earth's atmosphere and gravitational fields. Principally; these facts involve certain chemical imbalances which occur in the bodies of these men as they travel through space. Calcium and potassium are not properly assimilated and the body, in turn, robs the bone structure of calcium to supply the need for this mineral in the metabolism of the body. Curiously enough, supplementing this imbalance by the intake orally of these elements does not reconstitute the balance and the long-term effect of such imbalances could be greatly increased should the space flights continue beyond the limited number of days which man has succeeded in remaining aloft and away from the earth's gravitational fields.

All of this, of course, poses a great mystery to the scientists and those who are concerned with the health and well-being of mankind, either in space or more directly involved with our environmental factors as we so find ourselves in our daily lives. These very important facts could be very easily solved and the mysteries cleared up should the scientists learn to recognize and begin to work with the different electromagnetic fields which surround the Earth and which are a part of the solar system; some of which radiate from the sun and others are of a more fourth-dimensional nature which are actually the constituents of "inner" space which holds the galaxy together, forms planets and suns, and even is the motivating force as well as the constructive elements in the entire universe. However, the scientists of today are not aware of the multiples of the electro-magnetic fields as they are concerned either with the solar system or with the universe, and so the factors of metabolism which are upset when the forces of gravity and other electromagnetic fields are temporarily suspended, will no doubt remain a great mystery until the scientist does become acquainted with these different electromagnetic fields.

Hand in hand, so to speak, is another curious phenomenon which is common to all people who inhabit this planet, and while you may not see a direct relationship between this phenomenon and traveling through space, yet the underlying principles are exactly the same. This phenomenon of which I speak is the variance in weight which every person has during a twenty-four hour period. All persons may weigh from one to five pounds lighter at 4 A.M. than they do at 10 P.M. These fluctuations cannot altogether be attributed to the loss of water or common dietary influences, metabolic "burning" of food to maintain body temperatures, conversion of food to energy and such, during the course of the day. It might be surmised a person should weigh less at night before retiring than he would in the morning, but the reverse is always true.

Now again, if the total proposition of the different spectral electromagnetic fields which surround the Earth and which are part of our planetary system, together with the galaxy and the universe, if man's relationship to these electromagnetic fields were more properly understood, all of these mysteries would again be resolved.

In order to understand, we will revert back to our original consensus of our electromagnetic fields as they

154

exist either with the atomic constituents of our bodies or any other objects of the Earth, together with the many electromagnetic fields which surround the Earth. The chemistry or the metabolism of your body depends partially or wholly upon the relationship of these electromagnetic fields for this proper function and metabolism; that is to say, all atoms have an electromagnetic field. These atoms as they are compounded into molecules and cell structures, etc., again reradiate a magnetic field which contains a number of harmonics which are actually multiples of the original vibrations which surround the electrons of the atom. Now, according to phase or frequency relationship, these different electromagnetic wave forms can either repel or can be inductive to others or can combine with them, or they can also remain in a somewhat passive state—a quiescent state—depending of course upon frequencies and the harmonics which are regenerated within them.

The total sum of harmonics as they are regenerated in any human anatomy form, that has been commonly called in the ancient occultisms as the aura, are the radiating force fields which surround every human. It might be well to mention too, that this same aura surrounds every object on the Earth, even the stones upon the ground, or the mountains, the lakes, the oceans. In fact, the total Earth has a great and magnificent aura, this aura of course being composed of regenerative harmonics which have been regenerated in the general processes which are going on at any particular moment during the entire twenty-four hour cycle, together with the existing electromagnetic fields.

The picture here is rather complex and involves the entire solar mechanics: the revolution of the Earth around the sun, the revolution of the sun around the central apex of the galaxy, leading its flock of planets like a mother hen with her chicks. And with all of these different movements of the planets, the sun, the galaxy, and on through the universe, you can naturally see that an infinite number of magnetic lines of force are constantly being intercepted, passed through, or being in some way regenerated as harmonic structures within the net sum and total of our earth fields.

The metabolism of any human anatomy, or for that matter, any living thing on the face of the Earth, depends as I have said, on certain primary relationships with the total electromagnetic spectrum of the Earth, the solar system, and the universe. This is what is meant when it has been said in the Bible that even a sparrow which falls by the way is noted, because the movement of any particle or even an atom in the total spectral composite as it is in the entire universe, will, to a certain relative degree, affect its position as an inductive or a repellent capacity to this total spectrum of the universe. It can therefore, in its effectuation, be said to relay or to inject a certain variable degree of relationship even to the outermost edges of Infinity. When this total harmonic interplay is more thoroughly understood and envisioned within your own mind, complex as it is, then this will begin to give you a key to solving these mysteries which are now puzzling the scientists of this Earth at this time.

The weight of your body, for example, be it 150 pounds or 180 pounds or whatever, that weight is totally dependent upon the gravitational field, and this dependency or the relationship of this gravitational field with the Earth's gravitational field is, of course, as you can see, a relationship between the inductive properties of the electromagnetic field of your body and that of the gravitational spectrum of the Earth. We must also take into account that there are numerous other different electromagnetic fields which surround the Earth, and all but two of these are totally unknown to the scientist of the time. He knows only of the gravitational field and of the magnetic field, such as it might apply to the common horseshoe magnet. The gravitational field however, still remains quite a mystery to the scientist, chiefly because he has not concerned himself with the electromagnetic properties of the atom which constitute any object or body on the surface of the Earth, yes, and even the different layers of the Earth or of the total mass of the Earth itself—that this inductive field is force or induced force which has been generated by the total electromagnetic fields of the solar system, the galaxy and the universe—all done according to certain patterns generated in the principle of harmonics, and one of these harmonics comes out in the third dimension as the gravitational field.

So you see that as your aura fluctuates, as it does during the twenty-four hour period, the weight of your body will also fluctuate because it is either more or less attracted by the gravitational field, according to the principles which I have described. The inductive principles which attract certain harmonics in the net sum and total of your electromagnetic field or aura are likewise tuned, so to speak, to those particular harmonics which constitute the gravitational field of the Earth. The same principle is involved in complete totality to the entire metabolism of the human anatomy. While the psychic anatomy, which every person has, relays the necessary information or the compelling intelligence to the many different cells, molecules, atoms etc., which keep metabolism going in this human body, yet the necessary movements within the atomic structures themselves, as they constitute molecules or cells, would not be possible unless they had their relationship and their necessary oscillation with these fourth-dimensional electromagnetic fields.

This relationship is achieved constantly at all times through and with these different electromagnetic fields which I have mentioned, and as there are many thousands of them which, to some degree, can be said to be harmonically attuned or in a relationship with the cells, molecules and atoms which constitute your body, therefore their effect upon your metabolism can be quite readily seen. As you are sleeping, the metabolism of your body changes. That is why it is possible for you to rejuvenate your body much more successfully and completely during sleeping hours than it is during the waking period of your day. Also, many other accomplishments are achieved within your body, together with your psychic anatomy during sleep, which is not possible during the waking hours.

All of these functions are of course rebuilding, readjusting, recharging, renewing the different electromagnetic fields which are constantly radiating around the different atomic structures which constitute your body. You must remember that while your body is composed of countless trillions of atoms, yet the entire body is dependent upon the health and well-being of every single atom in your anatomy. And should one atom begin to fail, so to speak, that is, not to maintain its proper relationship with the total electromagnetic fields of the solar system, the Earth, together with the impelling intelligences or commands as they are reflected by the psychic anatomy, then this atom can be said to be cancerous, and it can affect other atoms. A number of atoms, as they comprise a molecule, are in turn, involved in the structure of a cell. This inharmony or lack of harmonic interplay, as I have described it, can regenerate a cancer.

Principally, however, we are concerned with the every-day factors of common living, such as they are expressed. So you see that by affecting the total metabolism of our body as it is involved during the sleeping state and toward 4:00 A.M. your weight will change. You will become lighter because the physical or that particular part of the aura of your body has somewhat less of a direct relationship or a pull to the electromagnetic field of the Earth. When you are awake and during the day, you regenerate a certain particular amount of physical oscillations in the total atomic structures of your body. These build up until about the time you retire at night so that your pull toward the gravitatiolial field of the Earth is somewhat greater at that period than it was at 4:00 A.M. When you understand this somewhat clearly you will have solved this mystery which has puzzled scientists and doctors since almost the beginning of the bathroom scale.

It will also solve for you why calcium is taken from the bones of the skeleton of a man in weightlessness in space, or that potassium cannot be assimilated simply because of the relationships in the net sum and total of the different electromagnetic fields of these atomic structures concerned with the metabolism of the body, the calcium and potassium itself and the net sum and total of all electromagnetic fields of the solar system, the galaxy and the universe.

Now you can readily appreciate that this has been a rather difficult concept to explain; however, you must also rely upon other ways and manners in which you can take principles which I have described to you and interject them into your daily life to explain why you have certain particular cycles of, shall I say, regression or progression in your own daily life; why some days seem to be better than others and vice versa. It is an expansion of this concept into what we will call planetary aspects which the astrologer of today relies upon. Here again, the astrologer is not conscious of and does not know about the different and numerous electromagnetic fields which are the composite of our solar system; neither does he understand, as I have described these electromagnetic fields to you, their effect upon the human anatomy or the psychic anatomy of every individual. Astrology therefore is invalid as it is so exercised today because it does not take into consideration the numerous other different factors which are relevant to your daily life on the planet Earth. That is the reason why any astrologer will tell you that astrology impels but does not compel. We are concerned in these compelling forces and motivations of your life and what makes it possible on this planet Earth.

As I have said, the total environment of any Earth world such as this is very hostile; it is hostile to life, yet strangely, this hostility in itself propagates and makes life possible on the basis that it selects the species according to the Darwinian principle of selectivity in its total evolution. Therefore, as a product of evolution, you as a human have learned to breathe the gas of the air even though during the first nine months of your life your lungs were entirely filled with water, and this water had to run from your mouth before you could breathe.

It will also explain to you, in understanding all of these mysteries as we are concerned in our evolution on this planet Earth, if we go into the basic factors which have not only made life possible, that they have engendered life and these principles have also constructed and reconstituted planets, suns and galaxies, etc. And I am speaking, of course, of the original consensus of principles as it involves the structures of electromagnetic fields, the harmonics which are therefore regenerated within the electromagnetic fields, how they apply to the inductive or to the repelling forces which make the difference between atoms, molecules, cells, human beings and every other form of life or any object on the Earth. You can very clearly see that there are no two objects on this Earth which are exactly similar in every respect.

Therefore, in the future, whether it is another space

flight to the moon or whether you read in the local newspapers about other mysteries which men have discovered in their daily lives and what makes it possible on this planet Earth, you can then resort to the explanations which I have given you: the properties of the electromagnetic fields, their relationships to each other according to harmonic structures, and bearing this in mind, will give you a great and added amount of wisdom which will help you in your evolutionary climb into the future.

It is only fair to note at this time that certain very important discoveries and developments have already transpired here among the scientific segment of humanity on the planet Earth. In Russia, for example, scientists there have made tremendous strides in what is more commonly known as ESP and as another factor in the total relationship of mankind in his life on the planet Earth, ESP is also made possible by the total electromagnetic spectrum of the fourth dimension. Notably in particular, a man and wife team have discovered what is known as the Kirlian effect. By using an oscillator-generator, working on frequencies between 30,000 and 40,000 kilocycles, certain objects animate and inanimate, life, plants, animals and even humans can be radiated to the extent that certain harmonics will be regenerated in the total auric emanations of their bodies, and these harmonics are photographed.

There are actually many thousands of photos of auras which relate to plants, animals, objects and people etc., and while this is a very important discovery and development which points in the right direction, there is still no indication that such explorations and discoveries will be pursued and followed into the adjacent fourth dimension, which is the seat and origin of all life, including the planet Earth and other similar untold millions of planets in the galaxy as well as the suns which warm these planetary systems and furnish power and energy to the life forms which are found on the surface of these planets.

Looking at our life here on Earth in sort of a totality, it could very well be said that any human, or any life form for that matter, is simply a little glob of energy in an infinite and great sea of energy wherein if we look at this energy closely and begin to resolve it into its dimensional form, we will see in the fourth dimension and all the adjacent dimensions, energy revolving in cyclic patterns and manners which are not comprehensible to third-dimensional minds. You, then, as a little glob of energy, moving about in this great sea of energy, can readily see that not only is your life here as you manifest it in your consciousness made possible by all of this energy, but that you are actually, at any given moment or any given time, merely relating yourself to any one or a number of different wave forms in a phase relationship to this total sea of infinity.

In consciousness or in a physical aspect, this relationship must take place constantly at all times; you are inductive or you absorb this energy in much the same manner and fashion that a radio or television receiver would absorb the energy from the transmitter. The number, ways and manners in which you absorb or that you reradiate energy are almost countless and without number—the absorption or induction into your psychic anatomy, into your physical body, into your consciousness, the re-radiation of different wave forms from the physical anatomy and your consciousness into infinity. You can therefore see that this is not only a complex picture but is one which must be, at least to some extent, understood.

Life without the physical body in any other dimension would not be possible unless you attained some of this understanding, and the degree in which you learn to understand will determine the net sum and total of your life in any of these future dimensions. If you have

162

no comprehension, then your life without your physical body, without the correlative factors which I have described to you, will be absolutely impossible. It is your physical body and your conscious mind, as it is constituted in the brain cells, which number anywhere up to 50 million or so, which make your life possible here on Earth.

However, divesting your psychic anatomy of this body in the way in which it expresses itself in relationship to all of the electromagnetic fields of force in the totality of the interdimensional consensus, then you can readily see that your life could very well be nightmarish. You would live in a vague, suspended, dream-like state where you would resort to such memories as were contained in your psychic anatomy, and some form of consciousness would be made possible only on the basis of these dreams. In other words, life without your body in another dimension could very well be one big nightmare unless you possessed some knowledge of the many different factors which relate to harmonic interplays of the numerous electromagnetic fields of the interdimensional cosmos, which I have described to you. So therefore, persist and do not be discouraged that you do not assimilate all of this knowledge in a few days or even in a lifetime. Remember, the assimilation of this knowledge is your future; it could well last the next hundred million years or so before you would arrive into any kind of a compatible position whereby you could live a really good life in a higher dimension. And when you achieve that life, you must also bear in mind that the common factors which you find palatable and necessary in your daily life now would be entirely foreign and unknown to you at that time. You might even look back on them in sort of a telepathic way into the past as one might read his own akashic record and you would wonder how you ever lived through being such a vegetative creature.

To further enlarge our prospective, therefore, on what has been discussed, it could be envisioned in another way: that as a human on an Earth planet, whether he is an astronaut, or Tom, Dick, or Harry, or whoever person he is, or for that matter, any animal, bird, tree, rock, etc., all life processes involved on this planet take place in what might be best described as a plasma; that is to say, the net sum and total of all electromagnetic fields which are concerned around the Earth, the solar system, the galaxy, the universe, as well as all other adjunctive relationships with the inter-dimensional cosmos, would form the composite of this plasma. The third dimensional constituents would of course be the harmonics and the more direct phase relationships which are third-dimensionally inclined or expressed. In this specified and constantly oscillating space-earth plasma, the average person has, through evolution, learned how to conduct and live his daily life.

From life to life, each life has added its own individual measure and which has gone into the psychic anatomy—that energy body which is the second person or more properly could be called the first person, as the psychic anatomy, being fourth-dimensional in nature, does not die but lives eternally. It also is dependent to a large degree upon certain infusions, I shall say, or direct radiations into, or being inductive into the net interdimensional cosmos. It finds within itself certain compatible relationships or frequencies which oscillate with, regenerate with, and totally build up with, and help to recharge from the interdimensional cosmos.

In common metaphysics, as is sometimes taught in earth world dimensions, it is said that God has created everything in infinite supply. Well, that is quite true; however, you must remember also that infinite supply and that Infinite Creation in whatever form you imagine has been done interdimensionally in cyclular wave

164

forms of energy. Each one of these large or small cycles contain within themselves certain idioms or quotients of intelligence, or they contain some sort of a form or embodiment which is of course, all as an oscillating component part of this cycle. It remains however for any individual consciousness such as is expressed in a human being, to incept this cyclic form and in a comparative ratio with his past that he can again re-manifest the intelligence or the quotient in this cyclic wave form contained in that cycle, into his daily life. For example; he may have, in a previous lifetime thousands of years ago, lived in a crude house constructed of stones on a hillside. Today, the same oscillating wave forms in his psychic anatomy could, when combined with a higher idiom or quotient of intelligence from a higher cyclic wave form in this oscillation from infinity, and combined with the two, develop into a much more modern house with indoor plumbing and all of the other amenities which are concerned with modern-day living.

Such is the way evolution is conducted. It is the constant re-induction or manifestation of the past into the present surface of consciousness, then added to with the infinite supply, or number of oscillating wave forms contained in an infinite number of cycles, and when so properly combined and expressed, become certain developments in the consciousness of each individual.

The sustaining motivations here, however, must always be remembered; that they are the past lifetimes; they are of the primary importance and no person can go beyond the precepts of what is being constantly radiated from his psychic anatomy and which is the determining factor of whatever he incepts or rejects into his daily life. A house, whether it is past or present, is a familiar object. Even though it was a hundred thousand years ago, it could still be, to a certain degree, a form sufficiently familiar to develop into a modern house.

So it is with the astronauts in space, when they are removed from all of the adjunctive oscillating electromagnetic fields which are concerned more directly with the evolutionary life on the planet Earth, then they become, to a certain degree, disoriented; their thinking is affected and it takes several days after they get back to Earth to adjust consciousness to the gravitational and electromagnetic fields of the Earth. Likewise, the same adjustments or maladjustments take place in the net sum and total of the chemical processes of the body or what can be considered to be the mineral metabolism of the body, such as in the assimilation of calcium or potassium. The same is quite true with all of the other inductions and processes which are concerned with our daily life, and we are concerned with them at any given time or any hour of the day, as can be seen in solar mechanics. There is a different relationship with the sun and with all other inductive or radiating sources in our planetary system at 4:00 A.M. than there is at 10:00 P.M., and you will have a somewhat different relationship to the total infinite cosmos on the same basis. Because of negative and positive polarities in harmonic structures, etc., as to your own particular position, your life, your thinking, your physical processes, all that is concerned with you will be affected to some more or less degree.

Yes, even wars and other types of human derelictions, famines, plagues, have been largely superimposed upon the facade of civilization by the same interdimensional cosmic processes; the changing of the different relationships to all of these inductive processes throughout the interdimensional galaxy will even adversely or conversely affect the weather of the Earth. It will affect the demeanor, the attitudes; even the stock market is affected.

A far greater understanding of astrology is needed than could now be considered, nor are any of these facts presently involved in our present civilization; they are as yet almost totally unknown although they may be vaguely recognized in different expressions such as extrasensory perception, mind telepathy, telekinesis and other factors of human expression which are still almost unknown to the present earthman.

In the future, many of these different aspects of life will be entered into more thoroughly and will be explained to you on the same basis of phase relationships, harmonic structures, isochronisms, and such, as it totally involves the infinite cosmos.

Physics of Matter vs. the Fourth Dimension

As long as we are on the subject of calcium versus astronauts, let us go more directly into the physics of matter versus the fourth-dimensional cosmos. It cannot be overemphasized at this time, that in order to make any headway in understanding these concepts you must first understand energy, at least to some appreciable degree. Again we will start with that familiar sine wave which is simply a bit of electrical energy which is moving up and down, say, from positive to negative and vice versa. In this cycle it is telling something according to its frequency. It is both the conveyance and the information; the frequency, of course, the times in which it goes from positive to negative, and is that particular information when it relates itself to any other sine wave. You might find some similarity or analogy in yourself when you walk to the grocery store; your legs are the conveyance and your consciousness is your intelligence. Well, the number of times your steps go from left to right, or we shall say, from positive to negative or vice versa is the frequency that relates you to the distance from your home to the store. Also, in your pocket, or bag, (or even piggyback) you can carry another person, or any other object. It is the same with sine waves. They too can carry, so to speak, other wave forms which are much smaller in frequency and which relate to certain kinds of information, such as is carried in the video and audio pulse in the television signal or wave form from the transmitter.

Now we are getting down to the proposition of the difference between what is solid and what is energy. Actually, there is no such thing as solid. All the world about you, no matter what it is, is actually energy.

Even the sidewalks upon which you walk to go to the store are energy. But what makes a solid? Well, Infinite Intelligence devised a little bit of something which is called an atom, or more properly, many kinds of atoms. Now atoms are just merely little anomalies or nuclei, or a tiny centrifuge of fourth-dimensional energy, and this little nucleus or atom has, I shall say, an exact line which divides it from the third to the fourth dimension—a very hard shell; not a shell like a walnut or a peanut shell, but is a shell made of certain frequencies of energy which are wave forms of energy which are very high frequencies or oscillations—so high, in fact, they won't combine with any other kind of frequencies or energies except that they are compatible with frequencies of other atoms and will adhere or cling without merging because certain positive and negative polarities mesh, like the fingers on your two hands can mesh in between each other.

In this we must again refer to that complex structure of wave forms and harmonics. What is a harmonic? Well, that is just a multiple of two plus, of all of these wave forms. Any particular up and down motion can, on the basis of this two plus, generate what is called a harmonic. In other words, it's just a little peak and is much stronger in many ways because it repeats the information much more loudly or strongly, so that any wave-form can generate on the basis of two plus, thousands of harmonics.

Now it's beginning to get a little complex. So the sidewalks that you walk on to the store are made of concrete. Now concrete is made up of little grains of sand combined with Portland cement, which is nothing more than ground up limestone and burned in a furnace which removes the carbon dioxide from it. Then when the water is mixed with it, the carbon dioxide reunites again those oscillating wave forms which are most necessary in this reuniting process. There wouldn't be any reuniting if the positive and negative polarities of these wave forms weren't properly phased or meshed. So all of the little grains of sand in the Portland cement which went into that fluid concrete to make your sidewalks that you walked on are actually made up of little atoms with little hard shells around them, so they combine to form molecules; the molecules, when combined with other molecules, became the grains of sand or the Portland cement, and we had a buildup of all those little hard shells. And those little hard shells of energy repelled the leather on your shoes; you could step right on those little hard shells of energy but you could go no further. So you called it concrete because of your association with the past, and it was built up from there—the stones, the rocks and other hard surfaces on which you walked in other lifetimes. But any of these so-called hard surfaces were actually little hard shells of molecules—energy shells, made up of countless trillions of little oscillating wave forms—all timed in their frequencies so they were in direct opposition with your feet or your shoes so that you wouldn't penetrate beyond the little shells.

And it's the same with anything else that you consider solid in your world about you—all made up of atoms, atoms into molecules, and molecules into different objects. And the net sum and combination of all of these molecules and atoms and their little hard shells made the surface of the material or object of whatever it was.

Now you are beginning to get it a little bit. And, as Einstein said, you can take any of this mass and, in theory at least—and proven in our atomic sciences—you can convert it into energy. Or, you can take your chair that you are sitting on and break it up and throw it into the stove or fireplace and it will burn. In that case, you have only combined oxygen with the original molecule atom forms to the extent that they were converted back into carbon dioxide, carbon monoxide and water vapor. So you see, what we are getting at here is merely a conversion of atomic forms as electrical energy.

It's the same with a DNA molecule. Scientists think that is the secret of life, but what he doesn't know is that the DNA molecule, in turn, is a recombination of atoms which went into that particular shape because of certain intelligent impulses or wave forms—messages, if you will—from the psychic anatomy which said that those little atoms should line themselves up in a certain way so that all the little polarities could express a certain quotient of energy, and that quotient of energy had its intelligence according to its electromagnetic field. It propagated this energy or information into other molecule-atom combinations about it and therefore, certain reactions or growths or whatever it was took place from the impulses which were originally sent to this atom-molecule combination (called the DNA molecule) by the psychic anatomy.

Well, it's that way with calcium too. If you have a little calcium molecule that goes into a man's body and it gets down into his intestinal tract, there are little protuberances which stick out from the intestinal wall which look something like sausages, only very, very small. These are little sensitive cells. Now, when that calcium molecule hits one of these sensitive cells, the net sum and total of the electromagnetic field around that calcium molecule is all timed in frequency, and is oscillating in a certain way with the net sum and total of the electromagnetic field of the entire body, the psychic anatomy and all other different electroplasmic fields of force. And so we can say then that calcium molecule was oscillating in a normal, quiescent condition so that immediately the little cell recognized this as a calcium molecule and it said to itself, "Oh, here is a calcium molecule; I want it," and through osmosis

171

the little calcium molecule went into the walls of the intestinal tract and eventually found its way up, like a brick in a wall, in the bone structure.

Now if we take this same little calcium molecule and give it to a man who is out in space, say a couple of hundred thousand miles away from the Earth and minus some of those very necessary electromagnetic fields which surround the Earth, then that little calcium molecule no longer oscillates the same as it would on the surface of the Earth due to the difference in the harmonics and in the interplays which are part of that molecule-atom combination. So when that little molecule, minus certain oscillating wave forms of information, or key oscillations, or isochronisms, or harmonics—whatever you wish to call the components of this total oscillating spectrum (certain of these quotients are minus)—gets down into the intestinal tract and that little cell "sees" that little calcium molecule, he won't recognize it because he doesn't have the same reaction or effect. The net sum and total of signals coming to the cell are not the same, and so the molecule passes on by, through the intestinal tract and is eliminated. So the body has to become parasitic; it starts feeding on its own bone structures to supply the calcium for the other metabolic processes in the body. That is the whole sum and the gist of it.

Well, the same proposition takes place with the leukocytes in the bloodstream. You know the leukocytes are those white cells which prey upon, or eat germs and other things that get into the bloodstream that shouldn't be there. And the reason there is exactly the same as it was with the calcium molecule in the intestine. The leukocytes are quite familiar with all the different oscillating wave forms in the cell structure and molecule-atom combinations in the body and they pass them on by; in fact, a leukocyte can pass right around in between the molecules very easily and apparently go right through cell walls or blood vessels, as well as to reach whatever objective he is called to go to. But if a germ gets into the body, into the bloodstream, the leukocyte immediately recognizes the germ as an enemy because that germ doesn't give out those familiar beep-beep signals or oscillations that are part of the life of the leukocyte in the bloodstream. So the leukocyte goes right to that germ and wraps himself around it and the little enzyme substances dissolve the germ.

So all of these mysteries really aren't mysteries after all if we understand the relationship between the radiating electromagnetic fields which are involved with every atom, every molecule, every cell, every human body, and the net sum and total of relationships of any human body and psychic anatomy with the inter-dimensional cosmos, as well as the third dimension. So there are a number of the basic secrets or facts of life which are still glaringly, apparently missing from our present-day sciences, whether they are in medicine, space technocracy, atomic technocracy or whatever field you wish to subdivide these things into. It's the same in the chemical field and there are thousands of men and women laboring in the fields of chemical research or biological research to establish certain relationships or to ferret out truths of the human body, the facts of life, here and hereafter. And they are laboring very blindly because they do not know the relationship and other factors between the electromagnetic fields which are built up in atoms, molecules, cells and other substances.

For instance, the nylon in your ladies' hose: this is called by the chemist a polyester molecule; it is long and shaped like a wiener and it has a number of atoms in this chain-like fashion which are adhering very closely together because of their total electromagnetic fields; the polarity, harmonics, et cetera, involved in the electromagnetic fields are meshed together, end to end

173

so to speak—all of the definite north to south, south to north poles lined up, similar to a horseshoe magnet so that in the end there is a long string of atoms which make a molecule which is called a polyester molecule. Now this molecule repeats exactly the same thing that the atom did; in other words, a similar polyester molecule is attracted to it, end to end, in a chain-like fashion, similar to a long chain of wieners. The magnetic fields on the ends of these different polyester molecules are very intensely attracted to the ends of any other particular polyester molecule and so they form long chains. So strong are these magnetic hook-ups that nylon, pound for pound, is 200 times stronger than steel.

So again the importance of knowing or understanding the electromagnetic fields; in fact, the whole concept or industry of chemistry itself could easily be resolved into one of these electromagnetic reactions or combinations. And all other things on the Earth should be more properly understood on the same basis; that they are reactionary or adhesive, or that they are inductive or they repel, according to the basis of frequencies, and how these frequencies—even as little hard-shell frequencies around an atom—can develop through the processes of combinations of molecules, into the hard surface of the concrete sidewalk.

And when all of this is somewhat mentally digested and assimilated by you, the student, you will have at your disposal and within your mind, concepts which are still just beyond the horizon of our present-day physicists and scientists. And yet, very vitally important, they have been part of your evolution since the beginning; they have been the principles which formulated the Earth and the solar system; they are the underlying principles which formulated the universe, or in the construction of new suns or stars, the destruction of older suns and stars. The changeover of chemical constituents, such as an acid eating a metal and so on, can only be resolved into the differences of electromagnetic fields which separate molecules from each other and separate atoms from each other on the basis that the electromagnetic fields are canceling each other out.

The same would be quite true if we were to build a spaceship which would have within it an apparatus which would reproduce all the necessary electromagnetic vibrations which are similar to those on Earth, in other words, a facsimile proposition. Then, calcium would be assimilated by the astronauts just as need be and on the same basis of learning and understanding the differences and combinations of electromagnetic fields as they were expressed by atoms and molecules, we could solve all of the very apparent and sometimes quite destructive derelictions which mankind is faced with on the Earth today.

For example: a heroin addict could be completely cured of his habit in a matter of seconds by super-imposing certain frequencies within his consciousness and into his psychic anatomy, which would cancel out certain oscillating wave forms which had been gener-ated within that psychic anatomy by the molecules of heroin as they reacted in the brain cells of the physical anatomy. The same basis here is analogous to sight, sound or any other inceptions which the human being experiences in the 24-hour life cycle.

So therefore, without question or without doubt, the secret to understanding life in any and all dimensions is clearly apparent that we must begin to understand energy. And if any person does not, that person is lost, lost in the purgatory of his own mind and in the ele-mental indispositions of a material world, lost until he can find himself out by beginning to understand the creative principles. Infinite Intelligence (or God, if you wish to call It that) is constantly manifesting Itself; It is regenerating, re-creating, and in the cyclic motion we could also say that It is being destroyed; yet, nothing is destroyed in Infinity. It cannot be. It is converted; it is converted from one form to another, even from one dimension to another.

If we split an atom, as we do in an atomic bomb through fissionable U-235, the atom is divided in such a way that two of its artificial components, a neutron and an electron, are left to fly off into space, so to speak, by themselves. It is these two frequencies which give the destructive force to the atomic bomb. In the case of the nuclear bomb or fusion bomb, there is an implosion where two hydrogen atoms actually merge into each other and form a helium atom. In so doing, they release a tremendous oscillation or vibration of energy. The interchange here is quite similar to that going on in the photosphere of the sun—that radiating envelope which radiates all of the countless energies into the third-dimensional space about it; energy which, in turn, is from these original sources or converted through hysteresis, through electromagnetic spectrums which are the structural form or the intelligence behind the vortical forms and, in this hysteresis are converted to such compatible frequencies known as heat and light, etc., which are so necessary and vital to life on any planet which has been developed through photosynthesis or other different chemical allegories through the evolution of time.

We can ceaselessly revolve within the precincts of our mind and we will never cease to get back to our original starting point—a cyclic terminus, if you will call it such, which dominantly re-creates the necessity within our own consciousness to learn to understand what energy is—the sum and substance of Infinite Intelligence, and the laws and principles which govern, control and manifest themselves through this Supreme Infinite Intelligence.

176

Misconceptions of Scientists Regarding
Astronauts' Sightings

There is one other aspect in space travel which has been discovered in the four journeys to the moon. This is in relationship to bright objects floating about the spacecraft and lights which seem to flash across the inside of the retina of the astronauts' eyes. On the first flight to the moon, astronauts mentioned there were bright objects or lights floating about the ship at about the halfway point to the moon. In successive journeys astronauts have seen tiny bright white specks of light which seem to float across the inside of their eyes. In the last (#15) flight, experiments were conducted and the astronauts deliberately blindfolded themselves, and again saw these bright specks of light which they believed were on the inside of the retina of their eyes. This, of course, is a fallacy. What actually happened in any of these dispensations or phenomena as they manifested themselves, either as white lights floating around the cabin, or as bright specks floating across the eye, is easily explained. It should be considered that none of these experiments have been conducted purposely here on Earth by the astronauts, or the same people who are involved in these experiments. And if they had, and had they been conducted under totally darkened conditions, there is no doubt they would have seen bright lights floating around the room and bright specks which seemed to be on the inside of their eyes.

Now let us consider the conditions under which astronauts travel through space. And as was previously mentioned, in such travel and as the ship is some 100,000 to 200,000 miles away from the intense electromagnetic fields of the Earth which are all directly involved in the various processes of hysteresis and other different transpositions which make life possible here on Earth, that it could be surmised that there was indeed a tremendous and intense electromagnetic plasma—if it can be called as such. Sunlight itself, or as it is manifested as light and heat—the energy from the sun in the process of hysteresis can be considered to be a very strong plasmic force, and as it is so converted through hysteresis, could conceivably be a force which was very disruptive to the transmissions of certain energy formations and phenomena from adjacent dimensions. It should be considered that there are many layers or astral worlds which are more or less directly associated through frequency, with life here on Earth, and in particular, to the people who live here, either past, present, or even to the future, and that such relationships have to be carried on in ways and manners which involve frequency transmissions, just as it is with sight, sound, radio, television, et cetera, and these frequency transmissions, by necessity, must be somewhere within the band of the in-between worlds. If this were not so, transmissions would be impossible. Telepathy or ESP, as it is more commonly known, is carried on through the different adjacent astral dimensions and this is one reason why there is little success in the direct application of ESP with the majority of people on the Earth; simply because they are not cognizant of the fact that they must have minds which are specifically trained to oscillate or regenerate with the psychic anatomy in bands or frequencies which are considerably higher than those which are the normal bands of frequencies in Earth life transmissions.

When astronauts or men are in a spacecraft out in the "vacuous" void of space, some of these very strong frequencies or electromagnetic fields are very greatly diminished or are completely absent, and under these conditions the astronauts can then be considered to be in sort of a cataleptic or trance state; they do not have the same normal relationship with all factors which are viable or in control of the reactionary factions of their life.

It is much the same proposition of the spiritualist medium who sits in a totally dark room and succeeds, to some degree, in temporarily suspending the very strong life force oscillations between the conscious mind and the psychic anatomy in conjunction with outside factors, such as lights, radiations, sight, and hearing. The same is true with the astronauts. In space there are no reflective surfaces from air and from countless terrestrial objects about them. Sunlight is absent except for a single ball of light which is the sun but which has no reflective surfaces in the total environment around them, outside of the spacecraft. And practically none is reflective on the inside, except under very controlled incandescent lights which do not radiate the same spectral intensities as does solar light. Under these conditions then, it is quite conceivable that the astronaut is in somewhat of a similar position to the spiritualist medium in the darkened room. Certain very strong earth like oscillations between consciousness, the outside world, and the psychic anatomy are to some degree suspended. There is not the same relationship with the very strong electromagnetic fields as there was on Earth. This, then, is kind of a trance or cataleptic state and is proven by the fact that these men will have to readjust themselves, reorient themselves, when getting back to Earth. They find a considerable degree of disorientation after landing on Earth.

It is the same with the spiritualist medium on emerging from the trance room; it takes several hours for the medium to assume a more natural and normal position to his daily life. So far as the bright lights, and as they were called cosmic rays by the scientists, this is entirely a misconception; they are not cosmic rays but are actually the more or less focused intensities of frequency radiations which are emanated by spiritual bodies from another world. They do not appear on the retina of the eye or on the inside of the eye but rather, in inner consciousness of the psychic anatomy and are oscillated back into consciousness where, in passing through the brain cells in the cortical layer, they again, as energy wave forms, superimpose in the facsimiles of wave forms, the image of a light speck. They are not really light specks, for if they could be seen consciously as they are reflected into the psychic anatomy by the spiritual being, or person, or the entity, they would be seen to be as a living embodiment of energy, perhaps formless as far as earth forms are concerned but, nevertheless, they are energy bodies which are living and very definitely personalities in a spiritual world.

So these misconceptions on the part of our modern-day scientists are doubly intensified when only one-half of the experiment is performed. Should they have been scientifically minded, they would have performed the same experiment here on Earth under simulated space conditions, that is; in a totally darkened room and, as much as possible, the participants in the experiment would have to be trained in the functions of the mind to the point where they could temporarily suspend these very strong, chain-like Earth oscillations which concern them in their daily lives.

That is one of the facets in training to be a spiritualist medium; that they very often sit in a totally darkened room. Even before their mediumship seems to open up, they purposely try to suspend the ever-present oscillations of the present earth life to the degree where they can incept the oscillations or vibrations from the spiritual world which will convey the message, the personage, or whatever picture it is which is being projected to them, or to which they can attune themselves, whichever the proposition is.

There is one other experiment which was connected with the third voyage to the moon which was an experiment in ESP. One of the astronauts was engaged in a telepathic communion with a scientist here on Earth from one of the universities in the state of Michigan, I believe it was, and a great deal of success was attained, in fact so successful that all of the messages received from space back and forth were reversed, and that too, is a common occurrence in all telepathic communications or whatever it may be called when telepathic communications are established with an adjacent or nearby astral world. Quite frequently such appearances or word forms or other messages, if they appear as symbols, et cetera, may be inverted and which is very simply and easily explained. Because the astral world will represent as a sending force, a positive polarity, and the Earth as a negative polarity, the recipient here on Earth will receive the inverted image as one-half of the phase reversal wave form impulse—again, facts which are not known to either spiritualists or other scientists here on the earth.

In my own particular dispensations in psychic science throughout the many years, I have quite frequently noted, and sometimes have even been intimidated to a large degree by the reversal of some image or message from a loved one from a different sphere or from an adjacent astral world. However, I have never been encumbered as is common with other so-called psychics or spiritualists of the world, to the degree that I had to sit in a dark room and suspend my consciousness in a trance, far from it. I have quite frequently described and conversed with people in spiritual worlds under bright sunlight and described them to other people and have given them very definite proof that these people were actually talking to me and conveying not only words but pictures to me, and through my mind I re-conveyed them back to the one to whom it was intended.

I have also received and worked with this psychic communication with other worlds, other times, in far distant reaches of this planet to the degree that houses, interiors of rooms, or letters that could be described to people (which still had to be written) even as long as three or four weeks in advance, all of which were later verified and proven by the recipients. So far as I am concerned, I have placed no limits upon the psychic science or my relationship to this, and my expression to psychic science in whatever particular form or manner as it has been deployed on Earth has never been encumbered by such limitations, except perhaps that it would be in my own physical dispensations and the intimidations of a physical mind which was strongly oscillating to some degree, in the normal contents of my daily life.

However, always superimposed on my life was a very definite pattern, a very strong, protective force. This directive pattern never failed and always materialized into whatever form or shape which was necessary for my existence and I lived by this. And so the laws of common metaphysics, psychic phenomena, and such, are well-known to me, far and beyond the point in which the earthman can understand them. I understand it as a direct and applicable science related, as I have explained, to the numerous third and fourth-dimensional interplays of electromagnetic fields and harmonic structures which make up the life force of every human here on Earth.

Therefore, whenever such particular expressions occur in the future as they may seem to waylay you or to mystify you to the degree that you might call them gifts or mysticisms, let it be known now, once and for all time, that there are no gifts, no mysteries! As I have

182

said many times before, that in Infinite Intelligence which some people have deified as the false configuration of a god, this Infinite Intelligence is infinite in nature and has made all of this infinite knowledge available to any person who seeks to find this knowledge on the common basic denominators which concern the correct structures and the deployment and expression of principles in energy formations, as they constitute not only the third dimension but the many, many dimensions or mansions which are beyond this Earth. There are no limits and no horizons which cannot be overcome or cannot be found and which cannot be extended, because infinity is just that—it is infinite, and do not presuppose at any time that you will reach any limits to this infinity except those which you superimpose upon your own mind.

So it remains as one of the facts or expressions of the future, a question in my own mind, if it could be called such—a question; yet, it is always completely resolved even before it is asked. What is the future and the destiny of the earthman from his present position of almost total chaos on the planet as it is today, to the imbalance of the population explosions, to the breeding of literally hundreds of millions of people who are incapable of sustaining themselves upon a planet whose sustaining life forces have already been depleted, exploited, plundered, raped and vilified? What is the meaning and answer to this? Yet, there is an answer; it has already been written upon the great wall with the moving finger of time. And it is predictable upon the common consensus of what has happened to previous civilizations, not only on this planet but on other planets throughout our galaxy.

Man is tremendously foolish in the assumption that he is godlike, or that God created him in his own image, for he already has constructed a false god and therefore his own imagery is false. To say that in infinity we can find any boundaries or any place in which we do not find an expansion of consciousness is, in itself, a kind of death warrant which writes out the doom of any person who limits himself under such conditions.

So far as my own position is concerned in regard to these explorations to the moon: first, they are totally unnecessary. It took $445 million to make the last exploration and the total expenditure of our space program is close to $30 billion. This sum of money would be enough to advance the cause of humanity not only in the United States but also throughout the world to a very appreciable degree; yet advancement must first be made upon a common consensus, an admission that man is fallacious in many of the precepts which he has laid down for his civilization, simply because people can and do breed promiscuously.

The total concept as it concerns the earthman, that he will spend hundreds of thousands of dollars to extend the life of an infant who has been born into the world under tremendous physical or mental handicaps, yet on the battlefield he will slaughter hundreds of thousands of the prime of his manhood in trying to propagate and promulgate certain political philosophies into the minds and lives of people who are totally unfit to accept such ideas into their minds, is of course, tremendously stupid. What is meant here is, rather than these tremendous explorations into space in a vain attempt to find the origin of the solar system, the answer to that is very apparent. And even if this answer is found, most certainly it will not solve the enigmas which now confront people on this planet.

It is a great sin—a travesty and a tragedy to bring a child into the world who is mentally or physically handicapped, for under our present economic systems, and in our defiled and polluted ecology—to expect that person to lead a reasonably healthy life is much more sinful than it would be to take a certain course of prevention of such a birth, and also, to spend these wasted billions of dollars into a more useful extension of knowledge which would push the frontiers of man's abysmal ignorance of his life on the planet Earth to a point where he could constructively live a life suited to the environment of his time.

Further Discussions re Weightlessness, Interdimensional Concepts, etc.

Judging by the current news media, the Apollo #15 flight to the moon is still very much in evidence; in fact, scientists and astronauts are eagerly beginning the examination of the various lunar rocks which were brought back on this flight, and in particular, that piece of black, glass-like rock called the Genesis rock which they believe to be about 4.7 billion years old. Astronaut David Scott also made a statement that these moon explorations should be continued, that it was very necessary and important. The 18th and 19th trips or flights have been cancelled and Scott believes these should be reinstated, etc.

To a person who has some insight and understanding of the interdimensional cosmos, such efforts and explorations, the belief that determining the age of a rock or the kind of a rock that it is will give them insight into the creation of the universe—such an assumption is ridiculous, asinine and elemental. It clearly points out the very obvious fact that these so-called scientists are trying to understand creation in much the same way as a blind man trying to describe the elephant after holding the animal's tail for a few moments.

To understand creation and in particular such elements of creation as earth worlds, planets, solar systems, galaxies and universes, etc., we must first understand the origins of the constituents which form these seeming solid masses and their capacities as radiating sources. As I have previously stated, all such seeming formations of masses and attendant phenomena such as radiations and so forth, must be understood as fourth-dimensional in their origins, not

186

reactionary third-dimensional elements.

Actually, any piece of moon rock or earth, any such composites of the terrestrial solar system or the galaxy which can be seen or envisioned by the scientist of this time or by any man, are atoms which compose these different forms and have no age. The universe, the galaxy, and our solar system or any of the planets are actually ageless; they have no beginning and they have no end, which is quite true when we understand that all of these terrestrial bodies or third dimensional bodies are the composite of atoms and atoms have no age. Of an atom, it can be said to be "formed" instantly and "die" instantly at a rate of speed which is beyond the comprehension of the human mind, an oscillating process, if you will. I have previously described atoms as being the central nucleus of a fourth-dimensional vortex of energy.

Let us go further into this subject that we may better understand. Certain oscillating energies in the fourth dimension which are all cyclic, or have a circular, self-contained oscillation within themselves, and according to certain polarities which they express within themselves to other similar cyclic motions, develop a sort of centripetal whirlpool of energy; that is, electromagnetic fluxes, as oscillating wave forms, generated as harmonics from these different oscillating polarities within the cyclic wave forms, and according to these different polarities can be said to precipitate themselves toward the center of such a vortex and develop as an oscillating pattern within the center of this vortex, a certain condensed wave form pattern which is the constituent of an atom oscillating pattern.

Within these rapidly oscillating wave forms are regenerated certain positive and negative oscillations according to the cyclic wave forms which generated them, and in an infinitesimally short space of time, they can be said to appear or reappear. This is the factor of time or the time consonant which is a very necessary expressionary element in the third dimension. Space now is also expressed in the net sum and total of these oscillations as they reappear and oscillate within the periphery of this nucleus, which gives us the space element. When all of these oscillating wave forms within this central nucleus are concerned in expressing a secondary electromagnetic field as a product of their wave form harmonics, this electromagnetic field, in turn, can also be synchronously attuned to other similar such nuclei or atoms, and, in turn, such similarities as they attract each other in the net densities of these electromagnetic fields would form a molecule, such as a molecule of iron or a molecule of hydrogen or any one of the ninety-two natural elements.

Now it begins to be quite clear just exactly how universes, galaxies, planets and planetary systems were formed; such formations being, of course, a grand scale reproduction of what a simple atom formation is. In other words, the interdimensional universe is just one huge centrifuge, or vortex of oscillating wave forms which forms sort of a nucleus which manifests itself as our terrestrial universe in such reactionary components as can be seen or visualized by astronomers in their telescopes, radio or optics. The universe, however, is vast and as of today is incomprehensible by the earthman. He is much more concerned with the immediate galaxy which is really a little bright speck in the total universe.

It takes light, so they estimate, something like 100,-000 light years to travel from one edge of our galaxy to the other. We can actually see through this galaxy to a certain extent on any clear night when we look up at the Milky Way, and which is looking out toward the edge of the galaxy. So we begin to grasp a small fraction of what is totally involved in the creation of the terrestrial universe, if it can be called a creation. Actually, the word creation is an anachronism which only adds to the net sum and total of all the materialistic derelictions with which science and the earthman are now concerned.

To more properly visualize our third-dimensional world as it would appear to a person from a higher world, the present atomic constituents which form this earth world, its attendant solar system and the astronomical universe, et cetera, are actually little energy particles which are constantly reappearing and disappearing according to their polarities and which maintain synchronously, either a relationship toward one another as attractive elements—according to their electromagnetic fields—or, by the same principle, a lack of synchronous attunement; or conversely, a repulsive synchronous wave form will repel other atoms. This is the net sum and total of the differentiation of the different atoms as they comprise the scale of atomic elements, as they are known to the present-day scientist.

A hydrogen atom is different than the helium atom, yet, if we merge two hydrogen atoms, we get a helium atom. Well, the reason is quite simple when we understand that two hydrogen atoms—while they may be synchronously attuned to each other and form part of a mass of hydrogen gas—do not and cannot be converted into helium until the electromagnetic fields of these hydrogen atoms are somehow changed. Changing the electromagnetic fields does also bring about a change within the atom itself; that is to say, we should change the net sum and total of the vibrating rate of the atom as it was concerned with its vortex or centrifuge, so that it was of the same attunement as that of the helium atom. This is the conversion principle involved in converting one element to the other.

In the hydrogen bomb this is an implosion process. Certain wave forms of the electromagnetic spectrum when released, create the tremendous energy of the hydrogen bomb as the net sum and total of all different hydrogen atoms which have been so imploded, one upon the other. Curiously enough, you might add; while two hydrogen atoms can be combined to make a helium atom, yet, in all of the mass hydrogen atoms used to implode or explode a hydrogen bomb, we get only helium atoms. Now wouldn't it seem that we might, under the same analogy, get one great big helium atom? No, it isn't that way because, as I've explained, in attunement, which attunes the electro-magnetic fields of each atom, one to another synchronously or that it repels them, these principles are absolute and cannot be changed.

It is the same as in tuning your radio or television set; if you get a misalignment there, you will get two stations. So if we misalign, so to speak, two hydrogen atoms, we can get one helium atom but the misalignment must be of a certain particular nature, frequency or oscillation so the changes within the hydrogen atom can reinstate themselves as a synchronous oscillation which is called a helium atom. Actually, all of these atoms which you see are rapidly appearing and disappearing, we might say, according to their polarities, so that it really isn't creation at all. All we are involved in, is in changing the oscillating frequencies.

Now this is quite true in your daily life. Your body is a composite of trillions of atoms, and there are about sixteen to twenty different kinds of atoms. All of the atoms of the same kind are synchronously attuned to each other according to their harmonic structures, such as the atoms in the calcium, which form the bones in your body. However, these bone atoms of calcium are not synchronously attuned to the atoms of iron in your bloodstream, so consequently, they do not merge. Yet, within the net sum and total of all magnetic energies, which are reproduced as the electromagnetic fields by these atoms, they are very necessary for the metabolic processes. It is sort of a catalytic action which takes place which makes all of the functions of the body possible. The instigating intelligence, the commands, the patterns for these different integrations, according to these catalytic elements are, of course, commands from the psychic anatomy. And here again we find very strong oscillating energies entering into the electromagnetic fields of the molecules and the atoms of your body and these different wave forms of energy, which are the command energy from the psychic anatomy, tell all of the little atoms in your body just what they are going to do, and what they should do, and make them do it. The energy from this conversion process is, of course, as I have said, contained in all of the net sum and total of the electromagnetic fields of force which are concerned with the atoms and which are in direct oscillation, as harmonic structures, with all of the oscillating electromagnetic fields of the Earth and the solar system, are again harmonically linked as patterns of oscillating wave forms to the total infinite cosmogony.

So you see it begins to be a rather complex process but one which, if you work at it long enough, you will begin to gain a little comprehension and you will see that you are—as I have said on numerous occasions—physically, or mentally, or any other way you wish to picture it, just a little glob or a polarity, so to speak, of energy which is oscillating with infinity. The Earth itself, or the terrestrial universe as the scientist knows it, is also such an oscillating entity. It isn't solid at all. The age, as it is called, in any particular rock formation or object as it is supposed to have been formed is strictly academic. It only means that a certain number of atom-molecule combinations have been, in effect, synchronously attuned to each other to the extent that they retained the mass formation of the rock over a given period of time and this period of time is strictly academic; it means absolutely nothing. And what they should be concerned with are the principles which engendered the formation of this rock or, as they call it, the creation. Actually, it wasn't created at all; it always existed in infinity and according to Infinite Intelligence and all of the oscillating principles within infinity, as the sum and substance of Infinite Intelligence had already created this rock billions and billions, yes, countless billions of years—long before it ever appeared as rock; the only difference was that it was oscillating wave forms.

When the proper conditions were brought about so that there was a combination of wave forms which were synchronously attuned to each other, they formed little vortexes of energy which formed the nucleus of certain atoms. These atoms, in turn, being synchronously attuned to other atoms which were likewise being formed, all got together to make some molecules according to their electromagnetic fields. These molecules, being likewise attracted to each other according to their electromagnetic fields and through synchronous attunements, made the formation of rock. It made little difference to these atom-molecule combinations if the rock was large or small, because within each one of these atom-molecule combinations, space and time was being expressed into one of the planes of expression which is called the third dimension.

Actually, the energy which was the composite of this rock, when we stop to consider that atoms are energy, then the age of the rock as it existed in any particular formation, shape or size was strictly an academic proposition and really didn't tell anybody anything. Likewise, none of the moon rocks or any explorations in space, so far as that is concerned, are going to tell the earthman anything about creation simply because he is looking in the wrong direction. He has the elephant's tail and he is trying to describe to himself and understand the entire elephant by the shape and size of the tail. What the scientist is trying to do in his analysis of moon rocks is to form a geological comparison with such existing sources as exist on the planet Earth. However, such comparisons will only lead to certain nebulous conclusions—actually, an impasse. Estimating a piece of rock at any given number of years is a totally incomprehensible conclusion. For example: Some scientists believe, or it is indicated that lava once flowed on the moon just as it does on Earth. Present earth-lava flows or past moon-lava flows are meaningless. Lava has been flowing on other planets for countless billions of years.

The value of time in any person's mind is a quasi-evaluation. The consensus of even a few years time, memory-wise speaking is, so far as the time factor is concerned, absolutely meaningless. A person may remember many incidents of his past life but so far as reliving them, so to speak, with the actual time consonant is impossible, because time, as it relates to any happening in a person's life, must relate itself harmonically to all life processes, past and present and in the combination of harmonic structures, the time element is the differentiation factor which separates these wave form patterns into understandable reactive components.

To look at a piece of moon rock and say equivocally that it is 4.7 billion years old is meaningless even if it were true because such elements as were at that time, 4.7 billion years ago, concerned with integrating atoms into molecule combinations which formed the rock— were then expressing the time consonant as the reactionary element in the formation of this rock, which could be quite analogous to witnessing a lava flow from a volcano. Perhaps the Earth scientists might get some satisfaction from this comparison and feel within themselves a great sense of accomplishment at having arrived at this meaningless comparison. In his limited thinking, he would not be concerned with the possible billions of years, time-wise, which were necessary to bring this atom-molecule lava flow up to its expressionary point or that such lava flows could recur hundreds of thousands of years apart. Yes, even the same lava could have been re-melted and cooled many times, again giving no information as to what form these atom-molecule combinations took and for that matter, what every atom-molecule combination takes which could be found anywhere in the galaxy or universe as planets or suns, etc. The 4.7 billion year age denotes a sharp and immediate creation from apparently nothing and imparts no information as to the total evolutionary consensus involved before and after the lava flow which formed this rock.

Finally, the scientist has apparently not been concerned with the tremendous forces which were necessary to bring about a lava flow or why planets, moons, and suns, etc., always appear as spherical balls. What are the forces and energies which keep the planets revolving around their respective suns? The admission of a single atom, whatever its weight, is an admission by all scientists concerned that they know little or nothing about this atom, even less about its origin, and absolutely nothing about the power and intelligence which engendered its origin. The explosion of Krakatoa, a submerged volcano, involved and released more energy than all man-made explosions combined; yet energy released in a thermal process—not atomic or nuclear energy. All energy must have a source. All the man-made laws of physics are based on cause and effect which is, in other words, source and reaction, yet science of today knows nothing of sources or origins and only an elemental superstructure of third-dimensional reactions.

We might well ask the scientist, "Was not the moon

already in existence and what made it possible for that lava flow to occur which formed the Genesis rock?" No moon, no lava flow. Then, where is the true beginning of the formation of the moon? Why not visualize the solar system as simply an anomaly or an eddy current, as it was regenerated within the infinitely dense, oscillating, cyclic wave forms which form infinity; the planets, in turn, secondary anomalies or eddy currents which, are called moons and which have an ageless, synchronous attunement, harmonically regenerating as substructures in such life forms as are found on planets.

So the scientist should know that here on Earth he has all of the answers to infinite creation within the simplest precincts of his everyday life. The metabolism of his body would give him very definite and conclusive evidence of what he calls creation. Creation is rather a limited word and actually means that something had to be brought into existence at a certain specified period of time. It's like the old fable of the Garden of Eden, which is strictly a fable and at best could be only an allegorical tale which related to the astrophysical concepts of the development of our own earth world and the exploration of our planetary system by other different people from other worlds in this galaxy. Again, it is of interest only as a point of history, and all the histories in the world, whether they relate to man in this terrestrial planet or relate to other races in other planets, are going to mean little or nothing.

We can invent time machines and we can, so to speak, go back in time and contact certain wave form aggregates which would—if they played within the surface planes of our cortical layers of the mind—regenerate certain scenes which have happened in the past. Of course, these past scenes or incidents, whatever they were, could never again exist as they did at that particular moment of their happening in the physical sense. That would be strictly impossible because, here again, we are concerned with the net sum and total of the time element or the time consonants as they are expressed by atomic energy nuclei. They express themselves synchronously, either to other atoms, or that other atoms are not in tune with them and each atom does in itself—according to this relationship of its electromagnetic field, in the relationship of all other electromagnetic fields of other atoms, express a space element or a space consonant. It can be said to be occupying space which is relative to all other atoms, or it can be said that the net sum and total of a certain mass of atoms, oscillating with and attracted to each other can form a molecule, and the molecule can again form an iron molecule, or a silver molecule, or a calcium molecule, or any of the ninety-two natural elements.

I am taking the trouble to re-explain this concept to you because it is most necessary and vital for you to understand the difference and the way in which time and space are expressed, so far as the atomic constituents of your third-dimensional world are concerned. The same is quite true when we consider that all other sources—such as the five senses with which you are connected to this third-dimensional or terrestrial world are concerned—are actually radiating, or emanating, wave forms which come from any one of these particular atomic elements. Again, according to their wave forms, they are expressing time and space; the time is the frequency in which they appear and reappear— such as light frequencies on the retina of your eye— and this frequency, or the time, gives it the space. So the two are actually the same. Time and space, so far as the third dimension is concerned, are analogous and mean one and the same thing and you could not have time without space.

In the fourth dimension, this is not the same because all oscillating wave forms in the fourth dimension express themselves in a cyclic or circular manner and contain their I.Q., their information, within the oscillating element which comprises their cyclic form. They can be synchronously attuned to other wave forms, or they are specifically in a spectral pattern completely out of tune; yet, in the net sum and total of all infinity, through these synchronous and harmonic attunements, infinity is all the same. It is boundless, limitless, and cannot be said to have a beginning or ending, and if it did so, it would not be infinity.

So you see how pointless and meaningless it is to go out into space and collect rocks from the moon or perhaps even in the future, collect rocks from Mars. What the scientist should be concerned with is finding out how these different molecule-atom combinations were formed, just what an atom is, and how it expresses itself as an oscillating entity into the third dimension; how time and space do, in a sense of the word, become separate as the expression of these atoms, one to another, either harmonically or synchronously, or they may be adversely expressed to each other; that is—they will not make any connection. For example, if you see an automobile going down the highway, that automobile is composed of a large number of different kinds of atoms and all these atoms go to make up the different molecules which form the steel body, the rubber in the tires, the iron frame, etc. Each of these atom-molecule combinations has a very strong electromagnetic field; strong, we say, because of the comparative size of these atoms and molecules. Now the rubber tires which contact the surface of the highway, as they are composed of different atom-molecule combinations which we call rubber, are adverse to the molecules which comprise the asphalt of the highway, so they will not merge. In effect, the rubber molecules and atoms actually ride on top of an electromagnetic field, an electromagnetic field which they have generated and the electromagnetic field which is generated by the asphalt atoms of the highway. So they aren't really touching the highway at all; they are riding on an electromagnetic field.

If we have a little grain of sand which penetrates into the molecular structure of the rubber under an impact or a force, what does it do? It merely separates a few molecules of rubber which disconnect themselves from the surface of the tire and the tire is wearing out. So the physics are very easy to understand. There isn't any fission or fusion involved; it's merely a molecular separation. Well, it's the same when we heat anything: for instance, if we put a piece of iron into a furnace, the atoms and molecules, in relationship to each other, have to open up a little in order to absorb the energy which is coming into them, or is inducted into them.

This energy is actually being forced into these molecular structures by a very strong contact with this thermal source so that the little molecules and atoms, and the spaces in between them, so to speak, must open up, and the electromagnetic fields therefore retain less of a hold upon each other; there is less affinity for them, so the iron gets a little larger inside and if you heat it hot enough it can actually change into a liquid state. In that state, of course, you can see that the molecules and atoms—the electromagnetic fields between them—have to some extent been very greatly weakened so that it can flow around, out of any respective shape which it may have had as a piece of iron.

It's very simple again, when you start to get down to the "nitty-gritties", which are the electromagnetic fields and which are so very, very important in understanding the hysteresis of the solar system, the galaxy and the universe. While we are very vitally concerned with all of the net sum and total of this hysteresis, as I have categorically described it to you as the electromagnetic field of the Earth in conjunction with the solar system, the sun, the galaxy and the universe, these electromagnetic fields are usually oscillated through the deployment of the electromagnetic fields of the atoms, but in many different ways. All of this hysteresis is made possible only because we have that infinite cosmogony which the scientist calls the fourth dimension and which is the originating source of everything.

As I have said, everything has already been created, everything which is far beyond the capacity of your mind to even very faintly imagine. You could never get to the end of it. In infinity, in this way, as you journey through infinity in your evolution, you are contacting, at any given point, a certain number of these cyclic wave forms and their information. Then, according to other different wave forms which you have contacted in this cyclic transference pattern from the past, you react and you form the basis of your present-day third-dimensional life.

You see, mind wave forms, as they are connected with the psychic anatomy and all other wave forms which emanate from the psychic anatomy, are more strictly fourth-dimensional in nature; that is, they, too, are cyclic. Part of this cyclic pattern is, of course the reaction between the electromagnetic fields of the different atoms involved, in other words, an oscillating process where we have both positive and negative.

Within the central portion of any magnet, there is absolutely no magnetism at all (whether it is a straight iron bar or whether it is bent into the shape of a horseshoe), that is, none that you can determine by touching a piece of iron to it. The reason for this is that regardless of its shape, any magnet is oscillating from one end of the magnet to the other and in this oscillation the electromagnetic fields of the atom-molecule combinations are expressing themselves in exactly the same way as they do anywhere else except, in this oscillating process, all of their electromagnetic fields are so synchronously or harmonically attuned to each other that they form a very large harmonic which is the magnetic energy or flux which emerges from either one or the other of the poles of the magnet.

Now it's very simple again, when you understand how it is that everything which is basically atomic in nature, or is formed of little atoms, is oscillating with all of the electromagnetic fields. The Earth itself can be considered to be just another little atom in the galaxy and, as such, is oscillating in the same harmonic patterns and magnetic fields of force as are all other so-called heavenly or astronomical bodies.

So, creation can be understood much more comprehensively on this basis. We can find all of the reactionary processes in the life of the individual or the collective evolution of any person or masses of people in any civilization or all the combined civilizations on Earth, the blades of grass, the trees, whatever objectivism you wish to achieve in your prospective. All of these things are made possible only by the fundamental principles which I have described to you and which are engendered in the net sum and total of the Infinite Intelligence which I have called Infinity.

Understanding these principles is extremely important to you. When you get over on the other side, or after death, as it is called, you won't have this physical body; you will be an inductive particle in this infinity. In other words, you will be just like a radio or a television set. You will be inducting into yourself at any given moment, an infinite number of wave forms of energy, and they can all mean something to you or they can mean absolutely nothing to you, according to how you understand them and are able to translate them into your consciousness.

So you can see how important it is. If they mean nothing to you, then they can set up a lot of oscillations within this energy body I have called the psychic anatomy in which you are now living, and when all of these spurious oscillations are set up, they can create pandemonium or a very hellish or nightmarish condition because these oscillations don't mean anything; they have no relationship to your past or to whatever it is you have contacted or developed as reactionary elements in your daily life. The reason why I am stressing this so emphatically at all times is because I know how important it is to you. Just to say that somebody is going to jerk you into heaven by the hair on the top of your head or by your chinny-chin-chin is ridiculous. You couldn't live there if you ever got there that way; you wouldn't be very happy.

Now, we do have spiritual communication—and don't get me wrong—I do believe in spiritual communication; as a matter of fact, I live by it 24 hours a day. As a matter of fact, everyone does. The difference between me and the general consensus of the public on this earth world is that I am totally conscious of this process and have developed my capacities to live as a spiritual medium to a much higher capacity or to a much more intelligent capacity than any of the so-called mediumistic efforts which have been promulgated on this Earth. The differences here are, of course, in the way in which I understand creation—not by chasing off madly in some kind of a rocket to a nearby planet to find rocks there which somehow have not had the same deterioration as have the earth rocks, and think that I can understand the creation of the universe by picking up a piece of rock.

Well, I would like to understand creation in a much more comprehensive manner. I would like to know where the atoms in that rock came from and how they were formed. I would like to know much more about the intelligence, the principles of creation, and such, which engendered the atoms in that rock. I would also like to know what it was that held these atoms together in that rock to form the molecules, etc. That's my approach to a comprehensive understanding of creation.

So you see, so far as I am concerned, the position of the average earthman is something analogous to a very elemental or very low-grade, expressionary way of life on some planet. During the course of my many years on this planet in this earth body, I have often felt like I was in the middle of a big zoo, and I was very avidly studying the reactions and the life patterns of different people about me. I never considered myself a human in the normal capacity that other people considered themselves. I didn't feel that way. I was never able to communicate with them on the same basis that other people communicate with each other. I never had the same rapport with them, and to top it all off, I radiated a tremendous energy aura which set me apart from all people.

Of course as you can well imagine, I had to develop a lot of different compensations and I had to, very definitely within my own mind, always hold uppermost the thought and the plan that I had come here specifically for the purpose of enlightening the earth-man on very definite concepts in which he would be very vitally interested in his future, to try to help him desist from the primeval elements of his life which were the worship of false spirits and gods, to try to get him to visualize within his own mind a constructive and comprehensive plan of evolution, and above all, to try to get him to stop praying to these false gods and doing lip and altar service and instead, to learn a much more intelligent approach to creation and infinity.

By understanding infinity and the principles which engender the appearance of all life forms on all planets as well as in higher levels and strata of the universal evolution, these principles in turn would give this lowly earthman a chance for immortality—a chance which he only very vaguely envisions within the closed confines of his materialistic world, or that he was seeking relief from the constant, ever-attendant pressure of death about him in some panacea or some escape so that he could visualize himself as living immortally. Well, there is an immortal life but it is only for those who achieve an intelligent relationship with Creation which engendered this immortality and this infinity which makes immortality possible. Unless this proper, intelligent relationship is achieved, any earthman or any other person, for that matter, will continually revolve on the wheel of karma, as it was spoken of by the Yogi. He will constantly reincarnate into the earth world and in each successive reincarnation, he will find that his position has become retrograde; he is regressing because he has not added any of the constructive elements which are most necessary for him to evolve and to progress in an evolutionary pattern. This is my purpose here on this world.

I am not indigenous to this planet; I have often said that I am an alien, but a benign alien; one who has come to give a life-giving message and a certain measure of intelligent, creative energy to any or all of those who participate in this earth life and especially to those who can attain a more direct relationship with the polarity which I express here into this world from the world from which I came.

We should not at this point become involved in any semantics which say that I am better or that he is better than the other, etc. We should be more constructively inclined to constantly inclinate and to assimilate into our daily lives the elements of a progressive evolution which link us more directly to the constructive forces which emanate from Infinite Intelligence to a more understandable relationship with the fourth dimension and to succeeding and progressive evolutions.

ESP, Mind Telepathy, Telekinesis, etc. Viewed Psychically

Now that we have entered into some of the more complex abstractions which deal directly with various interpolations of interdimensional movements, the formations of atoms, the relationship of an infinite number of electromagnetic fields, etc., this should prove a most opportune time to enter into associated fields of psychic interplay or extraterrestrial phenomena as they are sometimes called, to explain certain and as yet mysterious proclivities of human endeavor which are currently being very highly expressed and exploited—speaking principally on such factors as ESP, mind telepathy, telekinesis and such factors which are pertinent and relevant to mind expressions beyond norms of the reactionary materialistic earthman.

To begin with, a most fascinating field of exploration is sometimes referred to as fortune-telling, foretelling the future, as well as giving certain incidental information about the past which will prove to the recipient that the future is actually being foretold. This necromancy or occultism has been practiced since the beginning of man's life on the Earth and in the more primitive reaches and expressions of man's life, has assumed such channels as witchcraft, wizardry and associated expressionary elements.

As of today, the scientists to a large degree deny the existence of the ability to either communicate telepathically or to foretell the past or the future. Such assumptions are absolutely false; the future can be accurately foretold, and in my own personal experiences, I have foretold the future of many people, even to the last minute detail. Even at this time I describe past instances with minute details that may have escaped the memory or the observation of those persons involved. How is this accomplished? Well, in our previous discussions on the interdimensional cosmos, this explanation becomes relatively easy. We start first with what is called space, and as I have previously presented space, it is a false presumption. Space is actually infinitely filled at any given point with an infinite number of cyclic wave forms; that is, little or large circles of energy traveling around in a circle, each one relevant to itself to the degree that it impounds within its wave-form structures a certain quotient of intelligence or information and which can be harmonically, or by means of electromagnetic fields which regenerate these harmonics, transmitted to a degree to any and all other cycles of energy which exist in the infinite cosmos.

Now as a person progresses along his pathway of evolution, at any given moment he is directly in contact with any number of these infinite, regenerative cycles. Although he may not be conscious of this, yet this is true. Through the differences in harmonic structures, electromagnetic fields which regenerate and propagate these harmonics, this person is polarizing or implanting into the cyclic, fourth-dimensional wave forms, certain wave forms of his own. These wave forms are the actual information of the life experience which this person is undergoing at that particular moment.

Therefore, in the future, any person who has a mind which can tune into these fourth-dimensional wave forms, can attune himself through the frequency vibrations which are radiating in the aura of this person, into past lifetime incidents or happenings by merely contacting as a way of attunement, just as it is with the radio, the different little wave forms which were implanted by that person (unconsciously) at that particular moment. Then in the manner in which I have

205

described the functions of the psychic anatomy, the interplay of these wave forms recreating facsimiles in my own particular psychic anatomy which are again projected into the cortical layers of my brain is in effect, an energy structure which relates to me the exact picture of that happening in that past incident and it makes absolutely no difference if it was but a day or a thousand years. Time is of no particular importance in this dimension and if a person had experienced a certain happening in a lifetime, at any given moment in the last several thousand years of his life (as he has incarnated any number of times upon the earth), then I could very accurately tune in to any of these past instances and relate them to him in a comprehensive fashion.

Almost equally as important is the fact that with certain mind projections of energy which I would accomplish by means of my psychic anatomy and other related factors of which I am cognizant and can work with, I can project this picture accurately into this person's mind, even though he does not consciously remember the incident. He will then obtain a very strong rapport with the reproduction of this life incident, and as I have described it in the reverse-phase feedback principle, the difference in time frequency or the time consonant between this dimension at this time and that particular happening at that time, is a phase reversal and cancels out much of the pernicious effect of that life experience.

The same principles are quite true in predicting the future. Going back to our original consensus, all cycles in the infinite cosmogony are related to each other on the basis of harmonics; therefore, any past incidents which have happened to any person are harmonically oscillating in certain similarly attuned cycles in his future. That is to say, that at any given moment in your life at this time, there can be a contact with certain cycles which are similar to those cycles which you will contact in your future, and in that relationship then, the harmonic content which has been radiated to them from your past will then be regenerating in your future. You will therefore subconsciously try to reproduce these certain life incidents in your future life.

In my attunement to these future happenings, they are just as plain and realistic as those which you have had happen to you or that you have experienced in your past life. Now this has been very scientifically explained to you and is provable to you on the basis and the consensus of all existing electrical technocracy which is in existence today. They are provable to you in the laboratories of this world through oscilloscopes, generators and other such apparatus as is available to the scientist of this time. You must bear in mind that the oscilloscope, television, radio or any other of the electronic inventions or developments which we have at our disposal would not be possible unless the principles which I have explained to you were valid and in effect, and were working in these instruments.

The very nature of any electrical phenomena in any field in this earth-world dispensation is entirely synonymous, is engendered by, and made possible by the principles which explain creation itself and the proposition of infinity. One would not be possible without the other; as a matter of fact, there would not be a single blade of grass, a human, there would not be an earth world, there would not be a solar system, a galaxy or a universe. Nothing would be possible unless we had all of these very important factors in constant operation at all times.

As I have said, the third dimension is only one of the expressionary planes which are manifest in infinity; it is an oscillating and a pulsating plane of expression. It is constantly repeating the experience or the idiom, or the intelligence of the past into the future and in that way its own cyclic patterns are superimposed in the races of peoples and to individuals who are so involved in them. This will lead us more directly into what I have described in the first lesson course as the spiritual evolution—one of which Darwin did not know about. What it means actually is that any animate or living object, as it is going through its evolution—whether it is an amoeba, a tree, a flower, an animal, man, whatever this particular specimen, whatever it is, is also contacting infinity. It is, by the oscillating process, re-expressing its own life form and its life experience as a facsimile reproduction of Infinite Intelligence which is oscillating in these wave form patterns; or you might say that it is a preconceived concept which has been created or exists in infinity since the beginning of whatever infinity is.

Actually, as said, there is no beginning, so this specimen of life, whatever it is, manifests its own intelligence as it is oscillated from infinity and in the reverse process as polarized elements of experiences, reverses this oscillation back into infinity and propagates, on the basis of its own psychic anatomy, contact with the infinity which leaves its own oscillating quotient with those cyclic forms of infinity with which it was involved. Harmonically attuned, all infinity then can be said to be oscillating with, or resonating with the life experience of this specimen. Then, as the specimen progresses and gets to the point of death and reincarnates, or that another similar specimen is brought into the surface of life, this specimen can be said to be harmonically in tune with the past of this similar specimen and therefore inductive to it on the basis of frequency relationship. It will not only pick up the polarized idiom of these previous life experiences and will (just as you do) revamp them or reform them into its present life form and experience, but, through the proposition of harmonic attunements, it can very

208

easily pick up and reproduce or reform into the present, certain other different life experiences which have happened to other specimens of life upon the planet Earth. So again, this particular specimen has added a certain adjunctive to its own particular evolution.

It may be capable of performing a certain particular feat or function which it could not have done as a specimen in a previous lifetime. Now we must bear in mind that these two specimens were entirely different; they were not necessarily one and the same, nor did they contain the very same elements of life through the psychic anatomy from one life to another. This is strictly a proposition of harmonic attunement with other similar life forms or with those life forms which were even more remotely connected with any particular specimen but which could remanifest these life-form experiences into the present by means of a very remote system of harmonic interplay.

So this will again add a considerable dimension to the prospective of your own concept of evolution and could be called the more adaptive propensities of any specimen, particularly with mankind as he possesses a prehensile mind; that is to say, he is capable of fashioning within his own mind certain harmonics or interplays of wave forms from his past lifetime experiences which, when combined with the harmonic principle with other people's life experiences, he can then create certain imagery on the facade of his own mind. In that way he becomes more prehensile in the intellectual capacity of his daily life.

The inclusion of these discourses, such as they are, has always brought about at their conclusion a certain period of what I would call post-recriminations; that is, I may enter into a speculatory period of time where I might speculate as to the logic or wisdom of giving these discourses and the nature of these subjects to the earthman in his present state of evolution. I have very severely questioned the intellectual capacity of people to assimilate fourth-dimensional concepts within the confines of their third-dimensional world and to make them logical and viable in whatever life transpositions they are presently engaged. I am also concerned with other certain psychological factors which are involved in what might be termed the deflation of the ego, for the confrontation of the unknown to any person does immediately instigate certain subversive reactions which can cause specific repercussions to happen in the mind or even the physical actions of the person involved.

Moreover, the total evolutionary position of the world, as it concerns the populations of people as a whole unit, may be put somewhat in jeopardy by presenting these more advanced concepts simply because evolution itself mandates, at any particular time or moment in this evolution, that the life experiences of these people so involved are strictly confined within the closed precincts of their past life experiences, plus or minus some biases and interjections which they may desire and feel justified within their own reasonable dimension of their minds.

Beyond the immediate periphery of their own intellectual capacity however, is the great unknown, and this is the never-never land to every human who follows his own course of evolution on the planet Earth; and seldom if ever does he venture beyond the realm or the periphery of this closed dimension of his own life. He may combine any and all other elements or life experiences of other people to some degree or attain some relationship to them in the judgments he may arrive at in the dimension of his own mind, but these are all relative and adjunctive only to his life and do not extend into that never-never land of the fourth dimension.

It is also a point of conjecture, one which I have

often entered into, as to that oft repeated moment when any scientist arrives at that terminating point in any discoveries or in any particular developments of the science, that he will inevitably create the great and insoluble enigma in his own science, that he knows not the source, the cure, the origin or the manner and way in which it is manifest; sort of like a brick wall against which he is constantly butting his head and one which he refuses to climb over, yet the world of infinity beyond is limitless and boundless in all its dimensions and capacities. Yet he is closely confined within this brick wall of his own making, his third dimensional world which is that brick wall. Within this confine then, he is suitably placated in all of the factors of his daily life that he can, to a reasonable extent, deploy these factors, coordinate them and to otherwise satisfy his own ego with his own judgment in regard to them.

Fourth-dimensional concepts then could very seriously disrupt or could totally destroy certain continuities within the evolutionary position of any earth-man were he not suitably substantiated; or that he could not in some way bring a certain focus of his own limited introspections to render the necessary judgments, or to otherwise condemn and to flagellate any of these interdimensional aspects. I am always therefore tempered as to the extent in which I might extend these explanations. There is also one other limiting factor and that is the vernacular of the earth-man himself. Third-dimensional words are symbolic forms and, in themselves, are meaningless except that they have succeeded by the different consonants and certain tones and vibrations contained within them, into propagating certain subconscious reactions which give the form of speech, and the additive factors or associaions with the other five senses of the expressionary elements of the human being.

Yet, words are words, and in fourth dimensional

context are almost totally unsuited to explain such factors to the earthman, even assuming that he has the intellectual capacity to understand them; and should he have this intellectual capacity, it is almost useless to say that he would not need these explanations, that he would already have this information at his disposal. One is simply analogous to another; however, a starting place must be made. In my efforts here, I am attempting to polarize within the oscillating frequencies which have arisen from past lives of humans, to all present oscillating frequencies and to such harmonic frequencies which entail their future lifetimes—to instill certain polarizations which contain intelligent information which will be useful and viable to them on the basis that they can induct them into the periphery of their own intellectual capacity as something meaningful and viable to them.

Therefore, in the mechanics and the interplay of these harmonic structures, I am just as concerned with their past as I am with their future; one is coincidental and necessary to the other. In the future therefore, whether or not I shall enter into even more abstractions remains a proposition of total fulfillment of my life Mission. I most certainly will not extend beyond certain reasonable dimensions, reasonable in my own framework of logic and reason, as I know the inter-dimensional cosmos and man's present position in his evolution on this planet Earth. I am also quite aware that to supplant the deficiencies in such nomenclatures or word forms as they are used by the earthman with the power of projection or telekinesis, is by the formation of suitable harmonic energy wave forms, properly attuned to the individual mental capacity which can resonate within this psychic anatomy to the extent that they can be reconstituted and revitalized, or they can be harmonically attuned to in the future time and become meaningful to him as future life incorporations

212

into his daily life.

All of these factors are part of this post-period of recrimination of which I speak personally, one which is not entered into lightly and one in which I, in many ways, have to expose myself to certain incumbent dangers always manifest on the planet Earth which must be taken into consideration with regard to the reactionary elements in the nature of man himself; that he is quite prone to destroy, to vilify and reject the most necessary and vital elements in his life if they are not prefaced and prepared for him, in a manner of speaking, from such life experiences that he can correlate them into his present and accept them.

The ego of any person is supreme and is the dominant factor in his own life beyond any such judgments which will take place in his own mentality and which involves all of his life experiences in the past; he will adjure and condemn any of those to which he cannot harmonically relate himself. This is, of course, a very dangerous aspect to any person like myself as you might know by past texts and liturgies which I have brought into existence, that I am an alien; that I live in this world by virtue of a physical body which is master-minded by a psychic anatomy constructed of the different portions of six other psychic anatomies— lives of certain individuals of past lives. Respectively they are: Sharazar, Osiris, Akhenaton, Zoroaster, Anaxagoras, and Jesus, and there may be other portions of other lifetimes which, to some degree, may have been interjected. All of these were assembled in sort of a robot fashion by the Master Minds and Intellects of the Higher Worlds from whence I came.

It is this psychic anatomy which is constantly deploying its very necessary commands into the physical structures of my body and makes metabolism possible, and also presents in its entire strength and capacity, a certain duality of personalities. While I, in my true

213

Self, am one of the Organization or Brotherhood of Unarius in the Higher World, yet I must constantly live in this world by means and media of this physical anatomy; I must appear to others as a human like themselves, but beyond the radiating capacity of a very strong aura, there is little to suspect that I am not indigenous to this planet. Yet, the very life which this physical body lives and of which I am aware through certain capacities of my Inner Self, makes this life repugnant, even abhorrent to me at times, not that I deplore life as it is expressed on any particular level in the infinite, still there must always be these comparisons with life in the higher planets and this vegetative or animal life lived by people on this planet.

While inwardly—and from their capacities as attunements with Infinite Intelligence—they are quite capable of expressing a greater and much higher degree of life, yet they are inseparably bound to all the traditional capacities and expressions of the earth-world. Even their physiognomies, such as are expressed in their physical bodies, demand a constant and repetitious exercise of all the elements which are incumbent in an earth-life existence. Yet there is within each person this sublime spark, if we may call it such; the attunement with the higher capacities of intellects with Higher Worlds, to Infinite Intelligence Itself, which gives them certain aspirations, hopes, expressions of love and felicity to their fellowman.

Yes, even heroism is sometimes expressed beyond the normal capacities which could be expected on a more survival-of-the-fittest attitude which is so strongly expressed by the earthman. Yes, all of these and so many thousands of other factors, thoughts, speculations, analyses very frequently enter into the conscious surface of my mind, this earth-mind that must be the intermediary between this and the fourth dimension, this mind which is also the instrumentality of my

Higher Self—that Entity or Being which lives in company of the Brotherhood in the Higher Worlds. In these speculations and observations I have only sincerely and often hoped that I have not intimidated either this Higher Mind of myself, or those of my Brothers, yet I believe that all concerned are, in their intellectual capacities, sufficiently logical and envision within the scope and circumference of this intellectuality, an entire justification of what is necessary as a physical being or a physical life lived here on the planet Earth; that the necessary mechanisms—sex, defense, hunger, guilt, fear—all of these different physiological elements and reactions are most necessary to perpetuate the libido and sustain the physical body as a means and as a vehicle, or an intermediary, between this and the higher worlds.

In this respect then, I do not leave these judgments to others who may not know all factors involved, but remain absolute in them unto myself, and I might add, they are shared and understood by the dear one who is by my side—the only person in this world who does, to some appreciable degree, understand my position and the tremendous amount of conflict, as well as logic, reason and balance which must enter into the expression of this daily life.

To the future then, and to the evolution of man as he so finds himself in any planetary sphere, or under the influence of any governmental systems, socialisms or to whatever, this is one resource which is infallible and which he can constantly call upon even though he does not recognize nor is he conscious of these things, yet, even his prayers, though directed to a nonexistent god, do reach the ears of those who are vitally concerned with his welfare. To those Shining Angels who live in these Higher Worlds, to those of the Unariun Brotherhood who are the lifesavers of these material worlds and who, in their own intellectual capacities, do become a participating element in all of the creative facilities of the Universal Mind and Intelligence, this too, is the proposition which is always incumbent and should be foremost to every human who inhabits this earth; not to attain some position in his social structure which will bring him the adulation of others but rather, to concern himself with widening the prospective and the intellectual capacity of his own mind and beyond the dimension of his earth world to that point where he, too, can become a creative factor in Infinite Intelligence. To do otherwise is to centralize all form and motion within the closed confines of his own third-dimensional periphery of his earth life and brings ultimate destruction.

The factor of progressive evolution is inviolate and mandates that every atom, every molecule, every element which can be considered to be a separate entity which conducts life experiences, that this evolution must be progressive, that it must constantly in itself, recur in the cyclic motions through time and space as they are manifest in a third-dimensional planet. While they are individual constituents in this evolutionary expression, yet they too must contain polarized elements which come from the Infinite Intelligence Itself. To live beyond this is eventual destruction and dissemination of all wave forms and psychic structures within the psychic anatomy of any human and which would make any other reincarnations impossible and would relegate him back into one of the abysmal astral jungles which were so aptly described by Dante in his journey through Hades as it was conducted by the Angel Virgil.

To your welfare and well-being then, but especially to an evolutionary pattern into the future, to an evolutionary pathway which will lead you more directly into constructive elements. This science must always play a vital and important part of your life; it should become an all-consuming proposition—one in which, at whatever date you can relate your present life experience as an expression of Infinite Intelligence, this expression, in itself, carries its own morality. As you express this, and knowing as you do the harmonic content as it concerns the interplay with the infinite— this moment is indeed your future, a future manifest in a different form perhaps but nevertheless containing the same idiom or the same quotient of whatever your former life experience was. This then, is evolution.

Atomic Energy, the Red Shift,
the Doppler Effect, etc.

In a quantitative assessment of cyclic phenomena, the electromagnetic force fields which we have previously discussed have pointed out the primitive ignorance of this present-day science, in regard to the creative principles of solar systems, galaxies, universes and all life forms, all of which have led us directly into other fields and other interpolations where science has made colossal and stupid blunders in its assumptions when trying to view or rationalize such origins on the surface of their third-dimensional prospectus. Many of these stupid assumptions concern astronomical phenomena, such as believing the sun is a thermonuclear furnace. They believe the sun's energy comes from the fusion or implosion of two hydrogen atoms into one helium atom. What then of the other sixty-odd elements they have, through spectroscopic analysis, found on the sun? Apparently it is not known that this is an evolutionary process of atoms, as I have previously outlined. To change two hydrogen atoms into one helium atom, it is first necessary for certain changes to occur in all electromagnetic fields which are the formative pattern of the atom and which, in turn, are oscillating polarities with their respective fourth-dimensional centrifuges.

Now, to change these two hydrogen atoms, certain arrangements of harmonic pulses which are propagated by the centrifuge occur, and as these harmonics occur, the two atoms blend as one. At that exact moment of blending, a certain spiked pulse-beat, which can be called an isochronism, is released and as this pulse is a regeneration of harmonics or a combination of harmonics, it therefore beats on a much lower plane or frequency, which is synchronous to the third dimension and is radiated from the sun's photosphere as energy and is propagated through space as a cyclic wave form to be reconverted in the electromagnetic fields of the earth into our familiar heat, light, etc.

So you see, the energy pulses as they are combined en masse from countless trillions of merging atoms form the radiated energy, yet this energy does not come from the atoms. They are, in their total electromagnetic spectrums rearranged, and in these new polarities become helium. The energy and intelligence, so to speak, came from their fourth-dimensional centrifuge. The same process is true in exploding an atomic (fission) bomb. An atomic bomb is a mass of uranium atoms, U-235, made unstable by the addition of extra electromagnetic wave forms called electrons. A dynamite explosion generates the necessary wave forms of energy to harmonically unbalance these added wave forms and they fly off as energy, into space. A nuclear fusion bomb is exactly similar. A hydrogen isotope called heavy water is used and is unstable because it contains extra or added electromagnetic wave forms.

If an atom bomb is exploded in their midst, the necessary wave forms as shock energy release these extra wave forms and cause the hydrogen atoms to merge or implode, and again, on the basis of polarities and isochronisms, which are constantly regenerated by the fourth-dimensional centrifuges, there is also the added release of that third-dimensional pulse. So the hydrogen bomb is much more powerful than an atomic bomb because of the much greater release of energy, and this release, because of its rapid disbursement into the third dimension—traveling as it does in this resistive third dimension—is called heat and light and which again are merely false names and assumptions for the movement of energy through third dimensional plasma fields.

Another great and mistaken fallacy is the "Red Shift". On a spectrographic analysis, scientists compare the appearance of certain lines as they appear on the surface of the refractory, crystal prism. Like an ordinary triangular crystal of glass, the spectrograph divides the light spectrum into certain lines somewhat similar to a rainbow. It is assumed that all known elements found on earth are part of every star-sun being viewed, as these are similar to our own sun. The thermonuclear process, or burning (fusion) of these elements, radiates the necessary light viewed on the spectroscope. From very distant star suns, the red light appears at a different place than it does here on earth. The scientist thinks this is caused by what he calls the Doppler effect; i.e., the train-whistle receding away from you has a lower pitch than it does coming toward you.

The scientist thinks the star sun is moving rapidly away from the solar system and the galaxy because he is always looking out toward the outer rim of the galaxy and he cannot see toward the center because of the many more star suns and other conditions. He must always look out onto the Milky Way, so therefore he thinks that our galaxy and universe is expanding and this leads to the most ridiculous of all assumptions—the "Big Bang" theory; i.e., somewhere at some time, a huge ball of atoms collected together and when there were enough of them and they were compressed tightly enough, they suddenly exploded. The little pieces traveling outward formed the countless trillions of star suns of the universe.

Now, they have not yet explained why these little pieces, in traveling out, assumed that pinwheel fashion, or the rotating formation with which we are familiar from astronomical photographs. Logically, from an explosion, such objects would be propelled straight out from the center. Also not explained: why the universe is thicker at the center and tapers out to a thin edge. An explosion should hurl bits and pieces in all directions, up and down as well as sideways (360 degrees). Also not explained: why countless galaxies have formed in this universe, each one rotating pin-wheel-like, the same as the universe, and which again invalidates the "Big Bang" theory.

Pictures of our sister galaxy in Andromeda prove the existence of these galaxies—impossible to be formed in an explosion. What has formed the universe and these galaxies has been adequately described in the book "The Infinite Concept of Cosmic Creation", as well as elsewhere in these liturgies—a huge interdimensional centrifuge forming this universe—the galaxies being primary anomalies or eddy currents, generated from the net sum and total of this electromagnetic energy in this centrifuge. Here again, this same harmonic regeneration takes place in forming suns, planets, planetary systems and atom-energy forms again all remanifesting in their respective weights, the different electromagnetic energy and cyclic wave form patterns from their own particular vortexes or centrifuges. The net sum and total of all this inter-dimensional regeneration, electromagnetic energy force fields proves how wrong the red shift, Doppler theory is.

Einstein's mathematics showed how light is bent around intense magnetic fields. Energy as light combining from a distant star is curved in that space by the electromagnetic lines of the galaxy, and according to respective frequencies involved in the differences of light frequencies, the effect is to bend the shorter, or blue rays, more than the red rays; the yellow rays falling in between. So the scientist makes this big mistake: in his spectroscope he places his comparative graph lines to line up first with the blue light-ray lines, and the farther out on the scale he goes, the farther these lines appear to be out of alignment with his comparative chart which was made on earth-lines which were photographed and made into a picture-graph at a very short distance from their source and were unbent by any electromagnetic fields. So the red rays would naturally appear at a different place and farther out on the spectroscopic graph picture—not because that distant star sun was traveling at incredible speeds away from the center of the universe but because, just like with a prism, the light rays were bent to form an arc, and following the curved radial lines of the galaxy, the shorter blue rays were bent slightly more than were the red rays. The same process was duplicated by the spectroscope but, as yet, this stupid blunder has gone unnoticed.

Only one more fact should be noted: that all energy rays which are coming from our sun or from any distant sun are really not heat or light until they are converted in some relative degree by the electromagnetic fields of the earth. Again, this conversion takes place according to the total frequencies involved; heat coming out as one subharmonic, while our three primary light frequencies are higher harmonic frequencies.

(The following taken from the San Diego Tribune Aug. 19, 1971)

Present-day theory of light and heat produced by the sun is as follows:

"Inside the sun, gas particles, or atoms, are packed so tightly together that they break apart. An atom is made up of an inner part (or nucleus) and an outer part. Deep inside the sun the outer parts of the gas atoms have all been stripped away from the nuclei. A gas made up of atoms that are broken apart is called a plasma.

The temperature of the plasma at the sun's center is probably 27,000,000 degrees Fahrenheit or higher. At this high temperature, reactions can take place between the nuclei of atoms, which we call nuclear reactions. The nuclear reactions taking place inside the sun are nuclear-fusion reactions. The nuclei of two or more atoms point together, or fuse, producing a large amount of light and heat. Billions of atomic nuclei join together within the sun every second. These reactions are the source of the sun's energy.

The energy produced by nuclear fusion inside the sun has to escape or else the sun would explode. The energy flows from the center of the sun to the photosphere, (the sun's surface, which is a layer of gases a few hundred miles thick).

The energy is then emitted from the sun's surface as heat and light and other forms of radiation. A tiny amount of matter taking part in a fusion reaction produces a large amount of energy. Because the sun is so huge, it can keep burning for billions of years before it runs out of its nuclear fuel."

This article was carried in the San Diego Tribune, August 19, 1971, the very next morning after I gave the foregoing dissertations. Again, no reasons or causes were given why atoms condense so tightly as to form a sun and where do these atoms come from? Again, where or what causes these actions to take place? What causes the 27 million degrees Fahrenheit temperatures? Why does all the "action" take place in the photosphere and chromosphere and where pressures are less than in the sun's center? Rereading the transcripts I have just presented will give you all causes and reasons and will give you much more comprehensive understanding of what is actually happening in fusion or implosion processes and you can form a comprehensive understanding of the evolution of atoms.

Again, there is clearly indicated a complete and total lack of inter-dimensional knowledge which would give scientists and laymen a comprehensive understanding of not only the sun but of all creation and it could be taught to growing children in their school curriculums.

As a note of interest, the above essay, reprinted from a local newspaper is one of a series of daily essays composed by science students in different high schools throughout the area, a prize—not noted—being given for the essay chosen for printing. This article also quite obviously points out certain disparities, missing elements and certain other factors which should be included in this or any particular segment of science being taught to students, and a comparison with this article and previous presentations which I have just made will clearly point out all of the disparities, missing factors and elements.

When I was about the same age, (twelve or thirteen) and on entering my seventh grade science class, I immediately went on the mat, so to speak, with the science teacher about certain false concepts which were contained in our science book and which concerned the phases of the moon, eclipses, et cetera. In order to prove all points I constructed a crude working model of the solar system; a lighted candle for the sun, balls of different sizes and colors rotated by wires, which proved conclusively that I was right. As might be expected, this produced a tremendous upheaval and the banishment of these science textbooks, and a red-faced science teacher who left me strictly alone hence-forth.

Of course, this immediately suggests and brings to mind a certain obvious fact; about 99.9% of all students attending schools, meekly accept without question, all the established rhetorics which have been developed in the wind-up of our civilization—old wives' tales, claptrap, superstitions, vagaries, innuendos and a complete absence of the most important aspects and relationships of life on the planet Earth in regard to the interdimensional cosmos and the ever-creative principles constantly in action, all of which would give a new vitality to our educational systems, and if properly administered and taught, would present the incumbent total morality, which would mitigate or eliminate most of the insolvable problems now confronting our society such as drug abuse, sexual promiscuity, contempt for the basic values of this society, law, respect for the rights of others, et cetera.

Such knowledge and learning of all creative interdimensional faculties and principles would also eliminate the age-old superstitions which are covered and practiced by all denominational churches and their religious practices, again replaced by the new morality and an assuredness of future immortality, to be realized either in progressive reincarnation, or eventual development into an advanced life form, living in a Higher World.

To those few then who speak out against the rhetorics of their time, they who are the emancipators of ignorance and despair, may they live forever in the hearts of those who have been freed from these earth-world tyrannies, for they are the Shining Angels who go among the masses of humanity in these earth worlds to guide the way for those who have dedicated themselves to finding a way to live closer to the mainstream of Infinite Intelligence.

Electromagnetic Wave Forms, Fields
& Atoms vs. Mass

In the essay composed by the student in the news-paper, it is said that in the fusion process going on in the photosphere of the sun, an electron would be stripped from the nucleus or proton of the atom. Now, this would immediately suggest certain implications. As almost everyone knows or should know, an atom is extremely difficult to break apart, or to otherwise change—a fact which makes our third-dimensional world possible. Were this not so, the different reper-cussive forces and agencies which are constantly in motion about us would eventually subdivide all atomic forms into nothingness; so therefore, this leads us to an inevitable conclusion; that an atom, while it is extremely small, it is also extremely hard.

Also, an atom is energy, and so if it is not solid but is actually composed of oscillating energy wave forms, how is this solidity achieved? As I said: through a very strong shell of electromagnetic wave forms which are generated in harmony with the vortex which formed the atom as its central nucleus, on this basis then, atoms either repel each other or they are very strongly attracted to each other on the basis of this electromag-netic field. Some of these electromagnetic wave forms extend beyond the immediate shell of the atom itself and which makes adhesion possible. Also, an atom is oscillating at extreme velocities or frequencies. The scientist of today has not seen an atom; it is so small you could put about 200,000 of them on the head of a pin and still not be able to see them, and it might take anywhere from one to ten million diameters of magni-fication before an atom could even be seen as a tiny streak.

Remember the viruses? Well, science has taken pictures of viruses. They use an electron microscope which can magnify up to about 20,000 diameters; then, by using the photographs taken at this magnification, they can enlarge these pictures so that a theoretical 100,000 diameters of magnification is achieved. However, remember that a virus is composed of hundreds or even thousands of molecules, and each molecule in turn could be very easily composed of hundreds or even thousands of atoms and so on, ad infinitum. So the proposition here becomes a little more complex.

Now, what is the determinant in this oscillating frequency between atoms? There are certain similarities, in more familiar objectivisms, which can be achieved here about us on Earth. For example: looking at an ordinary motion picture, the individual pictures or frames, as they were photographed on the film, go through the gate of the projector and are exposed to the light at about 18 to 22 frames or pictures per second. Now, your eye cannot distinguish anything faster than 18 times per second, so that at 22 frames per second, the movement of the film through the gate becomes invisible to you and the subsequent differences in each of the succeeding frames gives the illusion that the picture is moving. It's pretty much the same with atoms versus mass.

Other similarities include the fluorescent light tube with which we are familiar, or the neon light which lights up our cities at night. The proposition with the fluorescent tube or neon light is quite simple: a glass tube is coated on the inside with a fluorescent material such as a phosphor compound and the air is then pumped out of the tube and replaced with one of the noble gases, usually neon. There are also other gases which serve this purpose such as xenon, et cetera.

Now, all of these gases have a certain peculiarity; that is, they can conduct an electrical wave form of energy according to how they are polarized—the scientist calls such polarization ionization—so that the gases inside the tube can actually become conductive to a wave form by assuming this certain positive or negative ionization, and so the electrodes fastened on each end of this glass tube contain an alternating current which oscillates at sixty cycles per second.

Now, on one-half of the wave form, the gases inside the tube assume a certain polarity and become conductive to the electricity on that end of the tube, and as the energy passes through the ionized gas to the other end, it completes one-half of the sixty-cycle oscillation. Then the ionization polarities are reversed and conduct the electricity on the other half of the cycle back to the other end of the tube. This goes on at the rate of sixty times per second, back and forth, to complete the total cycle. Meanwhile, the phosphorous coatings on the inside surface of the tube retain the impulses of light frequencies to a certain degree—a faculty called purveyance—and so the illusion of a steady light is maintained by your eye. However, if you move your head rapidly enough, you can synchronously attune your eyesight and actually be able to see one-half of this cycle as a subharmonic. By glancing rapidly across the top of the table for example, you can distinctly see the fluctuating impulses of light so that, here again, the fluorescent tube is actually dark for thirty times per second and is illuminated for the other thirty times per second. It goes off and on at the rate of sixty times per second.

It is pretty much the same way with atoms versus molecules as they compose the different mass forms within this world with which we are familiar except, of course, that all of these electronic impulses are electromagnetic in nature and sustain themselves on the

228

basis that they can either repel or attract each other. It is extremely difficult to break an atom apart, as any physicist (or for that matter even a high school boy) can tell you. At the big universities such as Berkeley here in California, they use cyclotrons or bevatrons to break up atoms and to attain what they call a neutron flow of energy. A cyclotron or a bevatron is simply either a circular or a long line of powerful electro-magnets. These are malleable iron cores wrapped with coils and they become saturated with electromagnetic flux when the electricity passes through the coil. So they start hydrogen atoms out at one end of this long line of coils and by successively alternating the polar-ities of these magnets, they can make these different hydrogen gas particles accelerate to tremendous speeds into what they call millions of electron volts.

At such incredible speeds, these atoms begin to collide, and as they collide, certain ones will break up or fall apart, so to speak, and as heavy hydrogen is simply a proton, a neutron and an electron, then the neutrons can, by means of certain deflection plates, be siphoned or funneled off this long line of magnets toward the end where it will form a certain line of neutronic impulses, very similar to what might be called a lightning bolt—except on a very small scale.

By studying such reactions which are involved in the net sum and process, the scientist hopes to gain some sort of a comprehensive idea as to what an atom is and what holds it together. As you see, I have that all down on paper and tape, so it wasn't really necessary to spend hundreds of millions of dollars to construct these bevatrons and cyclotrons and to pay fancy sal-aries to these physicists to try to break up an atom. An old boy like myself could have described the pro-cess of what an atom is and what holds it together very simply and very easily. Of course, it would take a little imagination on the part of the physicist, and it might strain his intellectual capacity to the breaking point and he would either very severely reject the whole thing and call me a nut, or he would in some other way be very seriously deflated in his ego. To say the least, he could very well lose his position and his high-paying salary while he was fooling around with his bevatron. And so the story goes.

Our physical world, as it is composed or comprised of atom-molecule forms, and in whatever shape, manner or form you wish to look at them—the table on which you eat your meals, the bed upon which you sleep at night, the house in which you live, the entire terrestrial atmosphere and environment—is a composition of molecules, and molecules, in turn, are atoms; in other words, the central nuclei or the central polarity of a fourth-dimensional vortex.

Well, you might wonder how all of this situation is maintained. How do atoms, for example, form a table and yet, seemingly, there will be a vacant space around the table, the nearest solid surfaces being walls or floors? Now, if you revert back to some of my original statements, you will see that I said that space—any space, the space around you in your room in which you are now sitting, or the space outdoors, when you are out on a picnic—really isn't space at all. It is infinitely filled with oscillating wave forms. They are so dense and solid that it would be incomprehensible to your physical, third-dimensional mind. Even more incomprehensible is the fact that all of these wave forms of oscillating energy can exist as they do, apparently within each other and all oscillating at incredible speeds far beyond the comprehension of your mind, just as it was with the motion picture film passing through the projector, and you were looking at the picture on the screen.

You walk through these infinitely dense, oscillating, cyclic forms of energy without being aware of them, simply because the atoms which comprise your body are harmonically in tune with them only on the basis of their own individual vortexes, of which they are the nucleus. In all other ways, however, so far as these interdimensional cyclic wave forms are concerned, you haven't the slightest idea that they are there and you would be astonished if you could, say for example, by some comparative means, weigh them on some sort of scale. As I have said, some stars in our galaxy are so heavy that a cubic inch will weigh 20,000 tons, or even several million tons.

Again we think back to our analysis of what gravitation is; simply the pull of certain atoms and their electromagnetic fields toward other masses of atoms and their electronic fields. The earth can be likened to one huge atom, having at the north pole a magnetic pole and at the south pole a magnetic pole. Every atom is quite similar in formation to this particular situation as they too have a north pole and a south pole, or a positive pole and a negative pole. Within the structure, as I will call it, of the atom, there are many millions of oscillating wave forms which are counterparts of the centrifuge or vortex of which they are composed.

As these atoms are madly gyrating around the central nucleus of the atom—which again is only a smaller atom on a subminiature scale—there are certain places where they cross each other and form parallaxes, just like when you go to the railroad yards, you will see many places where the different rails cross each other and are switched back and forth. So it is with atoms. As these different wave forms oscillate positively and negatively back and forth across each other, they produce certain pulses of energy, just as it was in the fluorescent tube. It is these pulses of energy which, in the net sum and total of all these impulses of energy as they appear and reappear within the atom, generate and maintain this very strong electromagnetic field which surrounds the atom and makes it impregnable and impervious to almost any but a superhuman effort to break it apart.

You could hammer on an atom all day long and you wouldn't hurt it, simply because the atom is too small to be affected by the concussion of molecules. The shell is absolutely impervious except on the basis that we can some way, interdimensionally speaking, actually interject certain electromagnetic forces within the structure of the vortex which forms the atom and which will change this atom's characteristics. So this "stripping off" a neutron from an atom is a bit of poppycock; something like this atom somehow caught itself on a nail going by somewhere.

What actually happened, as it would in the bevatron or the cyclotron; the extremely high electromagnetic fluxes—which were generated and which were synchronously attuned so that they propelled the atom very swiftly—were of such nature that certain harmonics were formed which were more fourth-dimensional in nature and could affect the centrifuge of the atom to the extent that other different harmonic regenerations occurred which changed the characteristic of this atom and temporarily left it "un-glued" so that it flew apart. Actually, you don't bang atoms together to make them separate. They have to be changed electro-magnetically, which is done, to a certain degree, by this bevatron or cyclotron.

This same process is going on in the photosphere of the sun all the time. As they are attuned, the countless trillions of vortexes of energy which form helium atoms, or any of the other atoms on the surface of the sun, undergo certain synchronous changes from within the fourth dimension itself as the synchronous pulses. As these changes occur, they change and affect the electromagnetic structures and the properties of the hydrogen atoms so that as they are changed, they can

232

be recombined by the same process of synchronous pulses and form helium atoms. When this is properly understood, then this business of stripping a neutron from the nucleus will indeed look very silly, stupid and elemental—which it is. It is the same in all different processes which involve atoms, molecules, et cetera.

One other bit of poppycock which scientists have to get rid of is the proposition of particles, which immediately suggests a tiny grain of sand or a pebble, or some such object. Well, there are no solid particles, either third-dimensionally, or fourth-dimensionally speaking and I am making this statement on the basis that all third-dimensional mass forms are composed of atoms and therefore aren't solid, even much more so in the fourth dimension where all these different cyclic wave forms, as they so infinitely fill Infinity, are not solid on the same basis. Here again this brings us to the term "time", and the time differentiation as I have pointed out is quite similar in our everyday life to that of the film passing through the projector.

If we use the camera and slow down the process of picture taking to say, twelve frames per second, then run it through the projector at a normal eighteen frames per second, then all motion on the screen will appear to be very greatly speeded up and the reverse process is true. If we take the pictures with the camera at the rate of thirty-two frames per second, then run them through the projector at eighteen frames per second, then all motion will be very, very slow; people walking will look like they are going at a very slow, crawling pace, with each step carefully measured.

That is very analogous to atoms versus the molecules, which form our terrestrial, third dimension. We are, to this degree, just as it was in taking the pictures with the camera and showing them with the projector, what could be called a synchronous attunement. We too, as part of this time element, maintain a synchronous attunement with atoms, molecules and the infinite cosmogony. This was, I will say, conceived in the Infinite Mind of Infinite Intelligence as a way and means in which the more primitive and more elemental life forms on a planet, such as the earth, could first begin to form certain cohesive elements in their life; that is, a certain chain-like series of reactions would form the life experience of, say, a human being and which would be retentively retained within the fourth-dimensional psychic anatomy. This fourth-dimensional psychic anatomy too, had been developed and synchronously attuned to the physical anatomy.

So here again, you must be impressed with the obvious fact that it is all extremely important that we first understand energy. The proposition of such an understanding will give us a key and an insight to the creative processes which have not only engendered or, shall I say (and using the word loosely) created the earth and all life forms but also the galaxy, the universe and the total interdimensional cosmos.

What is beyond the interdimensional cosmos would be, of, course, quite ridiculous for us to try and form some sort of an analysis or create an hypothesis, as it is, even with our relationship to the third dimension and its relationship to the fourth dimension in its constituents of atomic forms and other such electromagnetic phenomena, as is part of our daily life. And as all this phenomena is almost totally unknown to all mankind at the present time, we would indeed supersede the outermost precincts of even our strongest imaginative processes to try to envision what is beyond the interdimensional macrocosm.

The same situation is quite true to go into the microcosm, and we have already partly explored the nucleus or protons, as they are called by the scientist, which form every atom. And yet, each of these, too, is again a subminiature solar system of energy which, in all counterparts, is analogous to the parent atom of which it is a part. We can go on down, and down, and down, into sub-infinity and never come to the end of it. So how small is small or the smallest? It's much like saying that the people in Australia are walking upside down. Well, what is up, and what is down, so far as our terrestrial earth is concerned?

Again, it's simply a proposition of relationships and the integration of such facsimiles as we have developed in our evolutionary consensus in going from one life to another. We have immediately associated all of these atom-molecule forms into our daily lives and formed some sort of a sequence, a pattern, a chainlike day-to-day situation wherein each day is subdivided into hours, minutes, seconds, et cetera, and each particle of time, as we understand it, has its own particular connection with certain reactionary elements within the periphery of our life. These again are integrated and form cyclic wave forms within the psychic anatomy, which all adds to the total development of this psychic anatomy in either a forward or a retrogressive movement into the infinite cosmogony.

As I stated before, we are all just going about, making contacts every second of our lives with a certain number of these oscillating wave forms from infinity, each containing its own little oscillating idiom of intelligence or information and which, harmonically attuned through the electromagnetic fields, forms our own life experience and the world about us.

Abnormal Reactions of the Returned Astronauts

On making a general summary of our discussions of atoms versus astronauts, there are several very important facts and considerations which should be taken into account. First, one week after the astronauts returned from their exploration of the moon, they still complained of weakness, and medical tests have proven that they are still considerably under par. Also to be noted in reports published in newspapers, Scott and Irwin suffered brief spells of irregular heart rhythm while they were on the moon, as well as extreme fatigue. Erwin also suffered from spells of dizziness in space, and all three Apollo 15 crewmen have failed to recover from weightlessness as fast as was expected, Dr. Charles A. Berry, chief of the Space Center's medical office, told a news conference. The doctor described the heart irregularities as premature auricular and ventricular contractions which lasted only about ten heartbeats on both moon-walkers. These are usually associated with fatigue, he said. It has also been noted in instances of low potassium level and with increased adrenaline flow.

Also, the astronaut Scott said that upon returning to earth and sleeping in his bed, it felt like it was tilted about thirty degrees as he was lying down upon the bed. Of course, it may take many years to determine if there are any permanent effects on the physical anatomies of these spacemen. It can be almost a foregone conclusion in saying that the medical doctors or scientists will probably never know what effect these space flights have on the psychic anatomy and the general consensus of evolution as they concern these individual astronauts, as they were in a sense, projected from all known, existing forms in these evolutionary patterns, into an entirely different trajectory in which various unknown elements were interjected into their psychic anatomy as oscillating wave forms.

It should also be noted, with respect to the gravitational fields of the moon and the earth, there are several very important facts which should be discussed. It is well known that the moon has several of what are called hot spots, that is, where the gravitational field is hundreds of times stronger than it is over the balance of the surface of the moon. One of these hot spots in particular was sufficiently strong to deviate the space capsule in its flight down to the surface of the moon. These anomalies, of course, puzzle the scientists and there are many of these same gravitational anomalies or hot spots which are known to exist on the earth. In fact, there may be hundreds of them.

One in particular, of extreme intensity, is located near Santa Cruz, California, and is called the "Mystery Spot". Here, the gravitational field is so strong that it actually deviates and nullifies certain optical laws and creates an illusion which is very disconcerting to those individuals who move about over the surface of this spot. For example, two slabs of concrete have been laid on the ground and at exactly level positions—level, according to a carpenter's level; however, in standing on these two surfaces, one has the very distinct impression that one foot is higher than the other. Just above these concrete slabs is a shack or cabin which seems to be tilted at a precarious angle and is about to slide downhill; however, further examination proves that this is untrue, that walking through this cabin one has the very distinct impression that he is walking on a steep slope of a hill, yet a broom or a pole can be leaned equally well against either the upper or the lower walls which proves conclusively that this steepness of the hill is actually an illusion which is produced by the strong gravitational pull at this particular spot. This pull is so strong as to actually affect the total reactions of the physical anatomy to the extent that a person automatically begins to compensate when walking across this surface; he has the distinct impression that his right leg is uphill while his left leg is downhill, or that his left leg must compensate for the extra distance—that his right foot is walking across the upper portion of the hill while his left foot is traversing a parallel path at a lower angle—all of which can be proven to be simply an illusion produced by this strong gravitational pull.

The phenomena of these mystery spots similar to the one which I have just described is of course disconcerting to scientists, who believe implicitly in not only optical laws but all other associated laws of their sciences and physics. Some of these principles have been postulated by Newton in the seventeenth century. It should be quite apparent from our previous discussions, and in getting an enlarged prospective of the electromagnetic fields which surround the earth—and which are actually a part of the earth—that such physical laws are only applicable to the degree in which certain irregularities can be assumed in the transmissions of all of these different electromagnetic fields.

Some years before his death, Einstein postulated the theory that light is bent in bypassing the strong electromagnetic fields of a star or a planet. This was later to be proven true by certain astronomical observations and scientific tests conducted by astronomers at later periods of time.

Now if light can be bent in space by strong electromagnetic fields from different celestial or heavenly bodies, then most apparently the same principle applies here on earth; that we as humans, are entirely subjective to the regular interplay of these electromagnetic fluxes which form such a great and basic part of our life here on earth.

We might picture the earth simply as an energy body of countless trillions of atoms which have been formed from out a huge centrifuge of fourth-dimensional energy, and in this compressed condition, these little energy bits called atoms again assume—individually, within the constituents of wave forms of which they are made—the same irregularities of patterns as are expressed in the huge centrifuge which formed the earth. Again, there is a total affectation of all atoms as they are concerned on the planet Earth, whether they are of the surface or whether they are the atoms which make up the physical anatomies of humans. Certain electro-magnetic fields are very important and vital to the welfare and health of every human and make his life possible here on earth by virtue of the fact that there is a considerable transmission of energy and interchange of different fractional, spectral fields between the psychic anatomy and the total electromagnetic spectrum of the solar system, the galaxy and the universe.

This again is all part of that libido or life force or drive which every human has; his will to live, etc., all being part of the spectral energies which combine to make the electromagnetic fields of the terrestrial cosmogony, as well as the infinite cosmogony. So again, here we are, globs of energy which we call our bodies, and globs of energy which form our psychic anatomies, each one respectively combined and recombined of the proper constituents which are analogous to his earth life; that is, his physical body or the combination of atoms and molecules to form cells, et cetera; whereas his psychic anatomy is a combination of cyclic wave forms which combine within themselves the total life experience in all of the evolutionary life cycles which this human has had on the planet Earth, or, for that matter, it is combined with all of the total life moments which any human has had, either here or in the lives in

239

between earth lives. For surely, the psychic anatomy lives perpetually; it is immortal as it is developed by every human and remains immortal until any such time as that particular human being begins to dissipate the cyclic wave forms within the psychic anatomy by certain subversive life patterns which he has instigated within the expressionary elements of his own life.

In other words, by becoming centralized or selfish, to constantly reflect everything in life to the central ego is the necessary dispensating force which will gradually disintegrate the psychic anatomy; for surely, the psychic anatomy too, must be constantly replenished and refreshed, not only from the electromagnetic fields which form the adjacent fourth dimension and also as part of the third dimension, but also the psychic anatomy must be kept in tune, so to speak, with the inflow of energies from other different dimensions. In order to keep this attunement in progress, a person has to be constructively inclined, has to be consciously aware of the creative processes and all other moralities which might be included in a constructive life analysis. These, in turn, inspirational values or otherwise, such as they are called by humans, give the necessary polarities and biases to the cyclic wave forms within the psychic anatomy which make it possible for them to be harmonically in tune with the inflow of higher life forces from the higher dimensions and the surrounding electromagnetic fields which radiate from the higher dimensions.

Continuation of Einsteinian Theory
from Interdimensional Viewpoints

The total concept of the Infinite Cosmogony as a personal proposition to learn and to understand at least to a certain relevant degree, is indeed, without question, a mind-boggling proposition. All peoples, as they have so evolved on the planet earth, have conducted or incurred the total consensus of this evolution on a strictly third-dimensional basis, and except for certain inspirational values or occasional paranormal phenomena, the earthman has only recognized this interdimensional cosmos through such vagaries as superstitious beliefs, religions, et cetera, and has, to some degree, succeeded in strengthening such beliefs through the necessity to relieve and alleviate the fear of death, always incumbent in this mortal life about us.

As we have discovered in our previous presentations of the Einsteinian theory (the equation of energy equals mass multiplied by the square of the speed of light) all the familiar earth forms including our own personal physical anatomies are reducible to those energy forms classified in scientific nomenclature as atoms. These atomic forms universally, so far as the third dimension or terrestrial world is concerned, form a surface plane or a curtain, if you will, of energy upon which surface, man is beginning to learn the combination of certain factors not heretofore relevant in the more primitive stages of his evolution. In other words, he is learning to combine and recombine these atomic forms as the beginning of a facade of life which will later conceivably and predictably carry him into higher or more fully developed planes of life where all such attendant and relevant surface plane expressions, as he will then so find himself involved in, will be quite different than these third-dimensional forms in which he is now so entirely engrossed. The man who plays golf, the carpenter who builds a house, the housewife who is preparing a meal, the butcher, the baker, the candlestick maker—and what are they all doing? Well, they are taking the atom forms as they find them in their daily circumference of life and are learning to combine and recombine these different atom forms into certain reactive and meaningful components in the daily concourse of their lives. Atoms, of course, again synthesized into molecular structures, in turn, compose and comprise all familiar environmental forms in the world about us.

Beyond, as it is so called, is the spirit world where such atom forms do not exist and the total proposition of the earthman to evolve into such a state of personal consciousness that such surface planes will again be relevant to the concourse of his life, would be even more mind-boggling if he does not have some conditioning and training—a preparatory course of evolution which will enable him to function in some sort of a systematic fashion when he begins to arrive at that point. Actually, such an evolutionary course which would indoctrinate the necessary elements of understanding into this earthman's evolution and which would make such life possible in a higher dimension would most necessarily be the propelling force—if it could be called that—which would project him into that higher elevation of consciousness.

On the same basis then here on Earth and as we understand atomic forms and their molecular combinations, so again we must find in such electronic constituents, electromagnetic fields, et cetera, that all the varied and very much segmented fractions of life on planet Earth could be reducible to one common synthesis—the proposition of understanding such life forms and the components of our society as electronic motions and compositions of electronic forms. If ever such a synthesis did arrive upon the planet Earth, and man became totally involved in such a synthesis, it would be quite safe to predict that these most favored and sacred segments of our present civilization would have disappeared. I can mention many of these in particular, such as medicine, psychology, chemistry, in fact, the entire and total proposition of these familiar environmental forms and reactionary components would have largely or totally disappeared and we would have as a consequence, totally evolved this earth world into that higher state of evolution.

Again, to speculate upon or to more properly analyze, such a situation as this would never occur on the planet Earth or in any other such similar earth worlds throughout the galaxy or other galaxies. In their sequential levels, it has been so conceived and ordained in Infinite Intelligence that as life must be a progressive evolution, so must all of these planes be sustained, each plane relevant to that particular phase of evolution in which any particular person or society or the populations of such a planet en masse are involved, cycles of progression or regression, as they are concerned and manifest by the appearance and disappearance of civilizations, each one manifesting itself and progressing to a certain level of expression. These are all cyclic forms, all of which are minor in nature and do not foretell the total circumference of any evolutionary consensus as it involves the predictable future of the earth. Or, that is to say, we would progress through certain recurrent civilizations, each one becoming somewhat more advanced than the former civilization, with the ultimate end that we might arrive at some Utopian condition in our society. Such is not the case.

The principles and the total concept involved in reincarnation must totally substantiate and resubstantiate the life experiences of each person up to some theoretical saturation point in which that person, having reached this plateau in his third-dimensional evolution will become retrogressive or go back downward, so to speak, on the other end of the oscillating cycle of his progressive evolution. Should he not recognize these factors and that he is regressing rather than progressing, then most surely he will precipitate such evolutionary factors upon his own self and in this way diminish his capacity to reinstate his consciousness in future evolutions and which will eventually destroy his consciousness and his totality as a separate entity of expression.

Therefore, so far as these progressive evolutions are concerned, it behooves all persons to recognize and to be cognizant of these factors as they recur in his life and as progressive cyclic happenings so that he can more or less predictably insure a progressive evolution. On the same basis then, he could look forward into some higher life expression in which he would find that the old familiar segmentation of his former societies was no longer in existence; that other factors, now unknown to him, were relevant and that he should, as a denizen dwelling in this higher dimension, participate fully in all elements and factors so concerned. So again, he has arrived at a point where these concepts, as they were presented to him in former lifetimes, assumed mind-boggling proportions, yet now they were the sustaining and all-encompassing virtues and factors of his everyday life. This is Infinity and it is the promise of Infinity to every person who so recognizes this proposition of Infinity, that he can carve for himself, so to speak, any particular type of a life that he so wishes. We are always hopeful that whatever he sets for himself as a goal, it will be one of constructivism and that he will learn to become a more constructive participle in Infinite Intelligence.

So, again, as I have delivered these Messages to you and while you may seem to think that they are beyond your comprehension, yet persistence must be maintained in learning to understand these different elements. They are most vital and important to you and if you do not understand them on the surface of your conscious, third-dimensional mind, yet most surely they, as wave forms, and as you read the words from which they have been formed, will form oscillating constituents and components within your psychic anatomy.

At a much later date in your evolution, the time you lay aside your earthly overcoat and step over into the great unknown, you will already have a certain amount of preparation, a certain amount of the needs and the viable condiments which you will need to begin to form your new life, to begin to become more directional in whatever direction you wish to travel. When that day arrives, it is hardly necessary to say you will be most thankful for whatever you have been able to salvage and pick up in your former lifetimes, and especially to the messages and to the contents of these different documentaries which I am placing in your hands.

This is my Mission and purpose on Earth. I do not need, nor do I crave or want this physical life. It is quite possible that at one time I went through that same metamorphosis in some distant planetary system. If this is so, I do not at this time have any memory consciousness of this, yet every man must be so prepared for his advent into a Higher World by such indoctrinations in the more material worlds in which the atom forms have assumed the solid base plane of his frequency relationship. I am quoting my own particular position to you as a typical example and as some sort of a goal which you might set for yourselves; that we who are the Interplanetary Dwellers, who live, shall I say, in the more highly developed psychic anatomies which have been formed from our concourse and our constructivisms with Infinite Intelligence, then let whatever this is, as an example or as a goal, be most necessary and vital to you.

The earth world and its environmental factors, as they are linked to your evolutionary past and your previous lifetimes, are indeed the most serious threat to your evolution simply because they are the most vital and formative part of your everyday life and you are more securely linked to these past episodes and experiences in their oscillating wave forms as they are contained in your psychic anatomy. The proposition here then is quite clear. The psychic anatomy must be rebuilt as it is going to be your future home and your future self in that Higher World. It cannot and will not exist unless it is so constructed of suitable anomalies of energy which beat harmoniously in their frequencies with the spectral energy with which it is surrounded.

The proposition here is exactly similar here on the earth plane except that you have learned to accept and react to these different energy wave forms as emanations from seemingly solid substances or that your world is a solid world. You will have the same feeling in the higher world and that world will be just as relevant and seemingly as solid to you but in a higher capacity than is this present world. You will not do many of the things which you do here; likewise, you will do many more things there than you have ever imagined possible that you could do here. Mental telepathy or psychokinesis, teleportation and many of the other factors only now whispered about or dreamed about in the more fanciful connotations of science fiction magazines or such explorations of mediumistic abilities, are only very faint forerunners of what will actually be a part of your life in this future dimension.

Conversely, you can turn yourself into some kind of an astral entity which has been to some degree portrayed as a demon, a devil or such other ghoulish apparitions, and which in spite of their seeming fantasies, do have some basic truth in them, all of which again adds up to the inevitable proposition that we must learn to understand energy and the proposition of energy rather than simply as reactive mass forms in our environmental third-dimensional world, and which is most important and vital to you.

Now, I know I seemingly sound as though the needle were stuck in the groove, to use one of the clichés of this present time, yet my message to you is centrally encompassed in this single periphery of understanding; energy and the understanding of energy is most vital to you in your future evolutions. And again, into whatever dimension or into whatever segment of your environment you wish to carry your analysis or prospective, you will only wind up with that inevitable and inescapable conclusion that progression means learning to understand the new world in which you wish to live—a world and the proposition of evolution in that Higher World which is exactly similar in its principle to the beginning of your evolution in this world with the exception, of course, that all environmental factors including your own body, will be of a much higher and more fully developed evolutionary form.

Almost needless to say that in the future, and having achieved one of these higher dimensions of living, there will be ahead of you innumerable and countless successive evolutions into Higher and Higher Worlds. If we correctly understand the word Infinity, we can reasonably suppose that it would be impossible to reach the end of such an evolutionary course. Indeed, even to the most singular atom as it is found on the surface of this plane of expression, would have been utterly impossible had it not been so conceived and brought into being by this Infinite Intelligence, which is infinite in nature.

So let your life be one of a constant succession of analytical relationships to the Infinite or to the infinite macrocosm. Each seemingly reactionary component in your daily life always should be maintained in this introspective capacity, that you can directly link all of these reactionary components as they appear on your surface life as the beginning of your evolution and you should see in them the factors and principles which I have explained to you. All elements and the very necessary components of these expressionary forms, as they are linked to the interdimensional cosmos, are most important to you because it is in this phase of your progression that you are actually beginning to build your psychic anatomy; you are beginning to replace those anomalies of energy wave forms which you incurred in previous lifetimes.

In a certain way and sense, they may remain with you as sort of a memory consciousness, but as viable and useful condiments in your daily life, they should become less and less important to you and you should draw more and more, so to speak, from the proposition of evolution as it is supported in the infinite, interdimensional cosmos. Therefore, each act, each reaction, each connection which you have through your five senses with your life and the world about you in its reactionary forms should be supported and abetted by what is commonly referred to as ESP, combining the knowledge which you have incurred from these texts together with such elements as you will find within the secret closet of your own mind.

You will begin to replace those nefarious and deleterious anomalies in your psychic anatomy which have always relegated and, in a way, condemned you to successive reincarnations on this planet Earth. Should you not succeed in building and rebuilding this psychic anatomy to a more suitable habitation in a Higher World, then most surely you will, in successive incarnations on the earth, compile in a double indemnity fashion, all of these past negative experiences and you will be involved in what the Yogi calls karma—the sin of your past—to a depth which will completely submerge any logic, reason or intelligence in the circumference of that evolution.

To your success then, in the future! I and the Unariun Brotherhood, the Emissaries from the higher planes of life, will ever be in constant attendance with whatever aid and assistance we can most judiciously render to you; that we will be most logically tempered by what is most necessary, for uppermost in the formative stages of your evolution is always the ever-adamant proposition that you and you alone are the selective element. We do not wish nor do we have the power to consciously violate the precinct of your own selectivity. This must always be uppermost in your own mind and should we, in any of our capacities, change your course of evolution beyond the circumference and the periphery of your own choice, of your own mandates and desires, then we have violated—and if I can call it that —our most sacred trust to ourselves, and to Infinite Intelligence, for how well we know the principles of life, the principles of evolution which sustain this life. It is hardly necessary to say that we would not be people from this higher dimension of life had we not fully realized and encompassed all of these principles, the logic and the intelligence, into the dimension and capacity of our own existence.

And again, there is the example of what must be accomplished in what the religionist calls your "salvation", for salvation it is; not being resurrected, or with any other Messianic content, but rather, a logical evolutionary progression from life to life which rebuilds your true self, your psychic anatomy into the proportions of an intellectual status most necessary to live in this Higher World.

Cosmic Cycles, Astrophysical and Interdimensional Isotopes re the Wind

In our previous presentations and discussions regarding atoms, mass, the electromagnetic fields, et cetera, all of these factors were discussed in a more relative or quiescent condition—that is, it could be assumed that everything was stationary, such as the atoms which comprise the molecules of rock which form a large mountain. It would take thousands of years to make any appreciable difference in the contour of the mountain due to weathering elements; unless a very strong earthquake or volcano erupted, it might be, for all obvious purposes or visualizations, completely stationary.

Now you might well ask, "It is conceivable so far as each atom is concerned, and its relationship to the fourth dimension, and that it has a centrifuge or vortex of fourth-dimensional energy which forms and supports this atom," and you might well ask, "Well, what happens when the wind blows?" Then, there are a large number of nitrogen and oxygen atoms, along with the minor atoms of the noble gases which seem to be flowing past you at either a slow state or perhaps, as in the case of a tornado, wind velocities may reach 100 miles an hour, and you would wonder, "Are all of these little vortexes of energy which comprise the atom traveling rapidly in order to sustain each individual atom?" Not necessarily so, as we shall soon find out.

As I have stated before, any atom is being born and reborn at millions of times per second at incredible speeds; that is, the nucleus of a centrifuge of energy is pulsating at incredible speeds. The atom then forms certain basic relationships in each new reformation or oscillation, according to the polarities which are formed from these internal structures of the atom. There is a north pole and a south pole of an atom, and as the atom is oscillating, these poles are constantly being reversed with each oscillation.

Now, to build up the concept; as the relationship of each of these positive and negative poles change from north to south poles, so does the relationship of the atom change in respect to all other atoms which comprise the molecules say a molecule of oxygen or a molecule of nitrogen—of which air is composed. Also bear in mind that these oscillating atoms and their centrifuges are all suspended, so to speak, and are actively repolarized by the total electromagnetic spectrum, as I have previously described, this spectrum consisting of many millions of different oscillating lines of force of energy which, like the wheels of a watch, all cyclic in motion, are linked up according to their respective polarities to form large or small cycles around the earth or the composite of the magnetic spectrum of the solar system, or they may be involved as magnetic lines of force or energy around the sun. This is indeed a complex picture but some sort of a visualization must be achieved in your mind before you can understand all of the mechanics, if I can call them that, which are involved in the ordinary blowing of a wind.

Visualize, if you will, these countless millions of cycles which comprise the electromagnetic lines of force; within and adjacent to, as dimensional factors, are regenerated many other different anomalies or vortexes of energy which go to form the third-dimensional atomic mass. Now, think for a moment then, that this atomic mass—whatever it is, and comprised of molecules—will be, at any given time, affected by the total polarities which are involved in this rapid interchange of oscillations between north and south poles—not only between the atoms, but in the cyclic wave forms which comprise the electromagnetic spec-

251

trum. As it is so totally involved and say, concerned with the earth and the solar system, this entire electromagnetic spectrum is, too, but a small part of the magnetic spectrum of the galaxy. Again, that too, is but a small part of the electromagnetic spectrum of the universe. So you can easily see there are tremendous oscillations and movements, we shall say, in regard to the changing of polarities within all of these magnetic structures.

Actually, so far as the fourth dimension is concerned, and as each of these cyclic wave forms have, within themselves, their own intelligence or information, they really don't travel anywhere. Movements are confined, if we can call them movements, to the interchange of polarities, and in these interchanges of polarities then, of course, with the oscillations, remake certain harmonic oscillations which, in turn, help to link up and achieve total integration of the entire oscillating system.

Now that we have arrived at this point of our introspection, we can also very easily achieve the next step, which is to see that within the movements within these cyclic wave forms, as they form and re-form atomic constituents which, in turn, form the molecules of oxygen and nitrogen of the air, then the movement of the air is going to take place if the polarities within the electromagnetic structures change in regard to what I shall call, certain biases; that is to say, that the movements in the interdimensional electromagnetic spectrum, as it is constantly shifting or oscillating in many manners so that certain harmonics are regenerated, which replay back into the atomic field, constituents which comprise the atmosphere of the earth.

You have heard a meteorologist or weatherman talk on high or low pressure areas and we can include, on a certain basis what is called thermal currents or thermal expansion. A low pressure area merely means that we have a different relationship of positive and negative polarities in regard to all of the atoms which comprise the atmosphere in their relationship to the electromagnetic spectrum of the solar system and to the galaxy. Conversely, a higher pressure area is one in which we have a difference in polarity or bias with the net electromagnetic field. These changes in biases generate the pressures which activate our barometer, which is exactly similar to what affects your weight, and the difference in your weight in the A.M. and in the P.M. Also it explains, to a large degree, the fluctuations in human behaviorisms, the stock market, personalities, and so on, because here again we have achieved and remanifested certain positive and negative relationships with the electromagnetic spectrum.

As all atomic forms which constitute the planet Earth are subject in their net behaviorisms to this electromagnetic spectrum, then we can expect that, in the case of the atoms which comprise molecules which we call gas, they are sufficiently expanded to be mobile and move; that these mobile or movable molecule-atom combinations will follow these electromagnetic changes in polarities or biases—and which they do.

Sometimes you can see a puff or a blast of wind coming down the street although the surrounding air is quite still. There apparently is no reason or cause for this blast of wind, and almost as quickly as it comes, it passes; likewise, the whirlwinds which we have seen form in various areas during our lifetime; the rapidly revolving air currents whisk up straws, leaves and dust high into the air—all for no apparent reason. It's very easily visualized when we can realize that these, too, are differences in changes within the oscillating polarities of the electromagnetic spectrum in the immediate vicinity. As the space surrounding that whirlwind was actually infinitely filled with these oscillating cycles and lines of energy which form the electromagnetic spectrum, the changes in polarities or biases will most certainly reproduce changes so far as the space-time consonant is concerned with the atom-molecule combinations which they have formed. So it's all very easily achieved in the mentality of our own mind if we can form some sort of comprehensive picture of what is going on in the adjacent fourth dimension.

A thermal current, when air is heated, merely means that the different molecule-atom combinations have had to, within their own electromagnetic structures, absorb, so to speak, another external oscillating wave form, which is the heat energy wave form. In this condition they have, to a certain extent, partially cancelled out a certain positive-negative relationship with the vortexes and the electromagnetic structures which they are oscillating with in the next dimension. And when these are cancelled out, or to some degree nullified, then the air-molecules will rise from the earth, simply because the earth presents a heavier oscillating concentration and of a slightly different polarity than that in which this atom-molecule combination is, at that moment, oscillating in its own particular frequency—so that it is repelled away from the surface of the earth or that it rises up. This is the simple mechanics involved in the expansion of thermal current, and in principle, it is exactly the same as that we have described of the high and low pressure areas.

Also to be taken into account in the high and low pressure areas is more simply an explanation of what is called the ionization factor. As I have said, ionization is responsible for weather changes anywhere on this planet Earth. This is quite true, for ionization is merely a third-dimensional manifestation or demonstration in the changes in polarities which occur in the atomic structures of the molecules, positive to negative, and vice versa. The atom-molecule combination changes its net polarity and becomes ionized, and under certain conditions a majority, or say, 75 percent of the oxygen molecules may become ionized in a positive respect to 25 percent of the negative or vice versa and should be considered as merely a manifestation of the interplay of interdimensional polarities which are occurring in the adjacent dimensions, as the atoms themselves are formed from this very energy substance as it is oscillated. So you see, there isn't really any mystery in the movement of air as it concerns a flow of atom-molecule combinations. They are merely achieving their own relationship with the differences and changes within the electromagnetic spectrum and in the centrifuges from which they were generated.

Actually, so far as the fourth dimension is concerned, nothing is really moving in the sense that we would say any particular centrifuge which forms an atom would move from any one place to another, because any one of these centrifuges of energy is constantly generating and regenerating its atom forms. As the atom forms are part of the net sum and total of oscillating frequencies, then the appearance and re-appearance of these atom forms, in combinations of oxygen and nitrogen molecules, will form a flow of current, or a wind, as the appearances and reappearances of these atom forms follow these different electromagnetic lines in their net sum and total of harmonic phase shifts.

Yes, I know it's going to take a little digging to really get this, but keep going around with it. You have a third-dimensional mind and it isn't easy for that mind to achieve a relationship with the fourth dimension, especially in the matter of a few hours or even in a few weeks or months. It will take constant effort at every opportune moment to achieve some sort of a comprehensive prospective as to what is going on in this dimension in relationship to all other dimensions which form the interdimensional cosmos.

So the next time you see a rainstorm, you know that

every little drop of rain falling to the earth has been formed in a certain manner—the relationship of positive and negative polarities in the different molecules which form the water vapor of the cloud; and these polarities in turn, were remanifested harmonics of the atoms from which the atom-molecules were formed. As these different polarities change, so that part of the oxygen-nitrogen molecules were at a certain phase relationship to the hydrogen-oxygen molecules which formed the cloud, then certain atoms were attracted to each other, just as it would be with the horseshoe magnet.

On the basis of their respective polarities and as they were attracted to each other, so they formed a larger drop of water, and the same process, repeated many times with many molecules, formed that rain-drop which then fell to earth. It was not necessarily a little dust particle as the weatherman thinks. Dust particles too, as they are very small in the upper atmosphere, can be so ionized in their respective polarities that they too can create and regenerate the same condition, as I have described. They too can help form the little droplets of water.

A flake of snow is only a little drop of water which has been suddenly frozen by getting into a very cold stream of air and all the little molecules of water formed into little crystals and each one of those little snowflakes is different; there are no two snowflakes exactly alike. Of all the snowflakes that have fallen on the surface of the earth, all have been different. This too, is a proposition of understanding the phase relationships or the time consonant as the polarities changed and oscillated within the atomic constituents which formed the molecule of water compounds.

So again, it is very important; if we understand the composition and the mechanics of the interdimensional cosmos, it will give us an understanding of creation and what are commonly referred to as the secrets of creation. Just as your own body changes in weight from A.M. to P.M., so does the gravitational pull of the earth change within the 24-hour cycle. As the earth rotates around the sun, it comes into the different seasonal changes and this, too, forms a certain difference in phase relationships in the net sum and total of regenerations and oscillations as they are concerned with the electromagnetic spectrum and the transmission of solar energy to the surface of the earth. The seasonal changes or the position of the earth in regard to the sun does too, have a certain inductive capacity in many higher frequencies not known by scientists on the planet Earth and which relate to the general health and well-being of every human.

Along this same line of introspection, we can find out why it is that so many more viral forms, or viruses which cause colds, flu, pneumonia, et cetera, are manifest and incumbent during the winter seasons than they are during the summer seasons; because the relationship to the solar energy, the relationship to interdimensional energy as it concerns the electromagnetic fields is different in summer than it is in winter. Also, we must take into consideration that these can be visualized as cycles so that in the rotation within this cyclic system we are constantly, so far as the weather or the seasons are concerned, either ascending into, or receding from, a certain cycle.

On the basis of this ascension and descension, the health patterns of the peoples of the Northern or Southern Hemispheres can be somewhat predicted. The general physical tone and the health and well-being of the physical body is, as we have previously discovered in our former discussions, quite dependent not only on the food that we eat, but also on these interdimensional harmonics and interplays of energies which come to us, or that are radiated into us con-

257

stantly, from this interdimensional cosmos.

As I have said, we are a glob of energy revolving around in a huge and infinite sea of energy. When this energy is so subdivided into its various fractional factors such as the electromagnetic fields which form the gravitational fields and the magnetic fields and others, we are all harmonically in some way or another, linked to all of these interdimensional energy fields which are radiating about us and we cannot get away from it, no matter how hard we try. Even if we were to blast off in a spaceship and go to a distant part of the galaxy, or even into another universe, we would still be subjective to the same conditions and the same forces which we find here on the planet Earth, and we should be quite glad that all of these things exist because if they did not, we would not have life, and if we didn't have life, we wouldn't have that promise of immortality by achieving a constructive evolution.

So, in the vernacular, "Let's get with it." Let's spend some time on these very important concepts and try to visualize to some extent just what is totally involved in this interdimensional cosmos, just what our relationship to it is, and how we can divide and subdivide all the attendant factors of our physical life as simply remanifestations of the total harmonic interplay of the Interdimensional Cosmos.

In one way or another we are synchronously attuned —and don't let that word throw you; it merely means there has been a certain phase relationship achieved in a synchronous attunement, something like when you drive down the highway and there are a number of traffic lights and if the traffic lights have been regulated to turn red and green at intervals which will enable you to drive 35 miles an hour, and if you drive 35 miles an hour, you will pass through all of those signals when they are green. That is a synchronous movement or timing and is very simple to visualize. On the same basis, all of the harmonic interplays with which we are concerned with the interdimensional cosmos can be related into such synchronous movements.

An isochronism is another type of synchronous regeneration. For example; if you see six propeller driven aircraft flying along in the sky, the drone of their propellers will seem to have a sort of wawling, up-and-down sound as they propel themselves along through the air. That is an isochronism. Inside an ordinary watch, we also have isochronisms. We say that the total tolerances—such as the little wheels mounted in their bearings which were manufactured by the watchmaker—created by these mechanics involved in the watch in their total synchronous movements and meshing in and out of each other with their little gears, et cetera, also generate isochronisms just as do the aircraft. These isochronisms can upset the accuracy of the watch by introducing a minute and very high frequency vibration which will conversely increase the friction on bearings or will make the meshing of the gears more difficult. So the accuracy of the watch can be affected according to isochronisms—a fact known by every watchmaker.

It's the same in what we call our interdimensional mechanics. Even though we may be harmonically or synchronously attuned, yet in this attunement, due to the large number of these harmonic attunements and the synchronisms which are involved, they too can regenerate isochronisms which can, to a certain extent, affect certain behaviorisms which we might find in the world about us, and which might give rise to at least a few of the unexplained, or seemingly coincidental factors which arise in our lives and which seem to have no bearing or relationship with our pasts, or that we are not even logically or sensibly inclined to explain such happenings on the basis of ordinary analysis. Then you can remember that perhaps this is an isochronism. It is a generation of a number of regenerations which, according to the laws of harmonic interplay, will create certain variables within the structure of this oscillating mechanism, and it is these variables which can and do cause the most trouble.

One other way in which we can compare the movement of winds and of the total processes involved is to compare this process with what takes place in the cyclotron or the bevatron. As I have previously described this process, a long row of electromagnets formed by iron cores and coils are alternately and synchronously reversed in their polarities. By using hydrogen atoms, the scientist then can propel these atoms through this bevatron or cyclotron at incredible rates of speed by oscillating the polarities of the magnets. In this way, the polarities tend, just as in an electric motor, to first attract the atom toward them and then to repel it; in other words, with each oscillation, to kick it forward that much faster.

The same proposition is true with a flow of wind. Atoms of nitrogen and oxygen, as they constitute the air, begin to be kicked forward in the same manner as is done in the bevatron. First, due to the change of certain polarities in the electromagnetic structures in which the atom is encompassed, these polarities will attract the atom forward, then as the polarity changes, it repels the atom in the same forward-like manner.

The same proposition holds true with the electric motor which runs your vacuum cleaner; there is a difference of the changing of the polarities as they are involved with the fields which surround the armature of the motor. Analogous to this, the armature then is the molecule of air, while the field of electromagnets which surrounds it is the electromagnetic spectrum of the Infinite Cosmos. So now, when a certain mass of air which is comprised of molecules of nitrogen and oxygen with the noble gases is engaged in the same kind of interplay of synchronous phase reversals of polarities (within the magnetic structures) the molecules are first attracted forward then passing the central point, the polarities will be reversed; they will be kicked forward or repelled. So any given mass of air, even if it is a puff of wind or a whirlwind coming down the street, there is a certain very rapid synchronous interplay or oscillating condition within the electromagnetic structures of the immediate dimension in this interplay. As atoms form molecules, and as atoms are part of this total structure, they are quite subjective to all changes within the polarities of the total electromagnetic spectrum and they will respond to these changes according to the interplay or exchange of the polarities which formed the original vortexes of their respective anomalies.

So again, understanding all of what I have presented to you of the interdimensional cosmos will give you the explanations of all of the so-called secret mysteries of life, those secrets which have been extolled, sought after and worshipped; or otherwise, some sort of imagery was created to form sort of a symbolic content to represent such mysterious forces. All can now be subdivided and very harmonically integrated into your own life stream.

The Genesis Rock—Fallacy of the Time Concept

In our discussions and introspections into the interdimensional factors which opened with the discussions
on atoms versus astronauts, and reverting back to
some of the original statements made concerning the
moon flights and the great hubbub created over bringing back moon samples, including the Genesis rock
and others. While it is indeed a technological achievement for the earthman to have landed men on the
moon four times, however, the concept that he believes
he can achieve some sort of an intelligent formation as
to the embryonic period of the solar system, formation
of planets, the moon, from such existing specimens
of moon rock, will without question lead him into
another one of those insoluble enigmas, another one of
those anachronisms in which he has confounded himself in his numerous attempts to explore the created
world about him—simply because he has not as yet
lifted his efforts, his introspections and analysis into
the fourth dimension—to the origin of all things.

Let us create for a moment a hypothetical situation:
supposing in the scientist's mind, as he is concerned
with moon rocks and their origins, that the Genesis
rock would portray to him that at one time the moon
was either very volcanic or that it was entirely a ball of
molten lava. In either case the situation is quite clear;
that there was a huge mass of atom-molecules which
formed this ball of lava in existence for possibly hundreds of thousands or billions of years. So again,
the age of the moon goes up in, using a pun and say a
"puff of smoke", as we might see from the top of a volcano. And I don't go along with that "spin off" theory—
that all of the planets in the solar system were thrown

off from the mass of the sun by centrifugal motions or some other such forces which aided in this "spin off" process.

If you were to study a large whirlpool which had been formed on the surface of a large river you would, in the course of some fifteen or twenty minutes of viewing this whirlpool as it revolved around and around and made a cone-shaped hole into the center, observe that around the periphery of this whirling whirlpool a number of other smaller whirlpools of different sizes would appear and reappear, sort of like small anomalies of revolving currents. Now why should such a situation exist? Clearly, the currents of water as they were involved in rotating around in forming the central apex should not have, in a sense of the word, broken off their regular lines of rotation and engaged in the same kind of rotation by a very much smaller scale.

The situation here is quite analogous to what we have discussed about the wind and the currents of air. The same situation prevails in the fourth dimension in regard to the formation of the sun and the planets; that is, it is within the central vortex which formed the sun. And as the sun is the nucleus in the net sum and total of the different nuclei which formed the different atomic constituents of the photosphere of the sun, these too, so far as they are concerned, are actually appearing and disappearing in a series of oscillations which take place at incredible speeds, possibly within hundreds of billions of oscillations per second.

Now to more closely analyze the formation of any particular wave form as it involves the positive and negative phase reversal in an atom or anywhere else, for that matter, this is a condition in which the wave form is expressing a certain idiom or quotient of intelligence. That intelligence is contained in that phase reversal. Now if we study a sine wave, we will discover in the movement of the sine wave that exactly in the center of that phase reversal, there is a quiescent space or period in which apparently, so far as we can discover, there seems to be no movement at all in either direction. So how would this come about? Again we revert to the proposition of the fourth-dimensional centrifuge which formed this particular wave form, either as the nuclei of an atom or that it concerned itself in a large fashion as the centrifuge which generated the sun and was likewise the great anomaly which in secondary convolutions had regenerated the nuclei which we call planets; for the planets are simply that—simply large atoms, if they can be considered in the total mass content which they represent, either gaseous, liquid or solid. They represent, so far as the fourth dimension is concerned, a corresponding number of anomalies of centrifugal energy which formed the nuclei of each respective atom and, as such, are linked up to the respective electromagnetic fields and other components and constituents of cyclic wave forms which constitute the Infinite Cosmogony.

Just as it was with the whirlpool in the river and the smaller whirlpools around the periphery of this whirlpool, so according to the same laws of these whirlpools of water, the planetary systems are revolving around on the same basis of their interdimensional oscillations and frequencies as they are concerned in that vast interplay which I call the Infinite Cosmos.

Getting back to the earth scientist, all of this knowledge which concerns the mechanics of the Infinite Cosmogony and in its relationship to the planet Earth, the solar system and the visible terrestrial galaxy and universe, it is indeed pitiful that the American people should permit their life blood to be virtually drawn from their economic system in the furtherance and continuance of the exploration of the moon or for any other space program. The creation of the solar system or the universe will not be found in the age of a rock;

264

either here, on the moon, or on Mars. As I have previously stated, that considering the elements of space and time as they are integrated in the fourth dimension in cyclic transmissions, and as they are compounded in the Infinite Cosmogony, the element of time is a superficial anachronism. It means absolutely nothing; it tells nothing and it only leads those who seek the answers to the riddle of their life in this manner and form, down the garden path. They will only wind up— as it is said in the vernacular—"behind the eight ball".

Instead of spending his life's blood, the taxpayer's money, which could very well be devoted to other and much more productive channels in our economic system, man should begin to search for the riddle of life— if he must possess it—from within himself and this is virtually what we are doing in these discussions and introspections, for within the secret closet of our own mind we can learn to tune into the Infinite Cosmos to the Father which is within. And in finding this Infinite Cosmos, the creative Father, then we will indeed have the secrets of creation and we will have found our relationship to this Infinite Cosmos, to this Father and we will have formed a constructive position to our evolution in the future to become reproductive in a much higher sense and a much higher capacity.

So once again: to those who are concerned and, so far as I am concerned as well as the Unariun Brotherhood, in this mad-hatter's dance, sort of an "Alice in Wonderland" fantasy world, which seems to leave little in relevant values in the world about us, while our planet is steeped in all of the sins and iniquities and our ecology is polluted and filthy almost to the point in which life as we know it on this planet will be made impossible, yet man vainly searches for his origin in the most unlikely of all places—in the graveyards of our planetary systems, such as the moon! And, indeed, as he searches in these graveyards, so will he find his own epitaph carved upon the stone which he believes will give him the secret key to his life.

Indeed, if you must search, if you must seek, then let this searching and seeking be a logical continuity of life and the forces which propagated and made life possible; not among the ashes and dust of some defunct planetary system but rather, from the vital and integrating elements which formed and motivated the atoms within your body, the mechanics which engendered the movements of the planets and stars, the formations of the molecules and atoms which formed all of these celestial objects. Behind these are the mysteries of life and their solutions.

To all of those then, I speak these words: yours is an idle chase, a will-o'-the-wisp chase through the morass of your impenetrable and impregnable rhetorics of your earth-world mind, and until that day and time when you come upon the high ground of logic and reason, your footsteps will be constantly bogged down by the mires of your own indispositions and you will be constantly intimidated by the quicksands of your opinions and your own beliefs.

Infinite Cosmogony—the Facade of Immortality

It has been said that no man is truly ignorant until he stops seeking. Yet let this seeking—and man should always seek—be one of constructivism. If the efforts in space are in any way vindicated, then it must be upon this premise and this premise alone, that such efforts could be condoned—that he is indeed seeking. Yet we must again examine all psychological factors involved which are really behind the movements of such extrusions and such seekings. Do these really come from a desire to understand life, or would the understanding of life placate, in any way, the fear of death which is rampant in the secret subconscious of every human? Or that he wishes, in some way, to perpetuate himself upon the pedestal of immortality in the eyes of his fellowman?

The motivations, psychologically speaking, behind those who motivate, engineer and participate in such space explorations or even into other excursions of scientific endeavor, must be searched and questioned for such ulterior motivations as may exist within the confines of a subverted subconscious mind—complexes which have been developed in the insecurities and fears of this nether earth world and in the numerous incarnations which any individual may have been subjected to in these various indispositions. All, as they are compounded within the psychic anatomy, give a certain malevolence to the actions and to the conduct of any person who has such a complex—a syndrome of civilization, improbables compounded within the rhetorics of his own conduct, of his own mind produce as it has been quoted, an impenetrable jungle, more dense and with more thorns indeed than that which confronted any prince in his search for the sleeping beauty.

Truth is, indeed, when it is sought in the nebulous regions and horizons of life, an improbable; yet it must, at some time, become an element which has been substantiated in all factors of life to become valid in any person's personal evolution. To achieve immortality is a combination of elements and factors which are as yet beyond the horizon of the third-dimensional world minds and still assiduously sought for in temples and in churches, before altars and in other places.

Yet they will not be found there; neither will they be found in the halls of learning nor in the laboratories nor can any computer or any other electronic instrument which was so devised give the answer to the improbables of life's origin or to its sources, for these are not found in the exterior surfaces and protuberances of life but must be telepathically sought for and communicated with from within the innermost self or from within the psychic anatomy. For within any given moment of any person's life there is, on the basis of communication to that person, a constant and never-ending wealth of information which would most intelligently link him up to the normal processes and inductances of all life processes as they were concerned with not only his personal evolution, but to all animate and inanimate objects and their evolutionary consensus on this planet Earth.

Well, we might philosophize until we are short of breath and blue in the face yet, individually speaking, this remains the proposition of every human; to reach that threshold in his own evolution when he becomes inductive to certain radiations, to certain emanations which come to him from beyond the horizon of the rhetorical world. Then, and only then, if he recognizes such infusions and such radiations for such as they must be, and he begins to capitalize on them—he begins to seek what they mean and their true origins, then he is indeed facing his true evolutionary pathway —not one which will be filled with the stones of reactionaryism from his material world but rather one which will be paved as would be the fabled streets in the "New City of Jerusalem", with the gold of logic, reason and intellectual prospective.

Forward then, to all ways, manners and means which are logical in their conclusion and which have in themselves the morality of this progressive evolution. Let no man stray from his path, for surely he will be precipitated over the precipice of a bottomless abyss. His own strength has waylaid him in his purposes— his strength which he incurred in his past lifetime indispositions and which he has not securely locked within the Pandora's box of his past. I, who am an Emissary from a Higher World can only warn you of these dangers. I can only present to you the facade of immortality of the interdimensional cosmos. I can only interject into your consciousness, in the word symbols and forms of your earth world, the cardinal principles, the motivating forces and the activations which constitute the Infinite Cosmogony. Yet, this is done purely on the premise that it is a selective proposition, for you and you alone, can select and confirm within your future actions, a certain dedication to finding the promise of what has been presented to you in this facade.

I will not indulge at the moment in semantics as to the probables in responsibilities—as to my responsibilities or as to yours. These in themselves are obvious; they need not bear repeating. However, should any person shirk the burden of his own progressive evolution, then he has shirked the moralities of creation. He has foregone and denied this creation and he has denied the reason, the cause and the logic for his own existence, for even the atoms which constitute his physical anatomy are all, in themselves, a tribute to the manifestation of this Infinite Intelligence. No one can say more, no one can say less, for all has been encompassed, all has been foretold, all has been created, and we, as individuals, then must seek among this Infinite Cosmos for those elements and participles of life which lead us more directly toward the seat and the origin of Infinite Intelligence.

To your dedication and to the success of your efforts then, we, the Unariun Brothers, will always remain in the absolute as a proposition of integration according to your own efforts; that just as atoms must be in tune with the constituents of the Infinite Cosmogony, so you too, must be in all ways, manners and forms, in tune with those progressive elements which compound Infinity. Conversely, only destruction awaits those who seek to form their own citadel of life about them and who either mentally, within the precincts of their own minds, or physically rule the world and relegate the actions of all humanity.

To those who can see certain integrations, certain manifestations and the principles involved and capitalize upon such knowledge to build the horizon of the dimension of not only their own life but in the prospective of all humans who are struggling with the same aspirations—the same ideals. To all ends in their constructivisms, let us remain forever dedicated.

Sunspots, Hadron Light,
the New Heavy Light Photon

Since beginning our series of articles "Atoms Versus Astronauts", some very important scientific articles have appeared in the news media which are worthy of comment because these articles relate to the findings by scientists in regard to those certain particular and specific areas of introspection which we have been discussing in this series of articles.

Appearing in the San Diego Union this morning was an article written by a young high school girl in Tacoma, Washington, and is a summary of what scientists are finding in our present-day, twentieth century in regard to certain aspects of the sun. These findings are, of course, being currently taught to high school students in various grades throughout the country.

I will read you part of this rather short article: "The gases in sunspots are electrified. Sunspots are also magnetic. When sunspots occur in pairs, the two spots have an opposite magnetism. Astronomers are not sure why sunspots are electrified and magnetic. The number of sunspots are different from year to year. Astronomers have found a pattern in a changing number of sunspots; it increases for a few years, then decreases a few years then increases and decreases. This pattern is called the eleven-year cycle of sunspots."

The admission that astronomers and scientists know that the sunspots are magnetic and that they have polarities, yet they do not know why or how this magnetic property is acquired, is an appalling admission of ignorance. In looking at the creative universe as we find it about us, and in particular to the constant and ever-changing regeneration of cyclic forms on the planet Earth, and especially to the nuclear physics now in existence, it is almost an incomprehensible situation that any scientist, astronomer or otherwise could not at once link up the very obvious fact of electromagnetism with the very nature of atoms, of creation and re-creation as it is going on in the solar system about us and, in particular, the planet Earth.

We have found another article which is also of great importance here in our discussion, which is in regard to, and I shall quote the title: "Heavy Light Found at Stanford".

I shall read from this article: "A surprising new kind of light, "hadron" light, has been discovered by a team of their energy physicists at Stanford University. It 'shines' only inside the inconceivably small space of the nucleus of the atom. The photons (particles of energy of the new light) unlike those of all other kinds of known light or electromagnetic radiations, have the characteristics of protons and neutrons; protons and neutrons, the durable particles of matter of which the nuclear cores of atoms are composed, and the meson particles are called 'hadrons'.

"The Stanford researchers, led by Prof. Frederick V. Murphy, have discovered that light energy particles or photons within the atomic nucleus are like the "hadrons"—like the protons and the neutrons. So a new bridge between 'matter' and 'light' has been established. Visible light energy photons are weightless. But the 'hadron' light photons are enormously heavy. The typical new light photon has a mass (weight) of 765 million electron volts, compared with the 500,000 electron volt mass of the electron.

"Inside its region of activity, the space of the atomic nucleus, the new 'heavy light' photon is ruled by the 'strong force' which holds together the protons and the neutrons. This 'strong' force is 100 times stronger than the attraction or repulsion of electrically charged and magnetically operated particles. The finding of 'hadron' light was made by bombarding of the nuclear cores of various atoms such as hydrogen, carbon, copper and lead, with beams of electrons."

Again it is quite obvious that within these two articles, one as written by a high school student and the other composed from the findings of a physicist from a well-known and established university—all within themselves have compounded and exposed certain mysteries which the scientist of today has uncovered and is now presently engaged in struggling with to decipher what these mysteries are. Within our previous discussions—and it is only superfluous to go back into detail and to again enumerate the causes of these different mysteries—the nature of all atoms, as the nuclei of fourth-dimensional centrifuges must, by necessity, be electromagnetic. As they are composed of electromagnetic materials or energy material, they must, most necessarily, have polarities. Each oscillating wave form, as I have discussed it, has a positive and negative polarity and it is in the oscillations of these different polarities which give the atom its intelligence as well as its most constructive entity as a participating and oscillating element in the general consensus of Infinite Intelligent Creation.

So it was with the student in her essay on sunspots. Now, most everyone has seen the photographs of the sunspots; these too, assume that centrifugal, pinwheel motion which is expressed in the centrifuge of the galaxy and the centrifuge of the universe, and to other such photographs as have been photographed in our astronomical catalog. It's an obvious fact whether we are concerned with an atom or a galaxy or any other such structural entity as might engage us in some sort of an analysis or hypothesis, certain very obvious truths are most evident. If an atom is to exist and exist as it does, and as it is so described by these Stanford physicists in their explorations and discoveries—such findings must be most relevant to all structural entities which comprise the infinite macrocosm, together with the microcosm and which is, in itself, an extension of Infinity in one other direction.

So here again, by comparing facts and findings as they have so been written out for you and described in the previous articles which I have composed, it should be quite obvious to you that there are certain great disparities in our present-day scientific society. As scientists today, in whatever particular fields they are laboring—biological research, the nature of cancer, et cetera, on into such astronomical concepts which are theoretically the basic and motivating forces and principles which have engendered creation—all of these possess certain synonymies; a universal parallel in obvious facts, that creation must and does have, in whatever particular fashion or branch that we wish to introspect, creative expressions which are always found as oscillating components, and in different polarities and constituents which go to make up the total electromagnetic spectrums of all combined solar systems, galaxies and universes.

So again, how obvious must it get before these scientists can bridge that seemingly vast gulf, that impenetrable jungle, that hinterland which they have called the fourth dimension and which is, in its purest and simplest essence, the spawning ground for the third-dimensional worlds and also, within these fourth dimensional constituents, they comprise other dimensions and such subdivided astral planes. These are indeed the long talked of, long dreamed of heavenly reaches—those places where the religionist, in his wildest fantasies, has created the subliminal resources of some celestial city such as the New City of Jerusalem, or the utopian hinterland which is found in certain types of philosophies which particularly abounded in the Middle Ages.

Yet to all, the most obvious and necessary ingredients in formulating the constituents of life which would lead forward into a progressive evolutionary pathway are immediately on hand, so to speak, and they can be found in the face of every flower or blade of grass. They can be found within the coursing bloodstreams of our own bodies—in the intricate mechanism which is the transitory vehicle of this earth life.

"Seek and ye shall find; knock and the door shall be opened" are the words of one man who lived almost 2,000 years ago—a relevant philosophy and advice which is just as valid today as it was in any other day or time in the history of mankind; for no one escapes the horizon of his earth world until he can, within the precincts of his own mind, formulate an intelligent resource which is formulated from ingredients which embrace the entire Infinite Cosmogony.

The Laser Beam & Asininity of the Bible

On January 14, 1969, there appeared in the Los Angeles Times an article which dealt specifically with the laser beam. It seems that the scientists have now found out that the original incredibly short burst or pulse of the laser beam is actually composed of millions of even shorter pulses which are rated in the trillionths of a second! Moreover, these pulses contain incredible amounts of energy—millions of watts.

Of course, this discovery again leaves science and those particularly concerned scientists in another classical state of confusion as to time differentials, space-time factors, energy versus wave length, etc.

This is one of those typical ambiguous anachronisms which I have, through the years, taken time to point out; the incredible stupidity of those who are engaged in scientific endeavors and who have not as yet recognized the most obvious fact of creation—an interdimensional cosmos.

The situation here is analogous to a story I like to tell: a dog burying a bone had somehow thrust his tail through a knothole in the fence. At that precise moment, two visitors in a flying saucer had just landed close by; they saw the long board fence and the dog's tail wagging back and forth through the knothole. You can well imagine their difficulty on trying to describe what appeared to be an animate living animal standing on its end on a strip of cellulose material, many of which composed a long rectangle. And we can also imagine it would confuse everybody else when these visitors got back to their native planet and tried to describe this phenomenon to their fellow scientists.

This story hardly needs clarification. The board

fence is the interdimensional separation between this third dimension and all other dimensions on the other side, the dog representing the main body of life, his tail thrust through the knothole, analogous to the total third dimension.

While science and scientists have, through the many years, been constantly repeating these ambiguous anachronisms revealing this obvious stupidity, by far the greatest and most asinine stupidity was perpetrated on that memorable flight to and around the moon by three astronauts December 21-26, 1968. It is not necessary to repeat here that it was indeed the greatest and most successful attempt man has made to achieve this long-sought goal, nor will I enumerate the many years of efforts, experimentations, round-the-world space flights, the twenty-four billion dollars spent to achieve this goal—all done quite obviously for the main purpose of trying to understand creation better, how the world and the moon, yes, even the solar system was formed, etc.

Now, after the tenth orbit of the moon was completed, the astronauts gunned their rocket ship back onto a trajectory that would bring them back to earth. Then immediately after came the perpetration of this aforementioned great atrocity. These three astronauts did, while they were being heard and viewed through television by countless millions, actually read from the Bible the opening chapters of Genesis which describe the primitive, elemental way certain aboriginal people tried to conceive the creation of the heavens and earth! So great is this horrendous assault upon intelligence, logic and reason that its effect may not be immediately felt. Even after several weeks, Ruth and I were still in a state of shock. Here it is and so it will forever remain: three scientists on a spaceship, together with many thousands of other scientists and indirectly, the many millions of taxpayers who footed the bill, all engaged in what was the most obvious attempt to discover the true creation; yet, with victory a matter of hours away for the success of this space mission, they dug down into the vapid collection of ancient legends and fable called their Bible and resurrected the old, archaic, enigmatic fantasy—a ridiculous hokus-pokus, an irresponsible, incomprehensible act of creation performed by a self-constituted god, a god they have classically enshrined throughout this biblical collection of fables.

It is at this point that I become lost to find suitable and more adequate words to describe this incredible, asinine stupidity! The Bible itself is a total manifesto which is contradictory to any conception of creation. Even more totally confounded in the New Testament is the version of one man who tried to make one of the numerous attempts to defeat this primitive abracadabra god-concept, and the premise of intellectual decency was further violated when, after He was crucified for His efforts, He was actually enshrined as the son of this pagan god He had tried to defeat, later becoming the keystone in the arch of the great Machiavellian machination—the Christian hypocrisy!

And so at this moment, I will leave you to reflect upon the total circumference of this most incredible insanity. Will the peoples of the world ever evolve out of this sticky ooze of their material world, their superstitious beliefs which belittle and make flatulent, even destroy any comprehensive efforts or attainments to understand creation?

Yes, no doubt there will be many more of these ambiguous anachronisms, each one in itself will repeat this same vicious circle of anarchy—an anarchy which destroys logic, reason and comprehension.

Footnote: In deference to the proper use of the terminology, "ambiguous anachronisms" is a reference specifically pointing out a number of scientific discoveries which have occurred, particularly in the past two decades; more specifically the red shift, quasars, the DNA molecule, the laser beam, etc., and all such claims made purportedly as ultimates are therefore anachronisms. Such claims, when an interdimensional comparison is made, are completely out of place and time. Likewise, the term "ambiguous" becomes apropos when such comparisons are made, as such discoveries have neither the proper beginning or terminus and are, therefore, vague and not properly inclined for any fourth dimensional hypothesis.

Generally speaking, while these scientific discoveries have added to the scientific nomenclature, they have nevertheless, interdimensionally speaking, abrogated a comprehensive understanding of creation—more mystery, more confusion.

Addendum
(By Ruth Norman)

Although any added words to the voluminous texts which the Unarius Moderator, Ernest L. Norman, has given would be as straws in the wind, so to say, I would like nonetheless to express some thoughts that have so often come to me.

Part 1 & 2 of this volume are the last of the teachings of the Unarius Moderator, for as you have read in the format, He translated into the higher octaves of expression on December 6, 1971, to live amongst His Flame People. As He has related, it is doubtless that He and the Brothers feel, what with the voluminous amassment of teachings that has been brought into the earth dimension, and along with the great powers, the earthman can, with this help, work his way out of the earth bonds and ties.

Also as, man does now have within the combined texts of the Unarius Science more than sufficient knowledge to help him in his struggle toward self-overcoming, self-attainment and realization, if he will but enter into the study with open mind and remain ever steadfast to his goal of Infinite Consciousness. Whosoever shall thus become so dedicated to his own personal endeavor toward self-mastery will surely come to realize that the great and Infinite Creative Mind or Consciousness of the Moderator is without a doubt the greatest Mind to ever visit planet earth. The world shall long remember the life-changing teachings channeled by this selfless Soul—the true Mission of Jesus restored and added to, in great measure.

As has been written by this one in my book, "Bridge to Heaven" my life truly has been changed through His teachings and application—changed in so many ways that one would not recognize the present Ruth to be the entity she was B.N. (before Norman).

Most important, along with the concepts posed are the great and vast healing powers that He and the Brotherhood project as the student attunes himself through the study. Likewise have the lives of all students been changed for the better in some measure. However, all this shall be told in their own words and way in the next publications to be printed; in fact, there will be several of these volumes relating the students' healings, personal progress and psychisms of all natures and types, and which will be not only vitally interesting and informative but shall give opportunity to other students to relate to similar experiences which may have happened in their own pasts. These forthcoming books shall be titled "By Their Fruits" and will carry great and undeniable proof that our Teacher and Moderator, Ernest L. Norman, was (and is) indeed the reincarnate Jesus, Akhenaton, et cetera, and again, by His fruits shall He be known!

If you, the reader, may perchance feel that these words may have been uttered elsewhere, let it be said here and now that we could never—not ever in any one lifetime, sing sufficiently the praises to this great and beloved Master-Teacher. However, it is realized that words are but futile symbologies, and the vastness, the greatness, the monumental movement that Unarius is and shall become, can never be expressed in words nor described, and only through inner realization, the personal conceiving of the various principles and concepts contained, can any individual factually realize this monumental opportunity which changes man and helps free him from these carnal worlds and will prepare him to pass on to the higher spiritual worlds of Light when leaving the physical.

No, He did not want recognition while He lived in

the physical; in fact, He set it up before entering the earth world so this would not be, for were mankind to so recognize who He really was (and is), His work would soon have been forced to come to a conclusion in some one way or another.

It should be told too, how very closely does the Beloved One work with us now; as we carry on His Word and Work, He goes before and points the way, and His Light, His Love, His Guidance is sensed in all I do or express. The Light of the World shines ever the brighter for His having walked among us on Earth; He and the Brothers continue to radiate the Infinite Power unto us all—and we know these Powers shall exist and through this, my channelship, just as long as I personally can and do keep Consciousness attuned unto the Infinite. He is repeatedly proving the vital principle He taught us but a short time ago—that life is not terminated at so-called death, but yes, continues on in higher astral realms. Of this I can sincerely vouch, for I sense His Oneness, the great and infinite Love He has for all mankind, and He continues to aid all who are reaching toward the Light. And we say to you too, dear seeker, just as surely as you put forth the effort to conceive what He taught, you too shall receive His inner help from the Inner Higher Planes—the Spiritual Worlds— and which Powers are not affected by distance, time or space.

Let this book remain as a living memorial to His memory by all who love His Word (as it was printed and published after He stepped from out the flesh of atoms), the dissertations He had given previously. Thus it is with a special joy and pride that we add this important volume to His great and monumental works —wisdom to take man far, far into the future when he is thus able to conceive the contents and meanings. Surely, never has there ever been brought to planet Earth by any one mind such monumental and life-changing wisdom, a Herculean expression; knowledge, when made one's own, changes the dross to light, heals, lifts and transcends, and prepares man for his own time of translation into the Higher Worlds.

How very fortunate we are to have had the One to come again, and as He promised He would return, He has, and now He has ascended again unto the Lighted Worlds. And as He has fulfilled His promise made yea, two thousand years ago, He now renews the promise: "Seek and ye shall find; knock and the door shall be opened unto you, and ye shall live in the House of the Infinite forever."

* * * * *

Although this concludes Part 1 of this volume, it in no way is the end. Part 2 carries right on with these dissertations. They were so divided under two covers in order for more convenient reading. Part 2 shall be published as soon as possible. I feel it carries even more vital information than the first part of the book.

— Uriel

* Since the above writing, Part 2 has been printed and is now available.

Other works by Ernest L. Norman:

The Voice of Venus
The Voice of Eros
The Voice of Hermes
The Voice of Orion
The Voice of Muse

The Infinite Concept of Cosmic Creation
Cosmic Continuum
Infinite Perspectus
Infinite Contact
Truth About Mars
The Elysium (Parables)
The Anthenium   "
Magnetic Tape Lectures
Tempus Procedium
Tempus Invictus
Tempus Interludium Vol. II

Also a publication, now reprinted by
Unarius Publishing Company:
The True Life of Jesus of Nazareth (1899)

(The Sequel): The Story of the Little Red
Box